Developing Dialogues

Developing Dialogues
Indigenous and Ethnic Community Broadcasting in Australia

Susan Forde, Kerrie Foxwell & Michael Meadows

intellect Bristol, UK / Chicago, USA

First published in the UK in 2009 by
Intellect, The Mill, Parnall Road, Fishponds, Bristol, BS16 3JG, UK

First published in the USA in 2009 by
Intellect, The University of Chicago Press, 1427 E. 60th Street,
Chicago, IL 60637, USA

Copyright © 2009 Intellect Ltd

All rights reserved. No part of this publication may be reproduced, stored in a retrieval system, or transmitted, in any form or by any means, electronic, mechanical, photocopying, recording, or otherwise, without written permission.

A catalogue record for this book is available from the British Library.

Cover designer: Holly Rose
Copy-editor: Rebecca Vaughan-Williams
Typesetting: Mac Style, Beverley, E. Yorkshire

ISBN 978-1-84150-275-5

Contents

Acknowledgements	7
Abstracts	9
Chapter 1: Community Broadcasting Contexts	13
Chapter 2: Local and Global Perspectives	33
Chapter 3: Producers and Policies	49
Chapter 4: Audiences for Indigenous Community Radio and Television	77
Chapter 5: Audiences for Ethnic Community Radio	99
Chapter 6: Breaking down the Barriers	123
Conclusion	139
References	157
Appendix	177
Index	181

Acknowledgments

This book, like any major project, is the result of the contributions, participation and generosity of a wide range of people involved in the community broadcasting sector in Australia. It began with research into Indigenous media production and processes more than three decades ago. Many hundreds of community radio station managers, volunteers and media workers participated in our first-ever survey of the sector in the late 1990s. In our more recent work, there are several hundred more participants who represent community organizations using local radio and television services and, of course, the diverse audiences for these media who have been able to tell their stories for the first time.

We would like to warmly extend our thanks to long-standing supporters of our research endeavours. If we have inadvertently missed naming any of the myriad participants who have been involved with us over the past decades, then we humbly apologise in advance. We can identify the following organizations and personnel: the Community Broadcasting Foundation (Ian Stanistreet, Beth McRae and Deb Welch), the Community Broadcasting Association of Australia (Wendy Coates, Tamara Doncon, Joanna McCarthy, Barry Melville, David Melzer, Rebecca Pasqualini, and the late Mike Thompson), the then Department of Communication, Information Technology and the Arts (Ruth Ashe, Judy Hiscox, and Jen Levy), the Australian Indigenous Communication Association (Patrick Malone and Ken Reys), the Indigenous Remote Communications Association (Russell Bomford), Radio for the Print Handicapped Australia (Peter Luckett), the National Ethnic Multicultural Broadcasters' Council (Peter Ho and Tim Tolhurst), the Hunter Institute for Mental Health (Jaelea Skehan and Amy Laybutt), and Griffith University's Centre for Public Culture and Ideas (Andy Bennett and Jill Jones).

Thanks to colleague Jacqui Ewart who joined with us for the *Community Media Matters* audience study, and to Indigenous researcher Christine Morris who worked on that project in its early stages. Research assistants Jeremy Almeida, Heather Anderson, Stephen Cox, and Kitty van Vuuren all made significant contributions to our understanding of the sector over the past decade or more and we thank the interpreters and cultural guides who worked to translate and mediate our relations with Indigenous and ethnic communities. Special thanks must go to senior Indigenous researcher Derek Flucker. Without his insights, knowledge and good humour, it is almost certain that the Indigenous elements of the research — particularly during the *Community Media Matters* study — would have been impossible to conduct effectively and appropriately.

Susan Forde, Kerrie Foxwell and Michael Meadows, Brisbane 2009

Abstracts

1. Community Broadcasting Contexts

An overview of the book, arguing that it is the first to consider all major aspects of the community media production and reception process and the first to deal specifically with Indigenous and ethnic community media in this context. The chapter provides an introduction to the Australian community broadcasting sector, its historical development and the cultural context in which it has emerged. It outlines the scope and organization of the book.

2. Local and global contexts

This chapter offers a summary of the key texts and ideas that have informed scholarly debates around community media, particularly as it relates to Indigenous and ethnic community media forms. The authors argue throughout that much of the theorization and analysis thus far has taken place in the absence of any significant audience research.

3. Producers and policies

The authors outline in detail the nature of the Australian community broadcasting sector with a focus on producers of program content. This material draws from original research on Indigenous and ethnic community media undertaken by the authors and outlines the ways in which these particular elements of the Australian community radio sector have imagined their communities of interest and the ways in which they have responded to their perceived audiences' needs.

4. Audiences for Indigenous community radio and television

Indigenous audiences confirm that their community radio and television stations provide them with a first level of service in communities where they are active. Radio and television programming maintains languages and cultures and enables important kinship affiliations to be strengthened. For many, Indigenous broadcasting boosts self-esteem and plays a critical role in educating children. This sub-sector also provides a cultural bridge between Indigenous and non-Indigenous communities and as such, plays an important role in the reconciliation process.

5. Audiences for ethnic community radio

Ethnic audiences for community radio acknowledge the essential service nature of local stations in maintaining languages and cultures through specialist music and spoken language programming. Audiences emphasize the importance of local news and information to help them to establish and maintain local cultural connections. The chapter concludes that this sub-sector of the Australian community broadcasting sector is playing a crucial role in the settlement process for migrant communities. It creates opportunities for social inclusion rather than social division.

6. Breaking down the barriers

The authors offer a critique of current theorizing of community media and present their own dimensions, based on the data emerging from the Australian study of Indigenous and ethnic audiences. They consider empowerment as a primary element in the processes of community broadcasting, operating at the level of the media, the community and society. This argument is based on the notion of a collapse or weakening of the producer-audience boundary in community broadcasting.

7. Conclusion

The authors argue that the audience-producer relationship is a key defining characteristic of community broadcasting in Australia and that this idea might be applied more generally to alternative media globally. Importantly, it suggests Indigenous and ethnic audiences have identified community broadcasting as a key factor in creating community connectedness and a sense of community well-being. The chapter emphasizes the need for further qualitative audience research into community media internationally.

Appendix: Focus groups

A list of the focus groups and interview locations used to gather the audience data.

Chapter 1

Community Broadcasting Contexts

On the question of whether third sector media contribute to social cohesion or threaten it, the evidence points to the sector being an important factor in social cohesion and citizenship, particularly for minority ethnic communities and refugee and migrant communities (Lewis 2008: 7).

Audiences for community broadcasting in Australia identify it as the only media sector that is able to take account of the nation's social, political and cultural diversity. Community radio and television are playing an important cultural role in helping to draw together disparate elements of Australian society. At the same time, analysis of the processes involved in producing these media offers a powerful critique of mainstream media and their failure to contribute more actively to social cohesion. Nowhere is this dichotomy more apparent than amongst Australia's Indigenous (or First Nations) and ethnic community media audiences. It is one reason why we have focused on these particular segments of the community broadcasting sector in this book. The other, and perhaps more important reason, is to explore the processes which have empowered audiences for these multifarious minority media. Wherever Indigenous and ethnic community-based radio and television stations are active across the country, they provide a first level of service for their respective communities. They represent spaces where negotiation over the very nature of the audience-producer relationship has created new ways of conceptualizing 'community media' (Meadows et al. 2007).

Based on a long engagement with Native broadcasting developments and processes in Canada, Roth and Valaskakis have taken this idea further, arguing that the nature of Aboriginal community broadcasting, in particular, might provide a clue as to 'how to electronically recuperate public discourse and reconstitute public space in ways that will bear upon the future of…society' (1989: 233). Albeit in a more journalistic context, Deuze (2006: 458) underlines the importance of multiculturalism as a defining element of the 'occupational ideology' of modern communication. If, as we suggest, mainstream media remain unable to accurately reflect Australia's cultural diversity, analysis of the community media sector – and broadcasting in particular – offers an insight into how this process might evolve.

Although we undertook the first national study of the Australian community radio sector (Forde et al. 2002), our work was built on various earlier, albeit smaller-scale investigations (Bear 1979; 1983; Moran 1995; Thornley 1995; Barlow 1997; 1999). But what this book is able to include for the first time are the voices of the audiences for community radio and television, completing the production-reception cycle. The bulk of the analysis we offer here is based on what is arguably the first-ever qualitative audience study of an entire national community media sector. It has offered us a privileged glimpse of the processes that 'make' community radio and television in Australia.

Another book on community media?

Australia's burgeoning community broadcasting sector – one of the first established globally – received scant academic or government attention in the first 25 years of its development (Bear 1979; 1983; Moran 1995; Thornley 1995; Barlow 1997; 1999). This situation was reflected globally until the dawn of the new millennium when an outpouring of academic research began to identify community media generally as sites of innovative and participatory practice (Forde 1999; Ewart 2000; Downing 2001; Rodriguez 2001; Forde et al. 2002; Atton 2002; Howley 2005; McCauley 2005; Coyer et al. 2007; Carpentier and de Cleen 2007; Fuller 2007; Wilson and Stewart 2008). But voices of the audiences for these multifarious media have largely remained silent – until now. The handful of audience surveys carried out in the Australian community media sector over the past ten years or so have focused on individual stations – and virtually all have sought quantitative data. While the empowering possibilities of local media *production* have been canvassed and acknowledged globally in the past ten years, analysis of local audience *reception* has not received similar attention. Work with Indigenous media in Australia and elsewhere has tended to focus on specific production and reception processes within communities and have been guided by anthropological frameworks with media – or media audiences – not the primary focus (Michaels 1986; Ginsburg 1991; Ginsburg 2000; Deger 2007). Studies that have looked specifically at Indigenous media in Australia and internationally have not involved systematic audience methods, rather relying on analyses of production processes with anecdotal evidence of reception (Roth and Valaskakis 1989; Valaskakis 1993; Meadows 1994; Molnar and Meadows 2001; 2002; Roth 2005; Daniels 2006).

Although there has been significant research into ethnic communities in Australia and elsewhere, audiences for ethnic media have not been a specific focus thus far. For example, Australian research has included an audience study of mainstream media use by ethnic communities (Coupe and Jakubowicz 1992; Ang et al. 2002), the impact of media representation on refugees (Brough et al. 2003), and the relationship between community radio and diasporas (Cohen 2003; Chand 2004). Internationally, there have been numerous studies of ethnic media and their impact but again, audiences have largely remained absent as a *focus*. These studies include a global examination of ethnic and Indigenous minority media (Riggins 1992; Browne 2005) and investigations of the impact of ethnic media in terms of their impact on diasporas and majority community cultures (Downing and Fenton 2003; Tsagarousianou 2004; Shi 2005). A special issue of the international journal, *Journalism*, considered ethnic media from the perspectives of various authors (Deuze 2006; Guzman 2006;

Lin and Song 2006; Moran 2006; Ojo 2006; Wilkin and Ball-Rokeach 2006). Downing and Husband (2005) pooled their considerable research experiences in this area, identifying the importance of ethnic minority media in their global study of race and racisms. But apart from the audience analysis we offer in this book, there is virtually no other forthcoming audience research from international or local sources that might offer some sort of comparison. An emerging concentration in community radio studies at Sydney's Macquarie University has produced some encouraging new research, at this stage, confined to Thailand (Polnigongit 2005). But the 'absent issue of the virtually unknown' in community media – audience research – remains a challenge for scholars and practitioners alike (Downing 2003). The upshot of this body of research is essentially that 'minority', 'class' or 'progressive alternative' media play a critical role at various levels in their respective communities (Downing and Husband 2005; Gutierrez 2006). Perhaps this is best summarized by two key elements: the failure of mainstream media to become relevant to the lives of significant sections of modern, culturally diverse societies; and the ability of – in this case – Indigenous and ethnic community media to 'put people back in the frame' (Downing and Husband 2005: 37). This is clearly evident from our own investigations.

This book is the first to present detailed qualitative analysis of the ways in which diverse audiences for Indigenous community radio and television and ethnic community radio have adopted – and adapted – these media as essential communication services. We will draw from almost two decades of collective research into Australian and international community broadcasting, including the first Australian (and possibly global) qualitative audience research study of its kind which offers new models for audience research – particularly community and alternative media audience research (Lewis 2008: 23–24; 29). The research tells us a great deal about the nature of the relationships between such audiences, their media and society.

Our long and continuing engagement with the community broadcasting sector in Australia has revealed the extraordinary passion Indigenous and ethnic community media audiences have for their local stations and programmes, along with a belief that community radio and television provide them with an essential service. Community radio and television in Australia are providing minority audiences, in particular, with a first level of service with regard to local news and information, music formats and styles. Indigenous and ethnic community broadcasting networks play a critical role in maintaining cultures and languages, creating and strengthening notions of identity in the face of global, national and local stereotypes. These media more accurately represent Australian social and cultural diversity than any other outlets and perhaps inadvertently play an important role in educating the broader listenership about ideas and assumptions outside their usual frames of reference. The Australian community media sector is playing a significant empowering role for individuals, social groups and the processes that create 'communities' (Grossberg 1987; Rodriguez 2001; Carpentier et al. 2003; Bailey et al. 2008). The process represents a collapse – or at the very least, a weakening – of the traditional audience-producer barrier that defines media production, thus creating an environment which has enabled unique processes of identity-formation 'through dialogue' (Michaels 1986; Kulchyski 1989; Langton 1993). This suggests the need to re-think the role of community radio and television. Despite enabling spaces for distinct social and cultural groups to 'connect' and sustain each other, there is scant evidence from our studies to suggest that this process is producing significant division in the broader public sphere – in fact, quite the contrary. By virtue of its diverse and highly accessible nature, coupled with its ability to 'connect' local communities and individuals, Indigenous and ethnic community broadcasting is contributing to the idea of active citizenry and enhancing the democratic process. To emphasize this point, our work suggests community radio is enabling fuller participation in broader society through its provision of information – in language, and which migrant and remote Indigenous communities could not otherwise access – about government services, political and social issues, voting rights and so on. This content creates a sense within these communities that they are, indeed, an important part of a greater 'whole'.

A wide range of audiences access Indigenous radio and television across Australia with both Indigenous and non-Indigenous listeners and viewers identifying 'theirs' as an essential service that plays a central organizing role in community life. These media help people to maintain social networks and play a strong educative role in communities, particularly for young people. They offer an alternative source of news and information about the community and the outside world which avoids stereotyping of Indigenous people and issues. Both directly and indirectly, these media are helping to break down stereotypes about Indigenous people, thus playing an important role in promoting cross-cultural dialogue and in boosting Indigenous self-esteem. One of the key elements in this is the role being played by Indigenous community-produced radio and television in supporting the burgeoning Indigenous music and arts industry. From these multifarious ways in which Indigenous people engage with local radio and television, it is clear that these media are important cultural resources that are being effectively managed by the communities who 'own' them (Meadows 1994; Molnar and Meadows 2001; Meadows et al. 2007: 1).

Audiences listening to specialist ethnic programming on generalist community radio stations or full-time ethnic community radio stations are tuning in because station programming plays a central role in maintaining cultures and languages. Programmes help audiences to maintain community connections and networks and stations enable them to hear specialist music unavailable through other media. Ethnic community radio audiences want to hear local community news and gossip. They are particularly interested in hearing news and information relevant to their lives in Australia, along with that from their home countries and from neighbouring countries and regions (Meadows et al. 2007: 1).

The continuing circulation of ideas and assumptions about the world through Indigenous and ethnic community media contributes to the development of community public spheres which, in turn, interact with the broader public sphere, highlighting both common and differing experiences and issues. But importantly, Indigenous and ethnic media also act – most often quite deliberately – as cultural bridges between their own 'parallel universes' and mainstream society. They provide sites for public opinion formation; sites where citizens can engage in collective efforts to bring their issues to the dominant public sphere; and sites where marginalized communities can attempt to influence the policies of various governments through the pressure of public opinion. As Bickford (1996: 4) suggests, '*both* speaking and listening are central activities of citizenship' and it is clear that Indigenous and ethnic community broadcasting stations enable these activities in ways that separate them absolutely from mainstream media. These community-based media are most often the only sources of information – and communication – for their audiences. The mere act of listening becomes a participatory process because, as Bickford (1996: 141) reminds us, listening is 'a practice of democratic citizenship in a diverse, unequal social order'. Indigenous and ethnic community media continue to play a central role globally in offering a critique of mainstream media and its place in the formation of the broad democratic public sphere. Quite simply, Indigenous and ethnic media (and other community media) are spaces where citizens are encouraged to 'speak and listen differently' – and this truism summarizes their contribution to the public sphere and their challenge to mainstream media outlets.

This book is informed predominantly by our practical and research experience with the broader Australian community radio sector. For two of us – Susan Forde and Michael Meadows – it began as volunteer work with one of Australia's first community radio stations, 4ZzZ in Brisbane and involvement with Indigenous community radio and print media. Our collective research interest started with the first national study of managers, workers and volunteers in the community radio sector, resulting in publication of the report, *Culture, Commitment, Community* (Forde et al. 2002). This was bolstered by the most recent qualitative study, *Community Media Matters* (Meadows et al. 2007), which included Indigenous and ethnic audiences. During this period, there has been an increasing focus on community and/or alternative media from both the research community and Australian government policy circles. It is for these reasons that we offer – for the first time from an audience perspective – an analysis of why community media is succeeding in the current broadcasting environment.

Our project has been helped by an increasing level of research in Australia into community radio and television audiences, most notably, the McNair Ingenuity quantitative audience surveys in 2004, 2006 and 2008. These reveal that community broadcasting audiences have increased by 20 percent since 2006 and by 26 percent since 2004, with 57 percent of the Australian population over fifteen years old (around 7 million people) now tuning in at least monthly to a community radio station. More than 700,000 people are 'exclusive' listeners – that is, they do not listen to either commercial radio or ABC/SBS – and their primary reasons for listening are to hear specialist music and local news and local information (McNair Ingenuity 2008). Although there is no directly comparable quantitative data available for either the Indigenous or ethnic community broadcasting sectors, our own collective investigations over the past twenty years suggest that listenership within specific culturally and linguistically-defined communities is much higher than for the generalist community sector. We estimate that it varies between 60 and 90 percent, based on prior studies (Meadows and van Vuuren 1998) and recent qualitative data from interviews and focus groups (Meadows et al. 2007). The most recent qualitative audience research set out to explore 'why' Australians are tuning in to community radio and television and the impact it has on their lives. Neither the Indigenous nor the ethnic community broadcasting sector has participated in the McNair Ingenuity studies, believing that reducing an evaluation of their activities to 'numbers', along with the method adopted (5,000 telephone interviews nationally), is an inappropriate way of assessing their community and cultural contributions. Thus, the data presented in this book is the first to offer specific analysis of the sector's Indigenous and ethnic community broadcasting audiences.

There has been significant growth in international academic literature examining community media, in no small part provoked by the *official* establishment of the UK community radio sector and its steady expansion (Ofcom 2009). Based on its 30-year history, Australian community broadcasting offers an ideal case study from which its counterparts in the United Kingdom and elsewhere might draw. We hope that this book informs international community media practitioners and researchers of the strengths and weaknesses of the Australian community broadcasting network and the global implications that flow from this. While each broadcasting environment has its own unique set of variables and influences, there is still much common ground and we will attempt to highlight areas that illustrate this throughout the book.

Australian beginnings

Community radio began in Australia on 18 June 1972 when station 5UV, based at one of Australia's oldest universities, the University of Adelaide, was given the first low-powered AM frequency licence to broadcast educational materials on what was then called public radio. The nation's first FM public radio licence (and the first FM licence) was allocated in 1974 to classical or fine music station 2MBS in Sydney, quickly followed by a series of capital city FM stations that represented musical tastes at the other end of the spectrum. One in particular was Brisbane's 4ZzZ FM. It emerged from a civil liberties and anti-Vietnam war movement in Queensland from the mid- to late 1960s, first hitting the airwaves in December 1975, a few weeks after the elected Prime Minister of Australia, Gough Whitlam, had been sacked by the Governor General, plunging the country into a constitutional crisis. The station's first announcer, John Woods, proudly proclaimed its support for the sacked Labor Government before playing its first music track – The Who's anthem, '*Won't get fooled again*'. The alternative arm of the Australian community radio movement had well and truly begun.

The first Aboriginal public radio programme went to air on 5UV in Adelaide in 1972. However, there are reports of Aboriginal people being involved in commercial radio in Queensland in the late 1960s – 30 years after the first rudimentary experiments with wireless communication in the Torres Strait (Patterson 1938), a series of islands primarily populated by Indigenous people lying to the north of the Australian mainland. By the mid-

1970s, Indigenous-produced programmes were regularly broadcast on community radio in Hobart, Melbourne and Canberra, and by the early 1980s, Indigenous broadcasters were involved with community stations in the Northern Territory, Queensland and New South Wales. During this period, Indigenous people also began broadcasting weekly on the Australian Broadcasting Corporation (ABC) regional services and the Special Broadcasting Service (SBS). Ethnic communities had to wait until 1975 to first hear their voices on the Australian airwaves. The first ethnic community radio stations were 2EA (Sydney) and 3EA (Melbourne), operated by the federal government's Department of the Media and broadcasting in eight languages. Although both 2EA and 3EA were originally developed to operate for a three-month experimental period to explain Australia's new healthcare system to migrant communities, their popularity and community demand saw the continuation of both stations. They were later absorbed by the establishment in 1977 of the Special Broadcasting Service (SBS) and by 1978, 2EA and 3EA broadcast in 41 and 38 languages respectively. SBS remains Australia's national multicultural broadcaster, developing a television presence in 1980.

Community broadcasting outlets have arguably become the only media able to accurately represent the diversity of cultures that make up the modern Australian population through a philosophy of access and participation. Audiences for community radio and television in Australia are now amongst the largest per capita in the world with 27 percent of people over the age of fifteen – 4.5 million people – tuning in to a community radio station at least once each week. This number more than doubles (to 57 percent) for those tuning in monthly (McNair Ingenuity 2008). It is partly the result of phenomenal growth throughout the sector in the past fifteen years, mirrored in a threefold increase in station numbers since the 1990s. At the time of writing, there were 483 licensed, independent and community-owned and operated broadcasting services in Australia supported by an army of around 23,000 volunteers. The Indigenous community broadcasting sector has 96 community radio and television stations, located mostly in regional and remote Australia, with 123 radio stations producing content in 97 languages for Australia's ethnic communities across the country (CB Online 2008: 24–25). Indigenous and ethnic community broadcasting provides an important bridge between cultures and it is this process alone that could be one of community broadcasting's most valuable contributions to Australian culture.

Until relatively recent curbs in levels of government support, the Indigenous media sector has been the fastest-growing in Australia, relying heavily on community radio to get its messages across. A National Indigenous Radio Service (NIRS) has spanned the continent from 1996 in the same way as Dreaming Tracks – traditional conduits for information in Indigenous communities. A National Indigenous News Service (NINS) started in 2001 and serves a network that has the capability of challenging the Australian Broadcasting Corporation – the national broadcaster – for reach and diversity in the potential number of stations able to tune into its unique sounds. Despite its extraordinary reach, this network represents a vast untapped resource for programme sponsors ranging from the federal government (one of Australia's largest advertisers) to regional authorities and businesses.

Where they are active, Indigenous community broadcasting outlets are linked intimately with local community social structures. Indigenous people have long suggested this as an important framework for success as Aboriginal and Torres Strait Islander communities recognize the value of their intellectual property (including broadcasting) and devise ways of managing this more effectively.

The ethnic broadcasting sector has taken on the task of bringing to life the idea of multicultural Australia. A strong element that emerged from national focus group discussions was the way in which ethnic broadcasters around the country have embraced subsequent waves of refugees. The varied accounts of local initiatives which have sought to include the new arrivals in the face of sometimes public rejection of their status was one of the most moving and inspirational aspects of research into the sector we undertook in the late 1990s (Forde et al. 2002). It represents a different sort of reconciliation in action and one that ethnic community radio broadcasters demonstrated both through their passion and their expertise. The cultural and community service role performed on a daily basis by community broadcasting is incomparable to that played by commercial or publicly funded broadcasters like the ABC.

Community radio undoubtedly plays a unique role in the development of Australian culture in terms of its Indigenous and multicultural elements alone. Indigenous people would be a 'voiceless public' without the continued cultural and linguistic revitalization it provides. Ethnic communities are empowered by the operation of local stations broadcasting programmes in community languages. Children of immigrants maintain a sense of identity, of history, of belonging, with continued maintenance and production of their cultures and languages. The histories of ethnic Australians are not forgotten – they are embraced and celebrated through the efforts of community ethnic broadcasters. Acknowledgement of the Australian ethnic experience is at least implicit in the production efforts of community broadcasters. In Australia, these stations and programmes do much to represent and acknowledge the diaspora characteristic of established and more recent ethnic minorities. While for mainstream Australians this can seem of minor interest, for ethnic Australians this acknowledgement and representation of their past, present and future in an Australian landscape is critical to their capacity to live well and happily alongside other Australian cultures – a crucial element in the settlement process.

Seeking the audience: some notes on method

Perhaps the main reason why so few audience studies of community broadcasting stations – let alone entire sectors – are undertaken is because of the difficulties involved. Some discount this as an excuse, arguing that the pioneering days of developing reception research are long over and it is a 'pioneering spirit' that seems to be lacking in the application of available methods (Schrøder 2001: 34). Whatever the reason for its scarcity, audience research is usually more complex and time-consuming than studies that involve examination of media production practices, for example. And for all media – especially Indigenous and ethnic community media – the greatest challenge, perhaps, is identifying the audience. Coupled with this element is a decision about method – qualitative or quantitative or both? While there have been a handful of audience studies by individual community broadcasting stations, primarily in the United States, all those we have been able to identify are quantitative in nature – that is, they focus on *numbers* of listeners or viewers. We decided on a qualitative approach for several reasons. We were more interested in the 'how' and 'why' questions rather than in numbers per se. In any case, Indigenous and ethnic community broadcasting sector representatives were adamant that a counting exercise alone would not accurately reflect the 'richness' of the processes involved in the production and reception of community radio and television. In addition, the first McNair Ingenuity quantitative survey of the *generalist* Australian community radio and television sector was planned in 2002 during the same timeframe as our own research. This did not specifically include Indigenous and ethnic community audiences for the reasons outlined earlier although some data on these sub-sectors has been gathered. Nevertheless, we were able to have some input into a series of open-ended questions asked of the interviewees for the McNair Ingenuity national telephone survey and this contributed to our analysis. The responses to these questions enabled us to further pursue the issues raised in our own interviews and focus group discussions in greater depth.

Why qualitative research?

The primary aim in designing the audience study was to delve more deeply into the meanings audiences attached to their listening or viewing activities – in other words, the 'how' and 'why' of participation. Globally, there has been a significant increase in the frequency and popularity of qualitative research – and publications about these methods – for a wide range of projects across many disciplines (Seale et al. 2004). The primary methods adopted for our study – interviews and focus group discussions – have also experienced an increase in popularity. Albeit attracting criticism from some quarters, qualitative research, and specifically the focus group method, is principally a cycle of 'shared activities and understandings', enabling participants to offer various perspectives on the same topic. Relationships between the researcher and the researched are potentially transformed to enable a more democratic process (Gibbs 1997; Kitzinger and Barbour 1999: 18). Essentially, it is about shared responsibility, knowledge and power (Baker and Hinton 1999: 80). These became central elements in the research design, particularly because of the nature of the audiences we were seeking. This is reflected in Murdock's (1997: 191) pertinent observation that 'studies of emerging patterns of consumption and everyday creativity cannot be uncoupled from an analysis of the changing organisation of production of the altering contours of inequality'. Quantitative methods are not designed to take account of such contextual elements. Nightingale and Dwyer (2005: 124) remind us, too, that a demographic approach to audience research is unable to respond to 'the needs of audiences whose shared interests are defined in terms of any category other than demographics'. It highlights the weakness of quantitative methods alone if a search for meaning is a primary consideration. Qualitative studies assume that what we set out to examine is 'a creative process whereby people produce and maintain forms of life and society and systems of meaning and value' (Tacchi et al. 2003: 346). This approach, with its emphasis on process, sits comfortably with the Australian community broadcasting sector's own philosophies of democratic access and participation and indeed, their 'local' role in meaning-making viz a viz culture. A critical aspect of this approach is to find ways to channel knowledge and findings into practical ends. We set out to satisfy this cycle of participation and sharing by paying careful attention to the ways in which data were presented, as well as ensuring the research had empowering practical possibilities for participants.

At the level of policymaking, qualitative research enables application of an 'audience first' philosophy and looks beyond markets and statistics to obtain a clearer picture of community broadcasting services in local communities. As such, it tends to go against prevailing trends that see quantitative research in a dominant position in terms of influencing public policy formation. This is evident, for example, in continuing Australian federal government support for the McNair Ingenuity quantitative surveys. However, at the local level, qualitative research outcomes offer the potential for enabling community radio and television stations to better know their audiences and to provide them with 'richer' information for potential sponsors, other than simply numbers. Of course, delivering audiences to advertisers remains a key element of attracting sponsorship – local or otherwise – but a deeper understanding of how and why audiences 'participate' in their local community broadcasting communities of interest offers an important additional, and most often absent, dimension. This is an example of how quantitative and qualitative research can effectively work together.

Our primary field of theoretical investigation concerns notions of the public sphere and the emergence of 'community public spheres' in the Australian mediascape. As such, the democratic and cooperative nature of interviews and focus groups as a research method held great appeal. In devising a list of research priorities within the community research field, Gibson and Cameron (2001: 22) suggest priority should be given to 'researching and developing mechanisms for promoting active citizenship within all types of communities, especially in disadvantaged areas'. This was especially pertinent, given the focus of this book. We attempted to achieve this aim in part by involving Indigenous and ethnic media organizations in the process of research methodology development, design and application and by encouraging audience participation in discussions about 'their' media.

While market researchers in the commercial world have been the most enthusiastic proponents of the focus group method, they tend to see participants as 'consumers' rather than as 'citizens' (Cunningham-Burley et al. 1999). Some see the shift towards focus group methodologies as evidence of the 'commercialization' of university research within an environment where academics are expected to become more industry-relevant (Green 1999: 42). However, no research technology necessarily comes with specific instructions on how it should be used and in which contexts. Thus we used focus group research to explore a specific set of research problems. The group is 'focused' in that it involves the collective activity of debating and discussing a set of identified issues and questions. Crucially, focus groups are distinguished from the broader category of group interviews by the explicit use of group interaction to generate rich data (Kitzinger and Barbour 1999: 4). A defining feature of this approach is its rejection of 'statistical representativeness' in favour of a 'theoretical sample' (Glaser and Strauss 1967) which aims 'to generate talk that will extend the range of thinking about an issue' (McNaughten and Myers 2004: 68). This involved recruiting participants who were defined in relation to the particular conceptual framework of our study – people who already listened to community radio and who *wanted* to offer their views. Negotiating the difference between a 'theoretical sample' in qualitative research as opposed to a 'statistical sample' in quantitative research became an issue in negotiations with some of our federal government departmental representatives. Favouring 'theoretical rigour' over 'statistical rigour' raised the inevitable questions of 'bias' and 'objectivity'. Explaining that a qualitative research project necessarily involves some acceptance of 'bias' (as does all research, including quantitative methods) – as it actively seeks participants who will be 'willing to generate talk' (McNaughten and Myers 2004) – encouraged us to revisit the philosophical foundations of qualitative research and to clarify its validity as an appropriate tool (Forde et al. 2006). This was one of several 'critical moments' during the more than two-year lifespan of the audience research project and is an expected – and perhaps necessary – element of any study that adopts and applies qualitative methods. Horsfall et al. (2001: 4) capture the essence of this process:

> Critical moments are those times when researchers are impelled to negotiate between the theories and conventions about research and their lived experience of it. Critical moments tell us the truth of the research process…Good qualitative research includes critical moments, struggles, resistances, pleasure and a personal journey. These ingredients add rigour to our work.

The 'journey' which produced the audience data from which we will draw was long and complex. It necessitated taking into account the extraordinary cultural diversity of Australian society and, in effect, establishing a dialogue with each of the communities included in our 'theoretical sample'. Clearly, a methodological mélange would be the most appropriate way to take this into account and we applied different approaches in different cultural – and geographical – settings accordingly. We will outline the specific processes adopted later in this chapter. The sometimes delicate negotiations across cultural boundaries constantly reminded us not only of our ethical obligations as researchers, but also of the importance of maintaining this dialogue within the broad philosophical frameworks of the Indigenous and ethnic community broadcasting communities themselves. Community information and communication technologies (ICTs) – radio and television in this case – facilitate *existing* community needs, a process eloquently summarized by Ramirez (2001: 327):

A community defines what it wants to be, where it wants to go, and ICTs are tools to be harnessed towards those agreements. ICTs are part of a context, along with global markets, jobs, interest rates, tariffs, regulations, political parties, families, weather, and disease. They can be harnessed and put to work to reaffirm where a community wants to be. What is true, however, is that they create a new environment that was not there before...

By enlisting an approach drawn from 'systems thinking' – emphasizing the importance of the interrelationships among parts – Ramirez (2007: 89) suggests conventional policymaking is unable to respond to 'ill structured' or 'messy' problems that are often present in regional and remote community communication provision and development. A more flexible, 'soft systems thinking' approach is able to take into account uncertainty and conflict, for example, emphasizing the importance of consultation with different sources of knowledge and perspectives (Geurts and Joldersma 2001). This ongoing process of interaction suggests the need for 'negotiation, for learning and for adaptation'. Ramirez argues that when stakeholders come to understand the 'indicators' that matter to others, it is only then that they begin to recognize and apply them, enabling the development of 'a new common language' (2007: 90).

It was precisely this 'new common language' that was of interest to us and adopting a qualitative approach seemed most likely to enable us to achieve this. In choosing the focus group research approach, the primary consideration was that people attending would already be listening to either a particular station or language programme. This was the cohort we were seeking. And to reach them, we decided to use local community radio and television stations themselves, amongst other methods. Each of the eight selected Indigenous radio stations and ten ethnic community radio language programmes involved invited listeners through a simple broadcast message to participate in a planned focus group. Those interested registered either through a promoted toll-free telephone number or by leaving their details with their local stations. We then contacted potential participants in the lead-up to a focus group either in person (where they were confident in English), or through interpreters; and in occasional cases where translators were not available, through community station programme producers and presenters.

But how to choose a 'theoretical sample' from around 100 Indigenous and 120 ethnic community radio and/or television stations situated in capital cities, regional centres, rural and remote communities? This was resolved through negotiations stretching over almost eighteen months with our advisory committee members from the Australian Indigenous Communications Association (AICA), the Indigenous Remote Communications Association (IRCA) and the National Ethnic and Multicultural Broadcasters' Council (NEMBC). AICA represents mainly urban and regional Indigenous media interests while IRCA is focused on Indigenous radio and television being produced in remote Aboriginal and Torres Strait Islander communities. The National Ethnic and Multicultural Broadcasters' Council (NEMBC) represents all ethnic broadcasting stations, whether offering full-time or part-time ethnic programming. Our research engagement with the community broadcasting industry thus far has always entailed working with project advisory committees made up of representatives of sector stakeholders. This cooperative relationship has proven to be a crucial element in not only providing advice on research design, but also in facilitating access to communities, many of which are highly suspicious of 'outsiders'. The role of our advisory committee was particularly important in providing valuable feedback on interpretation of results and identifying nuances which helped to explain certain trends. Regular meetings of our committee – both in person and by teleconference – played a central role in mediating many of the particular and inevitable dilemmas of cross-cultural research. The role, importance and influence of this supportive, collaborative structure as a central element of our research design cannot be overstated.

Our approach to data gathering entailed three broad methods: interviews with key people (station coordinators, sector and language group representatives); local groups who use community radio and television (sponsors, local musicians, artists, etc.); and focus group discussions. The primary audience data is drawn from around 70 face-to-face interviews with Indigenous people in thirteen regions across Australia, eight Indigenous broadcasting focus group discussions and ten ethnic community radio focus groups (see Appendix A). The majority of the focus groups included six to ten participants. Although market research recommends focus group sizes of eight to twelve, sociological research suggests five to six participants as appropriate (Kitzinger and Barbour 1999: 8). Our approach with all focus groups was to initially invite participants to nominate *their* priorities for discussion before we canvassed common themes. This is more collaborative than other approaches (such as nominating the issues to be discussed) and is potentially empowering for participants (Catterall and MacLaran 1997; Criterion Research 2002). Our primary consideration was to promote an environment where Indigenous and ethnic community participants felt comfortable about sharing their experiences as listeners and viewers. We found this method particularly useful for allowing people to 'generate their own questions, frames and concepts and to pursue their own priorities on their own terms, in their own vocabulary' (Kitzinger and Barbour 1999: 4). Where required, translators or 'fixers' gave participants an opportunity to discuss issues in a vocabulary which was both familiar and appropriate. The location of focus groups was also important as it was necessary for us to go into people's communities in order to access their views (Kitzinger and Barbour 1999: 11). This meant choosing locations nominated by Indigenous and ethnic community station representatives. For most of the ethnic audience focus groups, we employed a translator to assist in its operation and to help locate potential participants whose English fluency was either weak or non-existent.

Audiences for Indigenous community radio and television

The Indigenous fieldwork involved several approaches designed to capture a wide range of audiences. We realized that the use of formal focus groups would be limited, given that

Indigenous people – particularly those in remote Australia – do not tend to gather in one place at the behest of researchers: either they have more important social obligations or are hesitant about participating in 'yet another research project' from which they expect no real outcomes. To overcome the problem of establishing trust with interviewees, local Indigenous people were employed in the interviewing process as research assistants, recognizing their specialist local knowledge. This approach has been used many times in seeking information about Native television audiences across the Arctic (Wilson 1993; Roth 2005). In our case, it clearly helped to put Indigenous interviewees at ease and minimized the potential for us to be told what people *thought* we wanted to hear – one of the many pitfalls in this kind of cross-cultural research (von Sturmer 1981: 27–30; Brady 1981; Lyons 1981; 1983; Eades 1985; Michaels 1985; 1986; Roy Morgan Research 1995 ; Meadows 2002; Meadows 2009). It underlines again the need to be aware of the subtle nuances involved, particularly if the notion of research is conceived within Western frameworks.

We organized focus groups where possible – at metropolitan and the larger regional radio stations – while in smaller and more remote locations we conducted either one-on-one interviews or small group interviews. The fieldwork involved a great deal of travel to metropolitan, regional and remote locations – sometimes several times – to access audiences from the selected Indigenous broadcasting organizations. We traveled tens of thousands of kilometers by plane and several thousand on the road, mostly in four wheel drive vehicles (SUVs) which were required to access remote communities. Altogether, we conducted eight focus groups with Indigenous audiences and collected data from a further thirteen locations around Australia (Appendix A). In remote areas, we found it was more effective to tap into existing cultural events – and existing community timeframes – rather than attempting to organize a stand-alone event of our own. This approach emerged based on advice from Indigenous advisory committee representative Ken Reys, senior Indigenous research assistant Derek Flucker and our prior research experiences with Indigenous people (Meadows 1988; 1994; Meadows and van Vuuren 1998; Molnar and Meadows 2001; Meadows and Molnar 2002). We identified a series of major events in the national Indigenous cultural calendar and interviewed Indigenous (and some non-Indigenous) people at selected locations with the help of local Indigenous research assistants. This greatly enhanced our chances of accessing a large number of people on their own terms and at locations where they were generally more relaxed and open to the research process.

Locally based Indigenous research assistants ensured we were introduced to 'ordinary' community members in the correct way according to local protocols, fostering a level of trust and 'authorization'. We were conscious, too, of the need for reciprocity – a form of gift exchange or sharing – in our dealings with individuals and communities (Morris and Meadows 2004; Meadows 2005; Marmot 2006). It also meant the local community received something back – for example, a wage for a community member to assist with the project and the associated work experience gained; advice on education and other matters within our areas of expertise; and informal media training advice. This concept of reciprocity underpinned this component of the research. An essential element was the need to develop local community contacts well in advance of a visit. This involved strengthening existing relationships with Indigenous media organizations and local communities and creating new ones to establish a dialogue with elders and local broadcasters (Michaels 1985). The contacts made with key community representatives and Indigenous media workers were integral to the success of later community visits and also helped us to identify upcoming cultural events that might be used as sites for data collection. In the few communities where we were unable to locate a local research assistant we found it very difficult – impossible in one – to collect substantial data because there was simply no-one to vouch for us and to assure community members we could be 'trusted'.

In addition to conducting focus groups and face-to-face interviews, we monitored discussions held over five days on the popular Indigenous-produced community radio programme *Talk Black*, broadcast by Bumma Bippera Media in Cairns. It included on-air interviews with project research personnel and was followed, each day, by an invitation for listeners to call in to comment on any aspect of Indigenous media. As a national talkback programme for Indigenous listeners, this represented an excellent opportunity to tap into a range of audience members who not only listened to Indigenous radio, but also interacted with other community members and the *Talk Black* host. Comments from twenty talkback callers who responded to our invitation along with transcripts from the Indigenous audience focus groups and interviews were analysed using the qualitative research software, NVIVO.

Ethnic community radio audiences

The need for a translator for most of the ten ethnic community language focus groups conducted meant a slightly different approach was required to manage this part of our research. As with the Indigenous focus group organization, individual ethnic community radio stations were involved in inviting listeners to participate. People interested in taking part either left their names and contact details on our toll-free telephone message service, or if there were language issues, they called their local stations and spoke to a programme presenter or production assistant in their preferred language. This approach initially caused some concern with our advisory committee member representing the National Ethnic and Multicultural Broadcasters' Council (NEMBC). It was suggested that presenters, who in many cases had an elevated position within their community due to their status as a broadcaster, could put unintended but nevertheless real pressure on ordinary community members to participate. In short, if the presenter asked a community member to attend a focus group discussion, in many cases it would be impossible for that community member to say 'no'. To negotiate this issue successfully, we made it quite a firm requirement in the ethnic community focus groups that an independent person from the community – usually our nominated translator for the focus group – contact potential participants who had registered an interest with the toll-free number or with the station to see if they wanted to participate. The programme presenter was able to encourage listeners on-air to participate, but did not make personal phone calls to community members to ask for their attendance at the focus group. Generally, this worked well with a good mix of people across most focus groups.

The need for simultaneous translation in focus groups meant that this element of the research was complex and time-consuming with discussions requiring full translation, commonly taking at least twice as long as those conducted in English. As part of the research process, we introduced a pre-focus group briefing with each translator to ensure they were fully aware of the aims and content of the project. This enabled them to better translate our questions and points of discussion during the conduct of focus groups. This briefing also gave researchers the opportunity to identify specific cultural protocols to be observed during discussions – for example, issues of seniority and status, preferred speaking order and issues around gender. This helped to improve both cross-cultural communication and data reliability.

Focus group participants were offered the opportunity at the start of a discussion to speak either in English or in their first language. Five of the ten focus groups were run primarily in a community language, and five in English, based on the wishes of participants. In our experience, it was preferable for focus groups to be run *entirely* either in English or in the language of choice. Focus groups in which some people spoke English and others their own language were generally less informative and contained less data than those conducted in either one language or the other. This mixing of languages had a tendency to cause some participants – usually those who could not speak English very well – to withdraw from the conversation.

Structure of the book

Our aim in this book is to explore *how* and *why* audiences for Indigenous and ethnic community broadcasting access their chosen media and the implications that flow from this in terms of a broader understanding of the role – both locally and globally – of this developing 'third tier' of broadcasting. Within this framework, we plan to explore for the first time, issues of empowerment, civic action, participation, access and community service from the perspectives of audiences for these media. We will pursue these questions by applying a series of participatory qualitative methods which have engaged both the sector and its assorted audiences. As the ensuing chapters will reveal, this methodology has evolved into an original and useful way for researchers, scholars, sector bodies and individual stations to evaluate the impact, role, community contribution and, indeed, the very nature of 'what community broadcasting does' in a broad range of contexts. We hope the audience research methods we have developed prove to be a valuable and enduring tool for broadcasters both in Australia and well beyond these shores.

In the next chapter, we review the local, national and international contexts in which community radio and television, in particular, are being produced and received. In chapter three, we will consider the producers of Indigenous and ethnic community broadcasting and the media policy environments in which they work. In chapters four and five we will present analysis of the detailed commentary from the real stars of this project – Indigenous and ethnic community audiences. In the penultimate chapter we apply a grounded theory approach to draw some conclusions stemming directly from our audience analysis. We will argue that there is strong evidence to suggest community radio and television for Indigenous and ethnic communities represent tools for empowerment at various levels. In the final chapter, we canvass the notion that the nature of the relationship between community media audiences and producers might be considered as a defining characteristic. In considering this, we explore the implications that flow from this body of research for the theory and practice of community media globally.

Chapter 2

Local and Global Perspectives

There are few, if any, audience studies of community broadcasting globally, apart from a handful of unrelated quantitative analyses which tend to focus exclusively on numbers of listeners and/or viewers. An extensive literature search, along with exploration of international community media networks has failed to reveal any significant qualitative audience research in this realm (de Wit 2007; Hollander 2007; Lewis 2007). But despite this absence, it is important to place the Australian sector and its current state of evolution within a global context to better understand how our findings might have relevance for other community broadcasting practitioners and scholars alike.

This study of community broadcasting audiences emerges at a particularly critical point in Australian media history. A perennial issue in Australian media policy has been a debate over ensuring adequate provisions to foster diversity of media ownership and content. At the heart of this issue are the needs of regional Australian audiences and, in particular, requirements for local news and information and local content. A key piece of legislation enacted in 2007 – the *Broadcasting Services Amendment (Media ownership) Act 2006* – represents a significant change in the Australian media policy environment. The legislation has relaxed existing cross-media and foreign ownership laws, allowing major media owners to own different media (e.g. radio and newspapers; television and radio) in the same market, and for foreign investors to own more than 15 percent of an Australian media enterprise. At the same time, the amendments have employed some safeguards to retain diversity and to ensure the needs of regional Australia are met by commercial broadcasters, including a requirement that at least five independent media groups remain in state capitals and four in regional markets, and that any merger may involve no more than two of the three regulated platforms (i.e. radio, television and the press) in any one licence area. The assumption is that the number of media owners in both metropolitan and regional Australia will decrease when the changes take effect (Gardiner-Garden and Chowns 2006).

Alongside this relaxation in ownership restrictions are increased roles for both the Australian Competition and Consumer Commission (ACCC) and the Australian Communications and Media Authority (ACMA) in ensuring compliance with competition regulations and local media content provisions. In relation to regional areas, the legislation specifically requires minimum levels of local content on commercial television, a minimum level of local content on radio and special rules pertaining to 'trigger events' such as changes of ownership which aim to ensure continued local content (Department of Communication, Information Technology and the Arts 2006). While the federal government has argued that information diversity will not decrease under the new laws – primarily because of increasing diversity offered by online and digitized media services – there are concerns that a further concentration of media in fewer hands will have a significant impact on the boundaries of public debate and discussion (Manne 2006). Within weeks of the announcement that Parliament had passed the new laws, major Australian media proprietors had initiated moves to re-organize their ownership portfolios. The prospect of increasing concentration of ownership in the mainstream media sector both nationally and globally suggests an even greater role for localized and independent broadcasting services typified by those in the community sector. This trend has the potential to impact significantly on minority audiences. And while community radio is well placed to take advantage of this change in power relations, a shift within the community broadcasting sector itself towards a more politically conservative outlook overall risks marginalizing alternative views (Forde et al. 2002; van Vuuren 2009).

Downing and Husband (2005: x) have identified 'continuing failures on the part of mainstream media, globally, to fulfil their potential to inform, enlighten, question, imagine and explain in this often troubled and dangerous field of ethnic diversity'. Further concentration of media ownership in the Australian market – already arguably the most concentrated in the Western world – will do little to address this shortfall. Representation of Indigenous people and their affairs in the Australian media reflects this global trend. It is usual for Indigenous sources to make up around 20 percent of those quoted in newspaper stories *about* Indigenous affairs in Australia (Meadows 1987; Hippocrates and Meadows 1996; Meadows 1999). Perhaps unsurprisingly, a study of Native Canadian newspaper sources revealed almost identical, similarly flawed sourcing practices (Meadows 2000). However, most commonly, Indigenous people – like ethnic minorities – are simply invisible in mainstream media agendas except in stories related to crime, financial mismanagement, and anti-social behaviour with the 'racialization' of such events transmitted uncritically to audiences (Meadows 2001; Downing and Husband 2005: 5). It is this kind of misrepresentation that has been a major impetus for the emergence of Indigenous and ethnic media in Australia, as elsewhere.

Another challenge – or opportunity – for Indigenous and ethnic community broadcasting is in the switch to digital broadcasting globally. Despite the commercial and government rhetoric around its benefits, Australian audiences seem far from enthused for digital radio services, in particular. Some indication of this is the rescheduling of conversion to digital from 2008 to 2010–2012. The United Kingdom, United States, Ireland and the Netherlands have also delayed their digital conversion dates (Commonwealth of Australia 2006: 6). In mid-2009 in Australia, community radio stations were not being greatly disadvantaged by their lack of a digital signal. And in any case, digital radio is not expected to fully replace analogue services: they will operate alongside each other, with digital radio acting as a supplement – rather than as a replacement – for analogue radio. While commercial media proprietors jostle for position to be the first, most profitable and/or biggest on the block (Knight 2005), audiences for community radio and television maintain their enthusiasm for local content that is relevant to local communities. This is especially the case for Indigenous and ethnic audiences who have few media alternatives. The imminent reduction in the number of media owners suggest that the services offered by community broadcasting services are entering a new age of importance. But what is community broadcasting and how can it be defined?

Defining community media

Throughout this book, we have adopted the term 'community' rather than 'alternative' to describe the broadcasting activities of Indigenous and ethnic communities, acknowledging the active global debate around the theoretical definition of this process of production and participation (Rodriguez 2001; Forde et al. 2003; Bailey et al. 2008; Gordon 2009). In our earlier national study of Australian community radio, we concluded that it is a significant cultural resource – 'a medium for representing, maintaining and reproducing local cultures' (Forde et al. 2002: 13). Commercial media are unable – perhaps unwilling – to deal with the diversity of cultures that characterize the modern Australian nation state. This is because of a perceived lack of profit stemming from smaller markets and the likelihood of offending audiences (thus losing advertisers) through the broadcast of unpalatable political and/or social viewpoints, Indigenous and ethnic language programming, specialist music formats and so on. Our approach is to consider community radio and television alongside broader concepts of democracy, citizenship and the creation and maintenance of 'community public spheres', an idea we will develop more in chapter six (Forde et al. 2003). We conceptualize community broadcasting workers as involved in a form of participatory democracy and active citizenship located 'within the everyday achievements of ordinary people' (Rennie 2002: 12).

In this chapter, we investigate different examples of 'community media', presenting our own Australian experiences within an international context. It is difficult to provide a single definition which encompasses the activities, and the local and global manifestations of community media. The ways in which the sector services a plethora of communities, alongside the different ways in which these types of media are produced, suggests a single organizational framework is difficult to sustain. Debate over definitions is indicative of the general status of theory surrounding the operations of community media in general. It is variously referred to as 'radical media', 'grassroots media', 'citizens media', 'alternative media', 'minority ethnic media' and so on (Downing 1984; 2001 ; Girard 1992; Rodriguez, 2001; Atton, 2002; Downing and Husband 2005). Different researchers focus on different aspects of the sector which generate different ideas about an appropriate definition. Howley (2005: 2) has adopted the term 'community' and offers a broad definition which seems to reflect many of the elements common to this array. He argues that 'community' can describe media that emerge from a dissatisfaction with mainstream media form and content with a strong progressive, participatory democratic element aimed at promoting community relations and solidarity. A tenuous consensus of what constitutes community radio seems to have emerged around four key elements: community ownership and control, community service, community participation and a non-profit business model (Fairbairn 2009: 7). An alternative definition – and one which resonates more with our own approach – emerges from a recent study of community media in the United States by the Benton Foundation. This focuses on the key defining characteristics of community media: localism, diverse participation, storytelling and deliberation and empowerment (Johnson 2007: 3–4). In particular, it is the latter concept – empowerment – that we seek to reclaim and reinforce as a fundamental dimension of all community media activity.

Although using the term 'class media' to describe the general field, Gutierrez (2006: 259–260) argues community media expansion has been driven by the growth of 'ethnic media'. He highlights two key influences on the emergence of this phenomenon:

> One is a growth in international migration and settlements composed of people from what were earlier identified as Third World countries to more developed nations. Second is the development of media technologies that facilitate instant communication across borders, cultures and languages to and through machines that are cheaper, smaller and easier to use than ever (2006: 260).

This emphasis on diaspora and technology is of particular importance to ethnic community radio in Australia. It is clear that ethnic groups use such media to simultaneously 'become part of and to distance themselves from other groups' (Deuze 2006: 271) – central elements of the processes of social cohesion and identity formation. But it is important to make a distinction here between ethnic and Indigenous media. The latter is sometimes referred to as First Nations media which perhaps affords it an appropriate status in the 'alternative' media hierarchy. Much energy has been expended by scholars – and, no doubt, has yet to be expended – debating the whys and wherefores of definitions and terminologies. At the 2008 Congress for the International Association for Mass Communication Research (IAMCR), for example, questions were raised about several forms of community communication – so-called 'local radio' in Japan and 'lamp post radio' in the *Favelas* (or slums) of Rio de Janiero – and whether they could actually be called 'community radio' (Yamada 2000; Ishikawa 1996, Medrado 2008). Perhaps it is because both rely more than other forms of 'alternative' media on local, community-driven commercial support. But does this make them somehow less 'community' in nature? There has even been a suggestion for some form of 'accreditation' for community media which would seem to effectively negate many of their 'alternative' claims. What is more important is understanding the *processes* involved. As Bickford (1996: 144) reminds us: 'Listening, like speaking, is a creative act, one that involves conscious effort.' This suggests that listening to community radio – or engaging with community media in whatever form it is produced – is worthy of our attention, underlined by this observation (Foundation for Development Corporation 2004): n.p.

> Media, too, plays an important part in cultural communication as well as in information dissemination. Local media can get close to the creators of culture, encouraging them to

express themselves in song, plays, festivals and stories, and conveying the people's voices and opinions to policy and decision makers at local, national and international levels. Citizens who feel they are being listened to are likely to participate with more vigour and enthusiasm in society than those who are treated primarily as a consumer there to receive whatever is offered from above.

Community-based communication operates globally in many different forms and by limiting this to a preferred – or 'accredited' – option limits the exciting possibilities which are emerging when communities with a 'will to communicate' adopt the most appropriate tools to achieve their aims (Hochheimer 1999). While local media access has the potential to empower audiences by giving them some control over representation – and thus enabling participation in the processes of the broader public sphere – the context in which these media are produced, distributed and received remains crucial to an understanding of their role and impact (Bailey et al. 2008: xi–xv). For example, Carpentier et al. (2003: 60) argue that the distinction between community media, the state and the market fosters social antagonisms which do not capture community media's actual or potential role in broader society. This suggests the need for a more open interpretation of what Elghul-Bebawi (2009: 29) has termed 'the alterity' of community media – one that can take account of the real-world processes of production and reception and the power relations involved. The term 'community', of course, is itself highly contested. Couldry offers a solution of sorts, drawing on cultural studies to resolve the apparent impasse over meaning:

> But the name matters much less than the way we conceive the purpose of that space, which, while falling short of the achievement of politics, should enact one of its essential preconditions: that is, citizens' mutual respect for each other's inalienable capacity to contribute as agents to the public sphere (2003: 17).

Nancy Fraser has suggested thinking about the public sphere in terms of multiple layers or 'public arenas'. We have termed these 'community public spheres' – places where particular 'communities of interest' such as Indigenous and ethnic peoples are able to engage in activities involving issues and interests of importance to them. As we will argue, this process fosters social cohesion rather than social dislocation. It echoes the idea of 'free spaces' (Atton 2002: 156) and 'autonomous public spheres [which] can acquire influence in the mass media public sphere under certain circumstances' (Downing and Fenton 2003: 188). Taking this idea further, Downing and Husband (2005: 22) highlight the importance of 'minority ethnic media', describing them as 'infrastructural prerequisites of a viable multi-ethnic public sphere'.

But however they are defined, community media have emerged from the margins in the past decade. Biennial audience surveys in Australia since 2002 reveal a steady increase in listeners for community radio across the country (McNair Ingenuity 2004; 2006; 2008). An outpouring of published work on community media by scholars, globally, is further evidence of this shift. Atton and Couldry (2003: 580) suggest four reasons for this:

1. A revival of social activism around anti-globalization in the late 1990s.
2. Loss of other critical traditions in media and cultural studies (ideological analysis).
3. Bankruptcy of Western models of democratic practice.
4. A re-focusing of global development organizations on the importance of educational, social and political empowerment to local and global peace.

It may also be due to what Mattelart (1994: 200) suggests as the 'fractured, incomplete and compelling' links between media and globalization. But at the heart of this is culture. He continues (1994: 241):

> Culture is the collective memory that makes communication possible between members of a historically situated community, creating amongst its members a community of meaning (the *expressive function*), allowing them to adapt to an economic environment (the *economic function*), and finally, giving them the ability to construct rational argument about the values implicit in the prevailing form of social relations (the rhetorical function, that of legitimation/delegitimation).

A global trend towards democratization has also created a challenge for societies in the form of 'oppositions and antagonisms' manifested in various forms of difference – ethnic, linguistic, national, religious, cultural – that have emerged (Benhabib 1996: 3). Community media in various forms have become communication tools for these and other communities of interest, creating for some an 'ambivalence of media that creates enclaves that threaten social cohesion but help to support social movements' (Downing and Fenton 2003: 189). But is this necessarily the case? Our experiences with Australia's diverse community broadcasting sector suggests a *strengthening* of social cohesion through these very media (Meadows et al. 2007; 2009). It alerts us to the importance of paying attention to the particular contexts in which these media forms are active.

Global trends

Since our initial national study of the Australian community radio sector from 1999, there has been growing academic attention directed towards community media research. This is evident in a significant increase in numbers of published journal articles, including establishment of the *3CMedia* electronic journal in Australia (published on the community broadcasting sector's portal, CBOnline – www.cbonline.org.au), book titles and special journal editions dedicated to community and grassroots media forms (Rodriguez 2001; Downing 2001; Forde et al 2002; Atton 2002; *Journalism* 2003; *Transformations* 2005; McCauley 2005; Howley 2005; Meadows et al. 2007; Chitty and Rattichalkalakorn 2007; Coyer et al. 2007; Fuller 2007; Carpentier and de Cleen 2007; Bailey et al. 2008; Gordon 2009; Rodriguez et al. 2010). This has been accompanied by growth in the number of local, national and international conferences with a 'community media' theme, along with an increase in the number of groups seeking membership as community broadcasting activists. This is especially evident within the active OurMedia (2008) network and at its recent international conferences. The official establishment of the UK community radio sector in 2004 is another indicator of change. By mid-2009, almost 200 licences had been issued (Lewis and Scifo 2007; Ofcom 2009; Gordon 2009; Scifo 2009).

The rise in community media research – and indeed in community media forms – could be quite simply attributed to increasing globalization and an increasing need for people to feel 'connected' to their local communities. Internationally, scholars are beginning to consider seriously the impact of the community media sector within the context of globalization and its potential impact on local cultures. The importance of community-based media is growing within the context of the ever-expanding global media industry. One impact, amongst others, is 'less competition and diversity, and more corporate control of newspapers and journalism, television, radio, film and other media of information and entertainment' (Kellner and Durham 2006: xxix). And despite some sign that large media corporations' expansion plans have been slowed by the US Senate (McChesney and Nichols 2008), the current state of global media ownership remains significantly concentrated to cause concern. This is especially the case in Australia which has amongst the most concentrated media ownership structures in the Western world. It underlines the importance of the community media sector in a globalized world where the representation of local cultures has increasingly become more of a commercial enterprise than a community service. In this media environment, audiences are perceived as 'consumers' rather than 'citizens'.

Dissatisfaction with mainstream and particularly, commercial media forms, appears to be playing a significant role in the growth of popularity in community media. Primary news decisions and content have become more heavily dependent on economic considerations, leading to a greater emphasis on infotainment, the rise of the celebrity journalist and an increasing focus on issues of interest to groups targeted by advertisers (Chomsky 1997; McChesney 2003; Hamilton 2004). This is occurring alongside trends which show a steady decline in audiences worldwide for mainstream news content (Davis 1997; Lewis 2001; Hamilton 2004; Project for Excellence in Journalism 2004 & 2006 ; Deuze 2006). The credibility of journalists working in Australian mainstream media remains firmly lodged around the level of 'advertisers, real estate agents and car sellers' (Australian Press Council 2006; *Sydney Morning Herald* 2007). Australian journalists were in twenty-fourth position on a 2008 credibility list headed by nurses, pharmacists, doctors and teachers (Roy Morgan Research 2008). British journalist Nick Davies' investigation into journalism practices there has revealed that around 12 percent of the more than 2,000 stories he examined were generated by reporters – the remainder had their genesis in wire service copy or public relations handouts, a process Davies describes as 'churnalism' (Beecher 2008: 15; Davies 2008). Public relations and journalism have never been closer bedfellows and the situation in Australia is no different. One study of Brisbane journalists in 2008 found that around half acknowledged that the biggest attraction of PR was its ability to 'identify' stories.

This is more than double the number identified in a survey two years earlier. One-fifth acknowledged that they relied on press releases to generate stories, almost three times the number identified in 2006. None of the journalists' surveys admitted that PR could *not* help them in their work (BBS 2008: 4).

But there could be other reasons for audiences turning away from the mainstream media. Almost half of all Australians surveyed in 2006 found it difficult to read text from newspapers, magazines and brochures (Australian Bureau of Statistics 2006). This suggests that the future of journalism lies in it offering specific content to increasingly fragmented audiences (Beecher 2008: 15).

There is little doubt that community radio, in particular, is playing a central role in enabling communities to find a voice in diverse environments around the world. Like most Western democracies, Australia has a system of community broadcasting that has managed to evolve without undue influence from the state, a stark contrast to other parts of the world such as Africa, Asia and Latin America where governments make it their business to control – or at least attempt to control – virtually every aspect of media (Camara 1996: 20–21; Mdlalose 1997: 14). Development radio projects such as those in Nepal (Radio Sagarmatha), Sri Lanka (Kothmale Community Radio) and the Philippines (Tambuli Community Radio) rely on support from NGOs or bodies such as UNESCO to survive in often hostile social and political environments (UNESCO 2003). Relatively recent government approval for community radio development in India offers NGOs and educational institutions new access to the airwaves with some estimating 4,000 stations could quickly emerge (UNESCO 2007).

One of the few examples of qualitative audience research into community radio use comes from Thailand where there are around 3,000 community radio stations operating around the country – 500 in Bangkok alone (Polnigongit 2005; 2007). Most perform the role of non-government organizations in terms of responding to natural disasters – tsunamis and crisis management activities, similar to the role performed by Japan's community radio during the 1996 Kobe earthquake (Kawakami 2007). The gradual and clandestine nature of the emergence of a community radio network in Thailand has some resonance with the formation of an Aboriginal public sphere in Canada and Australia where access to what now amount to alternative communications networks was won through stealth, rather than through overt government action. Now the community broadcasting networks in both countries offer a powerful mobilizing forum for alternative views. This, in turn, has acted to expose the 'cracks' in mainstream broadcasting, in particular, offering a powerful critique of mainstream media and its public sphere role. The station network in Thailand began as an educational tool but was seen to offer an alternative because of the government monopoly of mainstream broadcasting – 95 percent of television and radio is under government control. As an example of the growing influence of community radio in Thailand, former journalist and TV presenter Sondhi Cimtholkul was sacked in 2000 for criticizing the Thai government. He set up his own news website and in news reports during the 2006 coup, regularly used local community radio broadcasts as his sources (Chitty 2006). The lack of alternatives in Thailand explain why community radio has gained such a strong foothold there – readership of the country's newspapers is confined to the elite, around 5 percent of the population, with fewer than 10 percent having Internet access in 2006.

Polnigongit's (2005; 2007) study of Mukduhan Province's 'enterprise radio' near the Thai-Laos border found that it was welcomed by communities because of the opportunity to participate and to receive a better signal than other stations in the area. A survey revealed that two-thirds of the local population identified 'listening' as participation (Bickford 1996), and highlighting the importance of local information. Around 20 percent of the audience also actively participates through music requests, on-air competitions and volunteering. Audiences revealed that the station was playing an important cross-cultural role in bringing Thais and Laotians together through music request programmes (Polnigongit 2005; 2007). This reflects a similar role for music requests used extensively by Indigenous communities across Australia to maintain social and family networks (Meadows et al. 2007: 53).

Following the freeing up of access to the airwaves in 1993, around 150 community radio stations were licensed in South Africa within seven years (Tacchi and Price-Davies 2001). The possibilities offered by 'innovative and vibrant programming' in various local languages through community media has been identified as having a major impact on rural development in Africa (Onkaetse Mmusi 2002). Based on her case study of Bush Radio in South Africa, Bosch (2005, n.p.) argues that although community radio there is not becoming more powerful than larger forms of media, it is growing horizontally, 'creating ripples under the surface'. Drawing from rhizome theory, she likens its structure to that of an organism, 'held together by a complex set of interlinked structures', with the concept of community 'pulsating as its central life-force'. But in comparing Bush Radio to two popular Namibian radio talk programmes, Kivikuru (2006) has argued for the inappropriateness of Western notions of community and alternative media as frameworks for understanding the 'panorama of oppositional cultures' that are inevitably exposed by such stations. The author suggests that the Namibian stations are using community radio 'to generate dialogue', enabling people to talk to and understand each other. On the surface, at least, the processes identified here seem in tune with community broadcasting experiences in Australia – and elsewhere – particularly those emanating from Indigenous and ethnic communities. Continuing political machinations in Zimbabwe have led to calls for access to community broadcasting although this seems unlikely in view of unrelenting government controls over the airwaves in that country (Zhangazha 2002).

A 2002 study of broadcasting in Afghanistan – before recent deterioration in internal affairs – concluded that community radio is not only a viable option for that nation, but also a 'low-cost and effective way of contributing to medium and long-term efforts for reconstruction, development, democracy and nation-building' (Girard and van der Spek 2002). Although Latin American community radio is considered to be the most dynamic and diversified, like many other regions, it operates in a problematic legal and political environment (Girard 1992; Lopez-Vigil 1996: 8–9; Truglia 1996: 10–11).

Japan's community radio sector is based in many parts of the country around large shopping centres. Since relaxation of licensing regulations by the Ministry of Post and

Telecommunication in 1994, the number of community stations increased to more than 200 in 2006, with many of the licensees being local government authorities. Japan's emerging community television industry set up its first peak representative body late in 2006 – further evidence of a growing global interest in media alternatives (Yamada 2000; Ishikawa 1996: 10; Kawakami 2007). Some see these radio and television stations falling outside the definition of 'community', apart from a handful, preferring instead the term, 'local', to describe them. However, their commercial orientation does not necessarily override the clear community connections many have made. This may be more of a debate over a definition rather than a focus on role. A similar discussion has been underway in the United States where a resurgence of pirate radio reflects community dissatisfaction with licensed community broadcasters becoming 'less distinguishable from mainstream media' (Robinson 1997: 17). The United States National Public Radio (NPR) has an audience share of around 10 percent (McCauley 2005). In October 2009, the US Government House Committee approved a new Local Community Radio Act enabling the creation of potentially hundreds of low power FM community stations across the country. This will represent a significant boost for community media in North America (Prometheus Radio Project 2009). Further north, the community radio sector in Canada has been well established since the 1970s with more than 200 campus and community stations operating on miniscule annual budgets of around AUD$10,000. Native broadcasting in Canada makes extensive use of community radio, particularly in remote areas (Girard 1992: 10; Meadows 1994; Tacchi and Price-Davies 2001; Roth 2005) whereas state-controlled systems pervade the Pacific Islands and Papua New Guinea (Robie 1995; Alvarez 1997; Molnar and Meadows 2001). The innovative and expanding People First Network (PFNet) in the Solomon Islands, supported largely by international funding, continues to use wireless email communication to link hundreds of people in island communities throughout the archipelago (Biliki et al. 2005; Pipol Fastaem 2008). Along similar lines, emerging community radio in the Caribbean is looking at the Internet as a dynamic medium in the struggle for empowerment (Josiah 2000). The World Association of Community Radio Broadcasters (AMARC) facilitates a network of around 4,000 community radio stations, federations and community media stakeholders in more than 115 countries. Since its creation in 1983, AMARC has supported the growth of community radio internationally and has strongly advocated democratizing the media sector (AMARC 2008).

The recent surge in Western academic interest in community media has been spurred on, in part, by the establishment in 2004 of the UK community broadcasting sector and a sudden expansion of new community radio and television licensees. Experiments with 'access' radio in the United Kingdom began around the turn of the millennium with pilot projects achieving their 'social gain' goals (Everitt 2002; Gordon 2007; Lewis and Scifo 2007; Scifo 2007; Gordon 2009). Although yet to be the subject of an extensive audience study, early evidence suggests the growing UK sector is recruiting and training volunteers with most stations linked into existing community networks including local authorities. While this is a cause for celebration by community radio workers and the national regulator,

Ofcom, alike, Gordon (2009: 77) reminds us that sector sustainability will require stations to balance financial security against editorial independence and to continue to examine their relationships with their audiences. This parallels the modus operandi of community radio stations in Australia. Interestingly, too, already issues such as volunteer burnout and the difficulty of fund-raising have emerged (Everitt 2002; Gordon 2009). Ofcom is considering pursuing various audience research pathways to chart the growth and nature of the burgeoning UK community radio sector (Williams 2007). In its first annual report on the sector in March 2009, Ofcom acknowledged that the 131 stations on air at the time were meeting their obligations to deliver social gain to audiences by reflecting the diverse cultures, demographics and tastes that define the UK (Ofcom 2009). The same is true of community radio in Ireland where it has demonstrated its relevance, particularly for migrant communities in terms of both programme production and broadcasting skills acquisition (Moylan 2009).

While media activists in the United Kingdom have successfully lobbied for change, broadcasting legislation in Eastern and Central Europe has been in major transition since 1989 as nation-states shift from totalitarian to democratic forms of government (Kleinwächter 1995; Hirner 1996). Meanwhile, Western Europe has its own problems to confront with public broadcasting under threat from a creeping concentration of media ownership and its attendant limits on pluralism, diversity and quality of information (Peters 2004). While the European Broadcasting Union has committed itself to supporting public service broadcasting – the heart of an e-Europe (European Broadcasting Union 2001) – AMARC continues its efforts to advance discussion and debate on anti-racism and human rights through its European network of community stations. Countries such as France, with its 600 'free' or 'associative' radio stations, and the Netherlands, with 'local' radio, continue to support extensive community broadcasting sectors, with the number of stations steadily increasing. In 2007, Holland had 335 community radio and television stations as part of its community network now recognized as the country's third tier of broadcasting (Stevenson 2006: 2; *OLONieuws* 2007: 4; de Wit 2007; Hollander 2007). A study commissioned by the European Parliament's Committee on Culture and Education concluded that community media activity is highest in Europe's north-west states and is 'closely related to public awareness and legal recognition of the sector as well as to the existence of underlying regulatory procedures' (Kern European Affairs 2007: iii). The study found that the sector across Europe is highly diverse with audiences for community media varying 'significantly'. Importantly, the report identified 'low levels of awareness amongst policy makers regarding this sector and its potential societal contributions' (Kern European Affairs 2007: iii).

In July 2008, a report entitled *Promoting Social Cohesion: The Role of Community Media* took up the very issue of the contribution community media makes to society. Commissioned by the Council of Europe and authored primarily by long-standing UK community radio advocate Peter Lewis, the report urged the European Parliament to 'recognize the social value of community media and its role as a form of local public service', concluding (Lewis 2008: 33):

In a hugely changed media landscape, community media have an important role to play. The perceived need to communicate a sense of and participation in the European project at local and regional level, and the challenges posed by the presence of migrant communities – as well as the benefits they bring to their host communities – are issues that can be addressed most effectively at the local level. The sector is already making a substantial contribution to social cohesion, community engagement and regeneration. It is time to give it the support it deserves.

The European Parliament accepted the report in September 2008, acknowledging:

> Community media promote intercultural dialogue by educating the general public, combating negative stereotypes and correcting the ideas put forward by the mass media regarding communities within society threatened with exclusion, such as refugees, migrants, Roma and other ethnic and religious minorities…[and]…that community media are one of the existing means of facilitating the integration of immigrants and also enabling disadvantaged members of society to become active participants by engaging in debates that are important to them (European Parliament 2008).

The report acknowledged the importance of audience research, suggesting our Australian study and its methodology as an appropriate model for community media audience research in Europe and the United Kingdom (Lewis 2008: 23–24, 29). There is little doubt that community radio and television audience research in the United Kingdom and Europe, in their comparatively early stages of development, will add a critical dimension to our knowledge and understanding of the production and reception of alternative media. Most of this discussion necessarily has focused on community radio as it is the most widespread communication medium enlisted by various audiences globally, but we should remember that local television and online media are part of the mélange (Milioni 2009; Stewart 2009). Nevertheless, the technologies involved – radio, television, online, etc. – remain secondary in understanding the processes and relationships that create 'community' media.

Conclusion

An increasing global interest in community media – and research into its significance and impact – seems inexorably linked to the processes of globalization and a need for people to remain 'connected' to their local communities. The importance of community-based media is clearly growing within the context of the ever-expanding global media industry, producing 'less competition and diversity, and more corporate control of newspapers and journalism, television, radio, film and other media of information and entertainment' (Kellner and Durham 2006: xxix). It is indicative of the community media sector's importance in a globalized world where the maintenance and representation of local cultures through the media has increasingly become guided by commercial enterprise rather than being seen as a community service with links to ideas of citizenship rather than consumerism.

On a global scale, community broadcasting has the potential to reinstate the central 'community service' role of the media to revitalize public sphere debate at the local level. We acknowledge that there are 'degrees of success' in this pursuit. However, the research we have undertaken in Australia, alongside the mounting international efforts presented here, combine to indicate a development in the way communities encounter the media. As we discuss later in this book, the capacity of citizens all over the world to produce and receive local media heralds a challenge to the established processes of mass communication. This change to community-based production of their own media is, in part, a response to the forces of globalization – evident in global movements of peoples and the capacity of relatively inexpensive new communication technology to traverse national boundaries. The opportunity to address the challenges presented by Australian and international experiences of the diaspora is one of community broadcasting's key strengths. As First People's media, community broadcasting re/produces and supports Indigenous cultures giving meaning to their experiences of processes like colonization, enabling the appropriation of new technology to revitalize traditional cultures within the context of a global media environment. Particularly for Indigenous and ethnic audiences, community broadcasting facilitates social cohesion and harmony – by empowering these marginalized groups with the capacity to represent themselves to each other – and to communicate and validate their presence and place within the broader understanding of culture.

Our aim in this book is to problematize the current definitions of community media and, of course, to offer our own perspectives, based on evidence drawn from the first study to include the processes of community media production *and* reception. This has enabled us to investigate the nature of the complex relationships that define 'producers' and 'audiences'. We will argue that the very nature of this relationship is a principle defining characteristic of community broadcasting – and community media more broadly. In the next chapter, we consider the first element of this equation – the producers.

Chapter 3

Producers and Policies

Community broadcasting fulfils diverse roles in Australia. The sector represents a valuable cultural resource that contributes to the nation's rich and diverse heritage through its commitment to maintaining, representing and reproducing local cultures. That was the basis on which community radio was established in Australia more than 35 years ago and this philosophy persists. Despite a significant shift in emphasis during that period – from an early dominance by urban-based 'alternative' stations to today's predominance of generally more politically conservative rural and regional radio – the community sector overwhelmingly defines itself in terms of its commitment to local audiences (Forde et al. 2002). No other media sector operating in the public sphere in Australia has the capacity to do this.

The evidence suggests that the term 'alternative', used to describe community radio in its early years, may be misleading. This tag does not adequately account for the multiple roles now being performed by community radio and television stations and is quite overtly rejected by some in the community sector. While many community broadcasting employees, volunteers and audiences assert their commitment to contesting mainstream and dominant representations of Australian culture, they consistently identify the local roles they perform as crucial to their sense of identity. This perception highlights the empowering process facilitated by local access and participation and the relationships that exist both within stations and through their many and varied connections with local communities (Forde et al. 2002). We will address this in more detail in chapter six.

Community radio and television in Australia promote citizenship by enabling diverse cultures access to broadcasting opportunities and thus, access to the public sphere. It is one of the few places where neglected or marginalized communities can find a voice. The key to the success of community broadcasting success is its functionality – where local communities identify concrete outcomes from their involvement with stations at any level, then their participation will continue. It creates a sense of community ownership demonstrated time and time again in examples offered during the many national focus group discussions we have undertaken (Forde et al. 2002; Meadows et al. 2007). One of the processes we have observed is either a weakening or a dissolution of the traditional boundary between audiences and programme producers. These characteristics are most obvious with Indigenous and ethnic community radio and television. Audiences for such stations have become resources for the development of multiple and complex media and cultural literacies through participation on a localized and personalized scale. Indigenous and ethnic community broadcasting establishes a sense of personal and community power for audiences who have already expressed a desire to communicate (Hochheimer 1999). In these ways, the Australian community broadcasting sector plays an important role in encouraging dialogue between diverse cultural arenas – the process which is integral to sustaining community social structure.

An Australian sector snapshot

In Australia, discrete sections of the *Broadcasting Services Act* 1992 offer a legislative framework for community broadcasting. Amongst other principles, the *Act* requires that community stations be not-for-profit, represent the community they have been licensed to represent and significantly, that stations encourage their communities to participate in their operations and programme content. Unlike other media, community radio and television see their listeners as potential volunteers and perform a vital task in the Australian community enabling representation in the public sphere for those who would otherwise be denied access.

Three-quarters of those working in the community radio sector were born in Australia, which reflects almost exactly the proportion in the broader Australian community (Australian Bureau of Statistics 2006). A further one in ten community radio workers was born in Britain, which is slightly above the general population figure of 6 percent. About 2 percent were born in either Africa or Asia, with continental Europe comprising the most popular non-Anglo/Celtic place of birth (see Figure 1). Most ethnic groupings seem to be over-represented in the sector, a good indicator of its cultural diversity; and it also suggests some superficial evidence that the sector is fulfilling its legislative brief to be providing a voice for groups unrepresented elsewhere.

The Australian government established a dual radio broadcasting system in Australia in 1932. This consisted of the Australian Broadcasting Commission (now known as the Australian Broadcasting Corporation [ABC]) as publicly owned and funded, and commercial services which were privately owned, operating only in specific areas. This broadcasting arrangement remained relatively unchanged until 1972 when grassroots movements and other political forces joined to campaign for a third tier in Australia's broadcasting environment (Bear 1983). Dissatisfaction with existing broadcasters prompted music enthusiasts, educators, ethnic groups, religious groups, trade unionists, Aboriginal and Torres Strait Islanders and other interested parties to lobby for community access to the airwaves. Between 1972 and 1975, the Labor government granted the first low-powered community radio licences for the broadcast of educational material to universities (Moran 1995: 151; Thornley 1995; Barlow 1999). 'Fine music' or classical music stations in Sydney – 2MBS in 1974 – and 3MBS in Melbourne in 1977 – soon followed. In 1978, the new politically conservative coalition federal government enshrined the third tier of Australian broadcasting in legislation. Many authors have attributed the birth of the community radio movement to the reformist federal Labor government headed by Prime Minister Gough Whitlam. However, Thornley (1995)

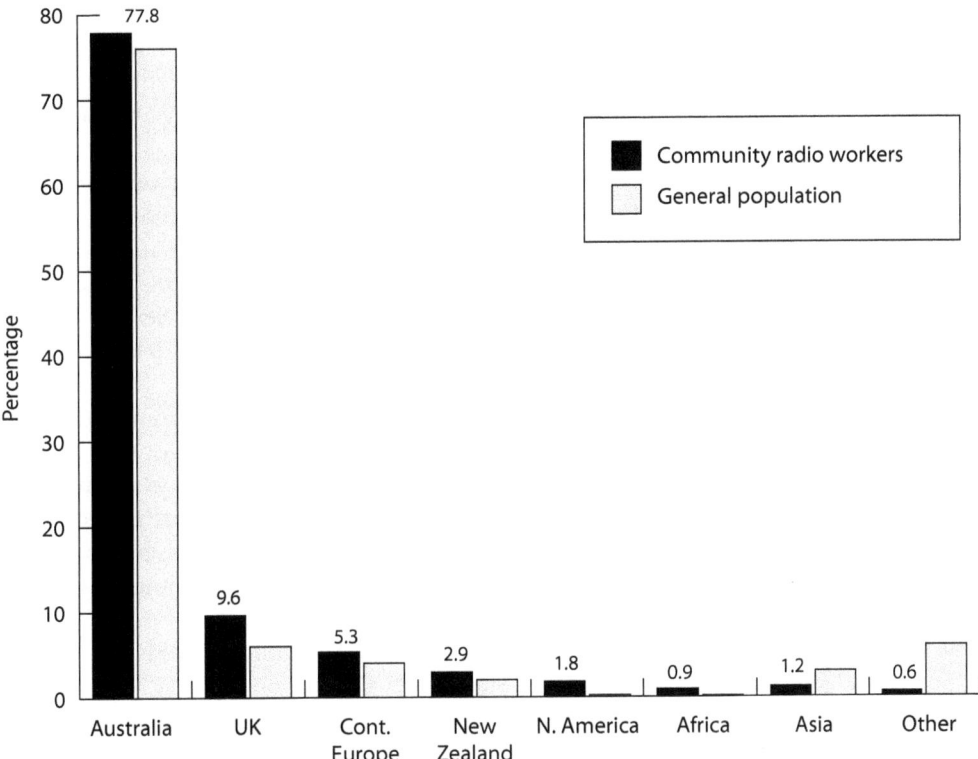

Figure 1: Countries of birth.

gives equal credit to both the Coalition (conservative) and Labor governments, but notes the first licences were granted during the albeit brief Labor era.

As is the case today, the early supporters and participants of community radio and television represented a diversity of interests. Bear (1979: 5–7) isolates four different groups that were primary participants in the development of the sector: fine or classical music buffs, ethnic communities, educational institutions and political groups. These four groups maintain a strong presence in the community broadcasting landscape and have continued to evolve over the past 35 years.

The first FM station in Australia, 2MBS in Sydney, demanded 'fine music' on community radio and significantly, better reception via the FM spectrum. In 1991, the Australian Fine Music Network was established for marketing and other purposes. Fine music stations (with a broader definition than 'classical music' – now including jazz, blues, folk, light opera and other formats) are established in every state in Australia and cater for musical tastes often absent in mainstream radio. Arguably the most successful of this group, 4MBS in Brisbane, stages Australia's largest classical music festival each year with minimal funding support from government or other sources. It has managed to harness an extraordinary passion amongst music lovers, local musicians, music and choral societies and has become a model internationally. Station manager for the past twenty years Gary Thorpe attributes the station's success to a recognition that it is 'merely one arm of a music community' (Thorpe 2006).

A second pressure group, ethnic communities, sought access to the airwaves to ensure programming in languages other than English and to undertake their own culturally relevant programming. In 1975, radio stations 2EA and 3EA went to air in Sydney and Melbourne respectively, although these were then operated by the Federal Department of the Media. They were later absorbed into the newly established Special Broadcasting Service (SBS) in 1977. Ethnic community radio stations were launched in Brisbane and Adelaide over the next three years (Moran 1995: 150–151).

The third impetus for the development of community radio came from educational institutions. The University of Newcastle and the University of Adelaide were the first to become involved in community radio. In 1975, the federal Labor government issued twelve experimental radio licences to groups generally associated with tertiary education institutions. Stations with an educational brief cover a broad range of interests by providing access to many communities including ethnic, educational, women, Indigenous Australians, youth, gay and lesbian and music groups (Moran 1995: 151).

The fourth element represented in the push for access to the public broadcasting airwaves was politically progressive (Bear 1979: 7). Stations in this group include stations 4ZzZ (Brisbane), 2SER (Sydney), 3RRR (Melbourne), 3PBS (Melbourne), 5MMM (Adelaide) and Canberra's 2XX. These stations enable access by Indigenous people, gays and lesbians, environmental groups, young people, anti-drug law campaigners and other politically marginalized groups. All stations in this grouping have adopted a strong commitment to local non-commercial music and have been responsible for launching the careers of many popular artists.

The Australian community broadcasting sector has experienced extraordinary growth in the past two decades in terms of both the number of licensed stations and the size of their audiences. At the end of 2008, the 483 licensed independent community-owned and operated broadcasting services included the following: 353 long-term licensed community radio stations and four permanent generalist community television stations. In addition, 46 aspirant organizations were operating with temporary broadcasting licences. Four long-term licensed community television stations produce 33 hours of ethnic programming in an average week. Community radio outlets have trebled in number since the early 1990s and almost all of them now broadcast 24 hours a day, seven days a week. Australia's commercial radio sector has around 270 operating licences with an estimated annual turnover of AU$1 billion dollars compared with the community sector's annual revenue of about AU$70 million. Community broadcasting's 23,000 volunteers contributed an estimated AU$300 million to the Australian economy in 2008 but perhaps more significantly, the community sector produces more local content, more Australian music and reflects a greater diversity of Australian cultures than its commercial and government-funded national broadcasting counterparts (CB Online 2008: 24–25).

The contemporary community radio scene in Australia retains the legacy of fine music, ethnic, educational and politically progressive stations and now boasts additional categories including specialist sports stations, Radio for the Print Handicapped (RPH), Indigenous stations, youth and religious/Christian stations. At first glance, it may appear that these diverse programming formats have very little in common. The *sine qua non* of community radio is its philosophy of community access and participation. A 'community' may be defined in terms of specific audience interests (musical style, for example), or is based on geographical or cultural boundaries. However defined, enabling local access to the airwaves is a consistent and central theme of community radio across the country.

The commitment to 'democratizing' the airwaves is particularly evident in the community broadcasting sector's Code of Practice (required under section 123 of the *Broadcasting Services Act* 1992). Amongst other principles, the code clearly states a responsibility to widen the community's involvement in broadcasting and to encourage participation by those denied effective access to, and those not adequately served by other media (See Figure 2). This is a key feature that differentiates community radio from its commercial counterparts. The capacity of community radio to provide access to groups not adequately served by mainstream media is a consequence of both their 'local community' and 'not-for-profit' status. Operating on a not-for-profit basis has traditionally allowed community broadcasters to pay less attention to audience share and to focus more on their community's profile and needs. However, the increase in audience data stemming from recent qualitative and quantitative sector research means that stations have become much more conscious of

---

There are a number of general principles that unite all community broadcasters across Australia. In pursuing these principles stations endeavour to:

- Promote harmony and diversity in contributing to a cohesive, inclusive and culturally diverse Australian community;
- Pursue the principles of democracy, access and equity, especially to people and issues under-represented in other media;
- Enhance the diversity of programming choices available to the public and present programmes which expand the variety of viewpoints broadcast in Australia;
- Demonstrate independence in their programming as well as in their editorial and management decisions;
- Support and develop local and Australian arts, music and culture in the station's programming, to reflect a sense of Australian identity, character and cultural diversity;
- Widen the community's involvement in broadcasting.

Source: CBAA Codes of Practice, available at http://www.cbaa.org.au/content.php/16.html.

Figure 2: Australian Community Broadcasting Code of Practice: Guiding Principles.

their listeners – who and how many there are – and are now able to address any perceived issues that arise.

The community broadcasting sector is a key cultural resource in that it offers ways of representing, maintaining and reproducing local cultures. In some ways, this is equally applicable to commercial broadcasting. The difference is that community broadcasting's commitment to the local and to marginalized groups *not* served by mainstream media means that it is able to represent a diversity of cultures in ways that are not possible elsewhere in the Australian mediascape. Commercial media are primarily concerned with selling audiences to advertisers and cannot afford to offend these by broadcasting radical political viewpoints, ethnic language programming or music formats with specialist appeal, for example. Besides, smaller regional markets do not offer commercial radio feasible returns for financial investment. A 2001 inquiry by the Australian Parliament into local radio found that although there had been a substantial increase in the number of commercial radio services to regional areas, networking and syndicated services from metropolitan centres, pre-recording and automation diminished a real commitment to local content. The inquiry found that the principal reason for the lack of local commercial radio services to regional areas related to commercial viability. Community radio can serve these regional and rural audiences and encourage them to actively broadcast their ideas for the simple reason that it has long been its primary responsibility to do so. The inquiry acknowledged that there were around 30 regional centres in Australia where the community radio station was the *only* local service available (House of Representatives Standing Committee on Communication, Transport and the Arts 2001).

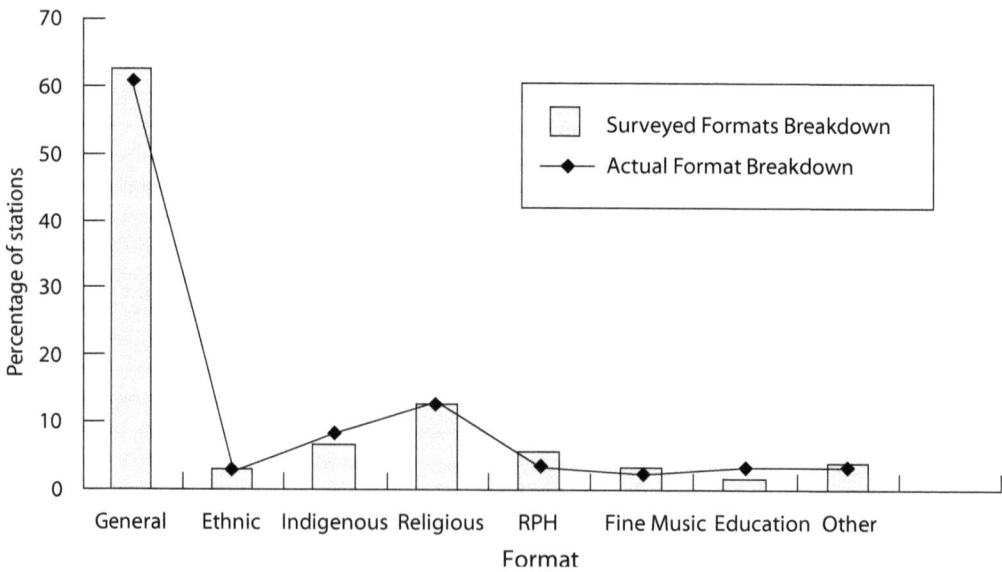

Figure 3: Station formats in survey and actual station formats.

While there are clearly differences between community and commercial radio formats, it is problematic to reduce the community broadcasting sector simply to an 'alternative' to its commercial and public sector counterparts. The danger in seeing community radio as providing an 'alternative' is the tendency to reduce all its operations to this simplistic dichotomy. In a similar vein, it is easy to perpetually define commercial media organizations as profit-driven hubs of cost-cutting and poor service. In truth, different sectors of the media landscape perform different tasks – the point here is that community broadcasting's value to its audiences and society has been, until recently, grossly under-researched and subsequently under-estimated. Data now shows us they are far more than simply an 'alternative' to the commercial and public sector broadcasters.

The areas of service represented in our surveys of community radio managers, news and general volunteers are indicative of the actual make-up of the sector, with the majority of stations – more than 60 percent – located in regional areas (Figure 4). While the metropolitan and sub-metropolitan[1] stations are often the largest in terms of staffing and audience reach, regional areas of Australia contain the largest number of community radio stations overall (Forde et al. 2002).

During the 1990s and into the early years of the new millennium, a headlong rush by governments globally toward economic efficiency and profitability prompted a concern

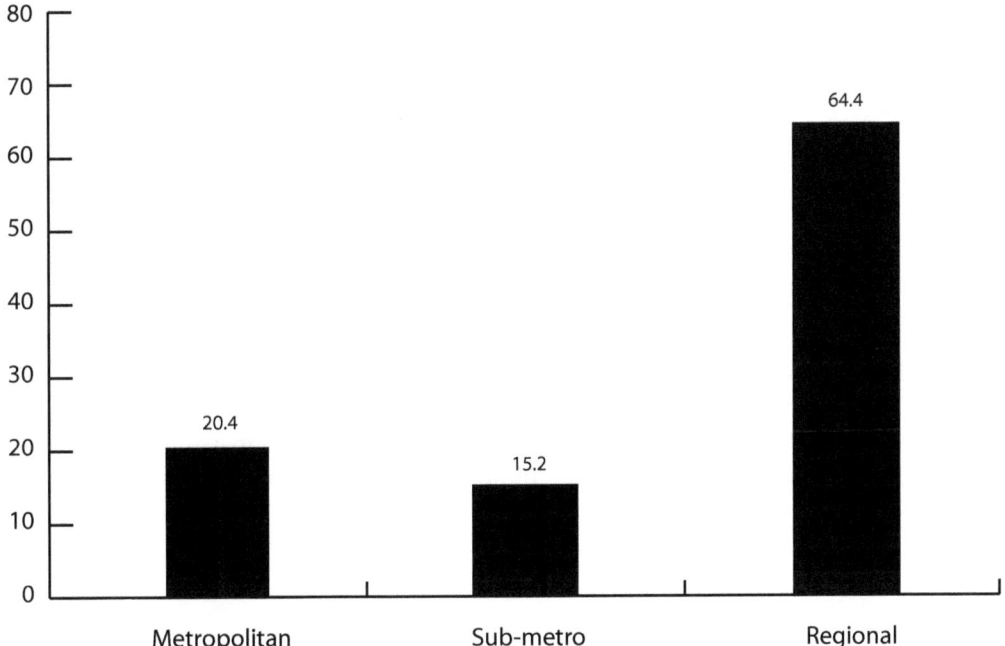

Figure 4: Areas of service.

that many of the altruistic ideals surrounding community radio and television and their role in 'broadcasting democracy' and 'citizenship' were being abandoned. Increasingly, the community radio sector in Australia was called upon to quantify its social and cultural benefits. Given the complex nature of its specialist, fragmented and diverse audiences, traditional audience research methods are deemed unlikely to produce results that impress inquiring government policymakers. It was in this environment that we undertook our first combined quantitative and qualitative study of the sector's managers, news and general volunteers, completing it in 2002. In this continuing climate of economic rationalism, where evaluation tends to be framed by ideas of profitability, efficiency, competition and numbers, notions such as social and cultural benefit still struggle to be recognized. Since 2004, regular quantitative audience surveys of the sector, funded by the Australian government, have provided strong evidence of a growing audience preference for the third tier of Australian broadcasting (McNair Ingenuity 2004; 2006; 2008). This has complemented the qualitative research in which we have been engaged during this period (Forde et al. 2002; Meadows et al. 2007).

Community broadcasting and cultural diversity

From its inception in Australia, community radio – and now, community television – was precisely about a fair representation of Australia's cultural diversity. It was concern over the need for the representation of minority groups in broadcast media that prompted initial investigations into the feasibility of a community radio sector. In 1975, the Whitlam government's Working Party on Public Broadcasting suggested that it was the responsibility of the new sector to provide neglected and minority interests with an avenue for participation in broadcasting. The working party asserted that access by trade unions, industry groups, professional groups, religious and all political, social, ethnic and cultural minorities would be effective in countering the discrimination these communities of interest experience in mainstream media. At the time, the capacity of community radio to foster democracy via access to broadcasting and its associated potential to 'extend the freedom of the individual, foster local independence and cultural enrichment' were familiar in both government and community literature and consultations (Barlow 1999: 86–87). Community television did not start in Australia until mid-1994 and remains a small sub-sector with just four semi-permanent stations operating in capital city locations in mid-2009. However, the fundamental philosophy involving both the rights of groups to broadcasting opportunities and the obligations of democratic governments to provide an environment conducive to public participation, still underpins the community broadcasting sector as a whole.

Community broadcasting now comprises a range of specialist sub-sectors, dispersed across the country. While educational, Indigenous and ethnic format stations are slightly over-represented, generalist stations are slightly under-represented as are religious stations, and those with a Radio for Print Handicapped (RPH) format. Generally, stations representing youth, Indigenous peoples and ethnic groups have a fairly high commitment to providing original news because of a recognition within the station that their 'community of interest' is not being served by mainstream news agendas. We now turn to consider each of the sub-sectors which are the focus of this book: Indigenous and ethnic community broadcasting.

Indigenous radio and television

> It's actually our only way of communicating. We don't have our finger in the pie of the big Murdoch stuff or Fairfax media or the big Channel Seven or Channel Nine networks and things like that. Murris[2] are sometimes left on the backburner or in the back room (Interview, Palm Island, 2005).

Community broadcasting is the largest component of Indigenous media production in Australia. It comprises 96 stations (including 21 dedicated Indigenous community radio stations), producing around 1,400 hours of Indigenous programming each week. This is in addition to 80 Remote Indigenous Broadcasting Services (RIBS) with community radio and television facilities, although most re-broadcast existing radio and television services (CB Online 2008: 24–25; AICA 2009).

The value of hearing local voices and stories is difficult, if not impossible, to quantify and is a distinguishing feature of all community radio and television. For Indigenous media in particular, this has been identified in academic literature from the early 1980s to the present (see for example, Michaels 1986; Ginsburg 1991; Meadows 1994; Aboriginal and Torres Strait Islander Commission 1999; Productivity Commission 2000; Molnar and Meadows 2001; Meadows and Molnar 2002; Meadows 2005; Deger 2007). The conclusion that emerges is that where local and culturally appropriate frameworks are used to structure community media, then these media become part of the local community – that is, part of local culture. For example, twenty different tribal groups speaking ten Indigenous languages are served by Umeewarra Media in Port Augusta, South Australia. Two languages were chosen for broadcast because of their relevance to local audiences, originating from local communities and others in the central Australian desert. The station prides itself on covering Indigenous issues in these languages and in 'plain English', thus accommodating those in the Port Augusta community for whom English is a second, third or even fourth language (Forde et al. 2002). This is not an isolated example, pointing to a role for many Indigenous media well beyond that of the generalist community broadcasting sector.

A central organizing function of Indigenous media is evident in the multiple tasks such enterprises undertake both within and between communities. One stark example comes from Indigenous audiences in north Queensland. In November 2004, Aboriginal people on Palm Island, near Townsville, stormed and burned down a police station on the island following the death in custody of a young local man. While mainstream media branded the incident 'the riot', Indigenous voices on Indigenous airwaves spoke about 'the resistance' with a Cairns-produced (Bumma Bippera Media) and nationally broadcast talkback programme, *Talk Black*, providing listeners with views other than those from sources such as state politicians and the police – in short: 'black voices and black issues' (Interview, Palm Island, 2006). The programme won an award for the best coverage of Indigenous Affairs at the 2006 Queensland Media Awards. Indigenous audience representatives have identified local radio and television as the only real alternative available to them in such times of community crisis – and indeed, in matters that concern ordinary people everyday. One avid listener to local Indigenous radio station 4K1G in Townsville captured the feelings of many when he observed:

> I think the only tool the community has to use is places like 4K1G to make sure that what was being brought out of the Palm [Island] community as a whole was projected in the right manner, not in a negative manner. That's only one part of the importance of Murri media or Indigenous media. It provides places like Palm, Woorabinda, the Cape [York] and other Indigenous communities, particularly the Indigenous population in the mainstream, with a voice, a balance, projecting our stories, our culture, our language the way we want to hear it but giving it to the wider audience too, people who live in the mainstream, people who don't often come in contact with Indigenous people.

It was not until the late 1970s that Indigenous broadcasters began to gain access to the Australian airwaves, largely through the emerging community radio sector. The first Aboriginal radio programme went to air on the generalist public radio station, 5UV in Adelaide, in 1972. By the early 1980s, Indigenous broadcasters were involved with community radio stations in the Northern Territory, Queensland and New South Wales. During this period, they also began broadcasting weekly on the Australian Broadcasting Corporation's (ABC) regional services and through the Special Broadcasting Service (SBS). The Central Australian Aboriginal Media Association (CAAMA) was one of the earliest Indigenous media groups to be established and it has been an important role model for many since. In 1985, CAAMA became the first Aboriginal community station in Australia. Since then, it has expanded to become a major production house for Indigenous audio and video. Several other regional Indigenous media groups such as Pilbara and Kimberley Aboriginal Media (PAKAM), Pintubi-Amatyerre-Warlpiri Media (PAW) and Pitjantjatjara-Yankunytjatjara (PY) Media have also become major production hubs. The ABC established working relationships with regional and remote Indigenous media associations throughout the 1980s, leading to several applying for their own community radio licences. The ABC employs Indigenous broadcasters to produce two national radio programmes – *Awaye* and *Speaking Out* – and the national television programme, *Message Stick*.

The Federal government decision to adopt satellite broadcasting for Australia in the 1980s raised the ire of Indigenous people in the bush. There was little negotiation with remote communities where English was not the primary language spoken. The Federal government held a series of regional inquiries, setting up four Remote Commercial Television Services (RCTS) with some caveats on licensees to produce culturally relevant programming. The successful licensee for the Central Zone RCTS was a consortium of Aboriginal organizations and people known as Imparja Television. It began broadcasting from Alice Springs in Central Australia in 1988. The opposition to satellite television from remote communities triggered two key investigations into Aboriginal use of media – Eric Willmot's hurried government-commissioned *Out of the Silent Land* and Eric Michaels' *The Aboriginal Invention of Television* (Willmot 1984; Michaels 1986). Based in the remote Indigenous community of Yuendumu, 300 kilometres from Alice Springs, Michaels worked with the Warlpiri to set up a pirate television station there and to broadcast locally produced videos shot and edited on the VHS format. It showed that Indigenous people could produce (or 'invent') their own kind of television. At the same time 800 kilometres south, the Anangu-Pitjantjatjara-Yankunytjatjara (APY) people in Pukutja (Ernabella) were involved in a similar venture. During the 1980s, each community amassed more than 1,000 hours of locally produced videotapes of social and cultural activities, most of which were re-broadcast to their audiences.

This flurry of production activity and inquiry reports influenced the Federal government to introduce the Broadcasting for Remote Aboriginal Communities Scheme (BRACS), designed to give communities some control over incoming satellite television signals – in theory, at least. Around 80 targeted remote communities were given a package of equipment allowing them to switch off undesirable programmes and to 'broadcast' their own. However, there was no money for training or maintenance and BRACS units quickly fell into a state of disrepair in most communities. The scheme, while good in theory, was mismanaged from the start with some suggesting it was set up to fail (Corker 1989). It remains in a modified form today but the vast majority of communities with a BRACS unit now use it simply to watch mainstream television – precisely what it was set up to avoid. By the early 1990s, a study revealed that just twenty of the 250 Indigenous languages spoken in Australia at the time of British invasion were being actively transmitted to and being used by children (Schmidt 1993). This is evidence of an opportunity missed to preserve and maintain Indigenous languages and cultures for future generations of both Indigenous and non-Indigenous Australians.

The Indigenous media sector in Australia emerged in a virtual policy vacuum. One underlying problem was that Indigenous media have been heavily dependent on government support – and seem destined to remain so. The first national review of the Indigenous media sector in 1998, *Digital Dreaming*, made 131 recommendations, including the establishment of a dedicated Indigenous broadcasting programme production fund. Two years later, the Australian Government Productivity Commission publicly acknowledged for the first time that Indigenous media was fulfilling a dual role – providing a primary level of service for communities and acting as a cultural bridge between Indigenous and non-Indigenous people (Productivity Commission 2000).

In the early 1990s, Yuendumu, along with three other communities in the Tanami Desert, experimented with compressed videoconferencing and satellite technologies creating the Tanami Network (Toyne 1992). Later expanded into the Outback Digital Network, it has been used to mediate a wide range of social and cultural activity, including successfully reuniting prisoners in Alice Springs prison with their families many hundreds of kilometres away. The cumbersome and high-maintenance videoconference units have given way to desktop technologies but at its peak, the network linked around 60 remote Indigenous communities in central and northern Australia. The convergence of broadcasting, computing and telephony has meant Indigenous communities have had to become familiar with digital technologies, appropriating these in many places to enable communication still largely based on traditional frameworks. Interestingly, some of the 'old' technologies like high-frequency radio have been enlisted again because they are cheap, trouble-free and enable communication over vast distances. In the Anangu-Pitjantjatjara-Yankunytjatjara Lands in central Australia, it is common for such old and new technologies to be melded to meet the needs of local communities.

From a Federal government policy perspective, Indigenous radio and television is considered to be part of the broader community broadcasting sector (see Figure 5),

---

This code acknowledges Indigenous peoples' special place as the first Australians, and offers a way to demonstrate respect for Indigenous cultures and customs, and to avoid offence with inappropriate words, phrases and actions. In the following section, 'Indigenous Australians' refers to the Aboriginal peoples and Torres Strait Islanders of Australia.

2.7 When reporting on Indigenous people and issues, stations will take care to verify and observe the best way to respect Indigenous cultures and customs by:

   (a) considering regional differences in the cultural practices and customs of Indigenous Australians;
   (b) seeking appropriate advice on how to best respect Indigenous bereavement customs on the reporting of people recently deceased;
   (c) using the appropriate words and phrases for referring to an Indigenous Australian and his/her regional group.

2.8 Broadcasters will seek to involve and take advice from Indigenous Australians, and where possible Indigenous media organizations and/or Indigenous broadcasters, in the production of programmes focusing on Indigenous people and issues.
2.9 Broadcasters will avoid prejudicial references to, or undue emphasis on a person who is Aboriginal or Torres Strait Islander.

Source: CBAA Codes of Practice, available at http://www.cbaa.org.au/content.php/16.html.

Figure 5: Australian Community Broadcasting Code of Practice: Indigenous programming and coverage of Indigenous issues.

something that Indigenous people see as ignoring their First Nations' status. At the time of writing, three national Indigenous newspapers – *Land Rights News*, the *Koori Mail* and the *National Indigenous Times* – target diverse audiences across the country and there is a growing Indigenous online presence. But community-produced radio and television remain the major communications media for Aboriginal and Torres Strait Islander people. Around 80 licensed Remote Indigenous Broadcasting Services (RIBS) – small radio and television stations – serve their audiences in remote parts of Australia with a further 21 community radio stations in regional and urban areas. Each represents a local Indigenous media association and many broadcast in local languages. Most of the small, remote stations are engaged in re-transmitting available satellite programming, with a handful having access to sufficient resources to enable local production. In addition, there are two Indigenous commercial stations – radio 6LN in Carnarvon in Western Australia and Imparja Television, based in Alice Springs. Two Indigenous organizations in Western Australia operate semi-commercial broadcasting licences – Goolarri Television, owned by the Broome Aboriginal Media Association and Ngarda TV, run by the Juluwarlu Aboriginal Corporation in Roebourne. There are two Indigenous community radio networks – the National Indigenous Radio Service (NIRS) and the National Indigenous News Service (NINS).

A regular Indigenous Community Television service (ICTV) started in 2001 broadcasting around twenty hours a day of locally produced television on a shoestring budget using a spare Imparja Television channel. It has included contributions from the Remote Indigenous Broadcasting Services (RIBS) PY Media, Warlpiri Media (now known as PAW), PAKAM, Ngaanyatjarra Media, Top End Aboriginal Bush Broadcasters' Association (TEABBA) and other local producers. Following a federal government policy decision in 2005, a National Indigenous Television service (NITV) controversially supplanted ICTV by taking over the only available community television channel in remote and regional Australia when it began broadcasting in July 2007. At the time of writing, the majority of Australian audiences could access NITV only through pay TV or a free-to-air community channel in regional and remote areas. The start-up of NITV in 2007 was supported by AUD$48 million in Federal government funds *over four years*. This amount pales when compared with the *annual* revenue for the Aboriginal Peoples Television Network in Canada (CAD$36 million in 2007, or by comparison, almost AUD$42 million per year) and Maori Television in New Zealand (NZD$34 million, or almost AUD$29 million in 2008). The significance of Aboriginal and Torres Strait Islander languages and cultures is ignored in Australia's *Broadcasting Services Act* – another key departure from similar legislation in Canada and New Zealand.

Indigenous media in Australia provides a first level of service for diverse communities across the country along with building a 'cultural bridge' between Indigenous and non-Indigenous communities (Meadows 1994; Aboriginal and Torres Strait Islander Commission 1999; Productivity Commission 2000; Molnar and Meadows 2001). Audiences for Aboriginal and Torres Strait Islander radio and television support the assertion that where these media are active they represent a central organizing element for local communities. They are essentially centres for community social organization.

Ethnic community radio

A post-war immigration boom has seen 6.5 million people come to Australia as new settlers up to 2007. Today, around 24 percent of the Australian population of 20 million people were born overseas (Department of Immigration and Citizenship 2008: 8). Continuing mainstream media misrepresentation of Australia's ethnic minorities has been a catalyst for many to seek access to alternative media with community broadcasting a preferred option (Hippocrates et al. 1996; and see further discussion below). And as with long-term coverage of Indigenous affairs, Jakubowicz and Seneviratne (1996: 20) argue that Australian media tend to represent ethnic affairs 'almost solely from a perspective of the problems they represent for the majority culture or to the dominant economic interests in society'. They conclude:

> The media present a picture of being 'reactive' rather than 'proactive' in relation to ethnic and racial conflict. For the most part, they seem unwilling or unable to recognise the implications of their construction of news and other stories, and broader entertainment offering, on race and ethnic relations. Despite recommendations of bodies such as the Human Rights and Equal Opportunity Commission through its 1991 report on Racist Violence, the media have done little to change their fundamental practices, particularly in relation to news (Jakubowicz and Seneviratne 1996: 19).

Partly as a result of continuing misrepresentation by mainstream media, ethnic communities in Australia sought access to the airwaves to ensure programming in languages other than English and to undertake their own culturally relevant programming. In 1975, the first ethnic community radio stations, 2EA and 3EA, went to air although these were operated by the Federal Department of the Media. They later became part of the Special Broadcasting Service (SBS). In 1979, 4EB went to air as a community-based ethnic radio station in Brisbane followed the next year by 5EBI in Adelaide, South Australia (Moran 1995: 150–151). The ethnic community radio sector at the end of 2008 had 123 stations (including seven producing ethnic language programmes full time) broadcasting around 2,400 hours of programming each week. Around 4,000 volunteers from 125 distinct cultural groups produce these programmes in 97 community languages (CB Online 2008: 24–25).

Ethnic radio stations receive a slightly higher proportion of government funds and senior figure in Melbourne's ethnic community radio George Zangalis has argued that the ethnic broadcasting sector saves the federal government 'billions of dollars' each year, with most ethnic stations raising 75–95 percent of their own funding:

> Ethnic broadcasting relies heavily on volunteers. Between seventy-five and ninety-five percent of the income of all stations broadcasting in community languages is raised by the stations themselves, by the volunteers. They pay to come and broadcast on behalf of their communities and the nation (EBAQ 2002: 97).

Ethnic community radio stations are providing an essential service to the new waves of migrants to Australia despite sometimes hostile mainstream media attention and it is clear that it is largely through community stations that the true nature of Australia's cultural diversity is being reflected (Forde et al. 2002). Indeed, there is a widespread assertion amongst media – and particularly journalism – scholars that the mainstream Australian media has failed to accurately report on political and social issues affecting ethnic communities time and again (Romano 2004; Dreher 2003; Marr and Wilkinson 2004; Klocker and Dunn 2003; Forde 2005). This highlights the importance of the service ethnic community radio stations provide. Antonio Castillo launched a well-directed attack on the mainstream Australian media in 2004 for the lack of cultural and ethnic diversity amongst journalism ranks which he believes gravely affects the media's ability to properly represent diverse communities. Castillo (2004: 16) wrote: 'apart from some minor exceptions and positive advances, the Australian news media, from reporters to management, doesn't reflect the ethnic diversity of this multicultural country. It's still a white, middle-class, English speaking business.'

Luckman (2004: 24) confirms that, generally, niche and community-based media tend to do a better job of portraying cultural diversity than mainstream media outlets, due to their proximity to their audiences. And because of a lack of connection with refugee communities, mainstream journalists overwhelmingly rely on government sources for information about refugees and asylum seekers which often slant stories towards the government policy of the time (Romano 2004: 58). A study in 2001 found that reporters from major daily newspapers *The Sydney Morning Herald* and *The Courier-Mail* rarely seek and report on the views of asylum seekers during incidents involving their communities which made front-page headlines in all major newspapers around the country for weeks (Pickering 2001). And confirming that the problem in reporting of ethnic communities is indeed a widespread issue of concern for mainstream media outlets, the Australian Press Council – the peak body which oversees print journalistic practice and reportage – notes that complaints about coverage of refugees and associated issues are numerous enough to warrant a special guideline (Guideline 262) being published to help journalists more appropriately and accurately cover refugee and migrant issues (Australian Press Council 2004: 35). The Press Council has a particular concern about consistent use of the term 'illegal immigrant' when referring to refugees and asylum seekers, most of whom have been found to have legitimate claims and subsequently granted residency in Australia (Australian Press Council 2004: 35–37). Press Council Chair Ken McKinnon further clarifies this:

> Readers of newspapers now know that in the 2001 election period the government got away with at least fudges, half-truths, and, it appears likely, outright lies over boat people in particular the 'children overboard' incident, which newspapers had dutifully communicated to the public…Was the press complicit in the fudging sins of omission by insufficient investigation?…why was the truth so hard to uncover? Are newspapers no longer sufficiently resourced or persistent enough to uncover lies and mischief? (2004: 3).

This suggests that the role community radio can play in correcting these 'half-truths' 'fudges' and indeed 'outright lies' conveyed by the mainstream media about ethnic communities is no minor issue. Undoubtedly, the understanding and application of Australian multiculturalism remains under pressure. The concept was borrowed from Canada in the 1970s by the Labor government but became official government policy under politically conservative Prime Minister Malcolm Fraser following the influential 1978 Galbally Report into various aspects of Australia's cultural diversity (Foster and Stockley 1988: 27–30). The National Multicultural Advisory Council (1999) defines Australian multiculturalism as a process which 'recognises and celebrates Australia's cultural diversity':

> It accepts and respects the right of all Australians to express and share their individual cultural heritage within an overriding commitment to Australia and the basic structures and values of Australian democracy. It refers to the strategies, policies and programmes that are designed to:
>
> - make our administrative structure, social and economic infrastructure more responsive to the rights, obligations and needs of our culturally diverse population;
> - promote social harmony amongst the different cultural groups in our society; and
> - optimise the benefits of our cultural diversity for all Australians (National Multicultural Advisory Council 1999).

Singh (2002) has argued that Australian ethnic broadcasters, through their multilingual media platforms, have created a dynamic environment where there is real dialogue around the role of community languages and their links to ideas of identity. He suggests that ethnic community broadcasters have demonstrated that it is 'not necessary to prescribe English-only broadcasting in order to create an egalitarian sense of Australianness that embraces Anglo-ethnics and all Other Australians':

> Australia's ethnic broadcasters are playing a significant role in developing their listeners' consciousness of the debates over the sustainability of linguistic diversity, sustaining egalitarian multilingualism; laying claim to and redefining constructions of Australianness (Singh 2002).

Singh argues that in this way, multilingual broadcasting plays an important role in shaping the day-to-day practices of Australian multiculturalism, including the following (2002):

- recognising and making explicit the power people have to influence changes in language use and identity construction in Australia;
- promoting a commitment to the sustainability of linguistic diversity within Australia and beyond, and

- encouraging a commitment to appropriating and remaking the Australian identity and Australian English(es).

Access to the airwaves for representatives from Australia's multicultural communities has not been easy – and it remains a challenge for many new migrants as a recent National Ethnic and Multicultural Broadcasters' Council study has identified. Even for new arrivals such as refugees, there are many barriers to access which include (*The Ethnic Broadcaster* 2002):

- lack of awareness of the existence of the sector;
- lack of awareness of funding and training available;
- lack of confidence;
- lack of mobility;
- making radio not a priority during the first stages of settlement;
- insufficient numbers of people from the community wanting to get involved to sustain a weekly programme;
- lack of resources and lack of airtime; and
- stations are under-resourced and therefore not proactive.

Our 2002 survey of station managers and volunteers identified many diverse and moving examples of community radio stations pursuing the idea of a multicultural Australia in their own particular ways. It is stations' ability to focus on a specific local audience that has enabled them to meet the challenges they identify. One of the recent themes that emerged powerfully from focus groups we conducted across Australia at the turn of the millennium was the relationship of community radio with recent refugees. While the federal government at the time sought solutions that focused on *removing* many of them from the community, radio station representatives spoke passionately about the strategies they introduced to *include* these 'new Australians'. One stand-out example is from manager of community station 5UV in Adelaide Deb Welch who describes the work undertaken by ethnic broadcasters in South Australia in 2001 to establish a dialogue with refugees there. The station set up a training programme for five refugees from West Africa and the Middle East to produce radio programmes and to learn the necessary skills. Welch eloquently summarizes the aims of the project (*The Ethnic Broadcaster* 2001):

> One of the key aims of community broadcasting is to encourage participation by those denied effective access to, and not effectively served by, other media. We've heard so much about refugees and asylum seekers – but how often do the people who have had this experience get to tell the story? Or determine how it will be told? Expanding the variety of viewpoints heard is to all our benefit and the underpinning of this project which came about through a partnership between our station and the Australian Refugees Association and is made possible through financial support from The Mercy Foundation. Here at

5UV Radio Adelaide we're also looking forward to expanding our awareness by getting to know these people with vastly different life experiences. The group includes journalists and a cultural tourism worker, and is shaping up to be one of this year's most exciting training projects.

This is one way in which ethnic community broadcasting fulfils a central community-building and cultural maintenance role.

In another example, Radio 3ZZZ in Melbourne became aware of a group of Albanian refugees brought to Australia to escape the Kosovo conflict. The station arranged an Albanian language programme to be produced and broadcast each day to inform them of happenings in their home country, as well as their status in Australia. In a similar way, Hobart's community radio station 7THE responded to the needs of Albanian refugees and managed to find some Albanian journalists within the refugee community. Members of the station drove 40 minutes each way to pick up the journalists to enable them to deliver their on-air programmes. This community radio station serves Hobart's minority ethnic communities providing programming for the Polish, Indian, Croatian, Greek, Dutch, Pakistani, Macedonian, African, Serbian, Spanish, Dutch and French people within its footprint. The station serves an audience of around 30,000 and its ethnic programming represents a valuable community cultural resource. Using new communication technologies, 7THE's Croatian programme regularly crosses live for an update on soccer scores. During the 2000 Sydney Olympics, the station crossed live to Croatian athletes for commentary and interviews. Using the Internet as a source, the station provides important news and current affairs information to a diverse range of ethnic communities. The Australian sub-Saharan African community has also acknowledged the importance of local programming. With a high number of illiterate refugees seeking solace in Australia, many rely completely on local language broadcasts through community radio as their sole source of information. This is particularly the case for those living outside the reception area for Special Broadcasting Service (SBS) radio services (Hobart Focus Group, 2001).

About the sector

The ethnic radio sector is perhaps the most diverse sub-sector in community broadcasting. In 2008 there were seven full-time dedicated ethnic stations, with a further 116 stations providing some level of ethnic programming – in all, providing about 2,400 hours of programming each week in 97 languages with about 4,000 broadcasters (voluntary and paid) involved in the sector. The generalist community radio sector broadcasts an additional 33 hours of ethnic programming weekly (CB Online 2008: 25). The attraction of ethnic media is evident beyond Australian shores: recent research in the United States has found that 45 percent of all African American, Hispanic, Asian American, Native American and Arab American adults now prefer ethnic television, radio or newspapers to mainstream media sources (Deuze 2006). Certainly, the annual US *State of the News Media* reports regularly find that the ethnic media sector is one of the few sectors of the news media with a growing, rather than a shrinking, audience and importantly 'they are closer to their audiences and less focused on profit demands, which makes them more flexible and more a leading indicator of cultural change' (Project for Excellence in Journalism 2004; 2006).

The McNair Ingenuity quantitative survey data provides a wealth of information both on and for the Australian community broadcasting sector as a whole, along with findings of specific interest to ethnic community radio. The most recent survey in 2008 confirms that community radio reaches around 28 percent of people who speak a Language Other Than English (LOTE) in their home on a weekly basis. As there is an estimated 12 percent of Australians generally who speak a language other than English at home, this indicates community radio is doing well in reaching a relatively high proportion of the non-English speaking ethnic population. Of all community radio listeners, 12 percent of them are LOTE speakers at home. This parallels general population statistics indicating, as our previous research found, that community radio listeners are representative of the general Australian population (Forde et al. 2002; McNair Ingenuity 2008).

A comparison of metropolitan and non-metropolitan community radio audiences indicates the importance of ethnic programming in metropolitan areas. While 17 percent of regular metropolitan community radio listeners are LOTE speakers at home, the proportion falls to just 4 percent of non-metropolitan listeners. This reflects the fact that most non-English speaking people live in metropolitan centres, and reinforces the importance of ethnic language programming in metropolitan areas.

The quantitative McNair Ingenuity survey also reveals that the provision of programmes in other languages is one of the less significant 'reasons for listening' cited by community radio audiences. The most cited reasons are 'specialized music content', 'local news and information', 'Australian music content' and 'announcers who sound like ordinary people' (McNair Ingenuity 2008). Across the nation, 7 percent of community radio listeners cited 'programmes in other languages' as the primary reason for listening to community radio. Not surprisingly, in metropolitan areas, this figure is slightly higher – at 8 percent of listeners – and in non-metropolitan areas, it drops to 4 percent. It is possible, within the McNair Ingenuity data, that some of the 'specialist music programming' listeners, which constitutes a sizeable proportion of the community radio listening population, are actually referring to specialist ethnic music. While it is impossible to determine from the quantitative data how important ethnic music programming is to those specialist music audiences, the qualitative findings presented in chapter four enable us to identify the significance of this element of ethnic radio production and reception. It is a good example of how these two data sets – qualitative and quantitative – can complement each other.

The Community Broadcasting Database is a resource comprised of information gathered directly from community stations across the country, managed by the Community Broadcasting Association of Australia (CBAA). It is a process managed by the community broadcasting sector itself although the quantitative data has been analysed variously by the

Australian Communications Media Authority (in 2005) and the CBAA (in 2006), aiming to provide a sector-based view rather than an audience perspective on the role and value of community radio. While the most prominent programme format for the community radio sector is music, ethnic stations are more likely to feature spoken-word content. This is indicative of the sector's importance as a source of local, national and international information for its audiences who often have poor English language skills or who are looking for news from their home country. Spoken-word programming comprises almost 64 percent of ethnic stations' total programming, while it makes up just 26 percent of programming on generalist stations (CBOnline 2006: 30; Australian Communication and Media Authority 2005: 2). Similarly, music comprises only 36 percent of ethnic station programming while it constitutes 74 percent of programming on generalist stations (CBOnline 2006: 30; Australian Communication and Media Authority 2005: 2). The figures are consistent, with minimal variation, with data from a 2002–2003 survey (Australian Communication and Media Authority 2005) and a 2003–2004 survey (CBOnline 2006). These findings very likely reflect Community Broadcasting Foundation funding guidelines which at the time, required programmes to run 50 percent language spoken-word programming in order to receive funding for particular programmes – ethnic programming featuring primarily music does not attract funding.

Ethnic stations are more likely to run a higher proportion of international satellite content than generalist stations. Radio for the Print Handicapped stations are the only sub-group more likely to run international satellite material (35 percent of total content, most notably from the BBC satellite service [CBOnline 2006: 45]). Ethnic station content includes 82 percent of locally produced programming and 15 percent of international satellite content. Generalist stations provide 77 percent locally produced content, 18 percent sourced from Australian satellite-delivered material, with just 5 percent international satellite programming (CBOnline 2006: 45). This is clearly consistent with many ethnic programmes' connections with countries overseas and their reliance on international news to match their audience's interests.

Volunteer numbers are highest at ethnic stations, averaging 271 volunteers per full-time licensee. This is well above the national average of 75 volunteers per station (CBOnline 2006: 64). The Australian Communication and Media Authority analysis (2005: 7) acknowledges that 'community participation in station operations is most evident within the ethnic, youth and fine music sub-sectors'. This is, of course, helped by the fact that most ethnic, youth and fine-music stations are located in capital cities, where volunteer numbers are traditionally much higher than their regional counterparts. If we compare ethnic radio volunteer numbers to metropolitan station volunteer numbers, we can perhaps elicit more accurate data – metropolitan stations attract an average of 168 volunteers, which still places ethnic radio volunteers at higher levels – but does not reflect the significant difference seen in the national average of 75 volunteers per station.

Ethnic stations also boast high subscriber numbers, coming in behind fine music broadcasters with the second-highest average number of subscribers per station. While fine music stations had an average of 2,724 subscribers, ethnic stations reported an average of 1,565 subscribers per station which compared very favourably with the average of 337 subscribers for generalist stations (CBOnline 2006). It should be noted that 'seniors/mature-aged' stations, which often fall into the category of 'generalist' stations, have subscriber numbers of 852 per station (CBOnline 2006: 71). These statistics are influenced by the fact that there are only seven full-time ethnic radio stations (and four full-time fine-music stations), while there are 173 licences held by full-time generalist stations, most of which are located in regional areas rather than the metropolitan areas (CBOnline 2006). Average subscriber numbers for metropolitan stations more closely reflect ethnic station subscriber numbers, with each metropolitan generalist station boasting an average of 1,373 subscribers compared to 1,565 for each full-time ethnic station (CBOnline 2006: 72). This still indicates more significant support for ethnic stations, but does reflect the benefit that all full-time ethnic stations enjoy in capital city locations with high population and potential subscriber/volunteer numbers.

Income levels for ethnic community radio is also relatively high, with each full-time station attracting about AUD$435,000 per year (CBOnline 2006: 87), compared to just AUD$89,600 for stations targeting a primarily seniors/mature-aged audience (CBOnline 2006: 89). Only fine-music stations achieved a higher average station income at AUD$670,000 per station (CBOnline 2006: 90). This indicates that relative to the rest of the sector, full-time ethnic community radio stations are reasonably well resourced and staffed, particularly when their high volunteer numbers are taken into account (National Ethnic Multicultural Broadcasters' Council 2006: 8). It should be noted, however, that full-time ethnic stations are more poorly resourced than their other metropolitan station counterparts – the average metropolitan station sees annual income of around AUD$601,000, compared to AUD$435,000 for the average full-time ethnic community radio station (CBOnline 2006: 91).

Communicating with those in need

Centrelink is an Australian government statutory agency, set up to assist people in the community to become self-sufficient and supporting those in need. It effectively deals with groups in society who require financial support to survive. It administers social security benefits for individuals and families in need, many of whom are from Indigenous and ethnic communities. The agency commissioned a study into the most effective ways of communicating with its target audiences and identified ethnic community radio as playing a significant role. As with our own study, Centrelink drew distinctions between 'established' and 'emerging' communities, acknowledging that the informational needs of these two sub-groups are quite different. The Centrelink study included members of the Chilean, Macedonian and Turkish communities as representatives of 'established' ethnic groups and the Afghani, Somalian and Sudanese people as representative of 'emerging' communities.

The research revealed that radio broadcasts in their own languages (which could include either community or the government-funded Special Broadcasting Service [SBS] radio) was the fourth most common way for people to access Centrelink information. We assume that the large bulk of this cohort is accessing community radio more often than SBS radio, as the community broadcasting sector produces many times more broadcast content directed at LOTE speakers than does SBS. Almost half of the Centrelink survey respondents obtain information through radio broadcasts in their own language, while one third get this information either through word of mouth, or through ethnic-language newspapers.

However, radio broadcasts in their own languages are the second *most preferred method* for ethnic communities to receive information about Centrelink. The most preferred media are translated brochures and fact sheets. Again, radio broadcasts in community languages rate above ethnic-language newspapers as a preferred medium to receive information.

These findings will help to contextualize our discussion of results from ethnic community radio focus groups which suggest that these audiences use ethnic-language radio widely as a source of local information and for 'community announcements' about government policies and services relevant to their everyday lives in Australia.

Ethnic community radio and mental health

There is an important link between cultural identity, cultural values and mental health amongst adolescents in ethnic communities in Australia (Sawrikar et al. 2005). In refugee communities, in particular, young people sometimes find themselves having to cope with parents who are suffering major emotional disorders as a result of trauma, for example. Young refugees employ a variety of strategies to deal with such situations – from talking with friends, family, medical practitioners and counsellors to becoming involved in sport, listening to music and participating in community events (Brough et al. 2003: 203). The 'community hub' nature of ethnic community radio in Australia means it is well placed to mediate many of these activities. Audiences for ethnic community radio programmes acknowledge their stations are playing a central role in maintaining culture and languages. In addition, they help communities to maintain community connections and networks and enable them to hear specialist music unavailable through other media. These stations play a critical role in providing local community news and gossip along with news and information relevant to their lives in Australia, from their home countries, and from neighbouring countries and regions (Meadows et al. 2007: 1).

Young people in Australia's refugee communities are active in constructing 'positive futures' for themselves by talking of their 'degree of connectedness within their family, their own ethnic community, their friends, and within Australian society at large' (Brough et al. 2003: 206). This pro-active approach was more likely than framing their lives in terms of 'illness boundaries'. The authors conclude:

This exemplifies the importance of promoting supportive social environments within public health approaches to refugee health. Biomedical dominance tends to highlight individual dysfunction in our understanding of health. Whilst this has a place, it is essential we also attempt to look at the larger picture. Community development strategies which connect young people to communities *and* communities to young people are of critical importance (Brough et al. 2003: 206).

Our research reveals the stand-out ability of ethnic and Indigenous community broadcasting, in particular, to facilitate identity construction in multifarious ways – an important process which is integral to managing mental health issues. The process involved is outlined in a study of ethnic Chinese communities and community media where the author (Shi 2005: 69) concludes:

Ethnic media provide socialising topics and contexts, and facilitate the imagination of a transnational Chinese community. They create a sense of cultural coherence and unity through symbolically reviving the memories of the past and retelling the history, which anchors the identification of the diasporic floating lives…'a shifting realm of differences and contradictions'.

The idea of 'community connection' is an important one identified by Tsagarousianou in her exploration of the understanding of diasporic phenomena so embedded in the history of modern nations like Australia. Although her study focused on communities in the United Kingdom, she is nevertheless able to draw attention to the importance of 'connectivity' and cultural politics that make 'the imagination and activation of the complex nexus of transnational/diasporic linkages and dynamics possible'. She observes (Tsagarousianou 2004: 64):

Diasporic cultures are therefore premised on the institution of diasporic imaginaries and communication infrastructures (diasporic media and cultural spaces) upon which multiple and diverse processes of identity and community are constructed, and depend on the production of narratives and discourses that reproduce and sustain relevant frames of self-identification, and collective action.

Ethnic media play a critical role in this process as an increasing range of studies suggest. For example, Chand (2004: 152) identifies a significant role for ethnic media – newspapers, magazines and radio programmes – in 'defining the identity of Fiji and South Asian Indians' in Sydney by providing local news and information. However, this preference is not universally held – Chinese and Korean immigrants in the United States, for example, seem to prefer to hear news about their home countries (Lin and Song 2006).

While preference for news content may vary geographically, it seems clear that ethnic groups use media in various ways to simultaneously 'become part of and to distance themselves from other groups' (Deuze 2006: 271). It is why we have argued that community media are more about social networking than programme production. As Cohen (2003: 146) suggests:

> The media, while undoubtedly a site of struggle over the 'community' and 'locality', are also where the diasporic experience is being constructed and particular identities are performed. The music, the cultural content of the programmes, their style of presentation and the ways in which their performances of 'culture' become a form of migratory gathering, enable the broadcasters and the audiences to construct a feeling of being at 'home' in the new place. Attempts to stay connected to their countries of origin are the means by which migrants come to understand and experience their life in a 'new' place. Such attachments are not merely an act of nostalgia or part of the effort to maintain culture, as depicted by multiculturalism. Rather, relations with the homeland are part of the ambiguity of 'home and away' that constitute the life experiences of many immigrants and construct their various ways of generating 'communities' in their new context.

There is compelling evidence that community media create an environment which can sustain 'a more engaged and participatory culture' (Deuze 2006: 271). But we would add one proviso – that an existing 'will to communicate' is the driving force (Hochheimer 1999: 451).

When it comes to the practical relationship between community media and health matters a 'compelling health story' is much more likely to be talked about and shared in ethnic communities. A study of Latino media in the United States concludes that these media can play an important role in helping this group to overcome and prevent health problems. Importantly, the study also reveals that that the Latino population is engaging with these media with the expectation of gaining health information (Wilkin and Ball-Rokeach 2006: 314). Our research thus far suggests a similar role for community broadcasting in Australia both in terms of what is happening now and its potential for further development by health care agencies.

Conclusion

Community radio and television are possibly the only media able to accurately represent the diversity of cultures that makes up the modern Australian population through a philosophy of access and participation. The many hundreds of broadcasting stations and programmes that provide an essential service for Indigenous and ethnic communities across the country also act as an important bridge between cultures. This process alone could be one of community broadcasting's most valuable contributions to Australian society.

The Indigenous media sector is amongst the fastest growing in Australia and relies heavily on community radio and television to get its messages across. The National Indigenous Radio Service (NIRS) criss-crosses the continent in the same way as Dreaming

Tracks – as a conduit for information. A National Indigenous News Service (NINS) has the capability of challenging the national broadcaster – the ABC – for reach and diversity in the potential number of stations able to tune into its unique sounds. And in 2007, the launch of National Indigenous Television (NITV) represents a bold new step for a section of the Australian community craving for stories and images that reflect their cultures. As the 1999 *Digital Dreaming* review of Indigenous broadcasting concluded – and as many focus group participants have reminded us – this network represents a vast untapped resource for advertisers ranging from the Federal government (one of Australia's largest advertisers) to regional authorities and businesses. Where they work best of all, Indigenous community broadcasting is linked intimately with local community social structures. This was particularly evident in the Indigenous Community Television (ICTV) service, unfortunately in a hiatus in mid-2009 because of a federal government decision to usurp its broadcast channel for the NITV signal. Nevertheless, several Indigenous observers have suggested this as an important framework for success as Aboriginal and Torres Strait Islander communities recognize the value of their intellectual property (including broadcasting) and devise ways of managing this more effectively.

The ethnic broadcasting sector has taken on the task of bringing to life the idea of multicultural Australia. This continues to be evident in the way in which ethnic broadcasters around the country have embraced new waves of refugees arriving in Australia. The varied accounts of local initiatives by communities to include refugees and other immigrants in their everyday lives in the face of sometimes hostile public reaction was one of the most moving and inspirational aspects of our earlier research (Forde et al. 2002). This represents a different sort of reconciliation in action and one that ethnic community radio broadcasters continue to demonstrate both through their passion and their expertise. Evidence of the shortcomings of the mainstream media in this regard – particularly their inability to provide journalists and other media personnel who have any connections to ethnic communities – further reinforces the role that programming in the community ethnic broadcasting sector can play in the future moulding of social structures and harmony. The real connection that ethnic broadcasters from the community sector have to their audiences is an invaluable resource that most mainstream media organizations could perhaps only dream about. The cultural and community service role performed on a daily basis by community broadcasting is incomparable to that played by commercial or publicly funded broadcasters like the ABC, despite the rhetoric – and in some cases, the good intentions – in their charters.

Community broadcasting undoubtedly has a unique role to play in the development of Australian culture in terms of its Indigenous and multicultural elements. Indigenous people would be voiceless without the continued revitalization provided, particularly through Indigenous radio and television. Ethnic communities would be powerless without their local-language radio stations and programmes and, quite probably, would be increasingly isolated from the rest of society with long-term repercussions. Children of migrants would be losing their sense of identity, of history, of belonging, without continued maintenance and production of their culture. In the past few decades, Australia has embraced multiculturalism and has moved some way towards empowering Indigenous peoples – the Prime Minister Kevin Rudd's apology to the Stolen Generations in 2008 stands as a significant milestone although much still needs to be done to put his words into practice. But it is community radio and television through which Australian cultural diversity is being affirmed and applauded. Commercial media and the national and multicultural broadcasters alone cannot provide the local diversity in programming sought by Australia's multifarious audiences. The first voices of these audiences to be heard in the next chapter are fittingly those of Australia's first peoples.

Notes

1. Sub-metropolitan stations exist in areas just outside major metropolitan areas – they are not far away enough to be considered 'regional' or indeed 'remote', but also do not service a strictly metropolitan audience.
2. 'Murri' is an Indigenous term generally used to describe Aboriginal people living in and around the state of Queensland.

Chapter 4

Audiences for Indigenous Community Radio and Television

Audiences for Indigenous radio and television in Australia reveal a great appreciation for the 'ordinary' nature of *their* media, evident in the strong connection – in fact, an absence of a barrier – between these media producers and their audiences. There is an acknowledgement, too, that music and information programming produced by Indigenous broadcasters is unique – there is no other source that Indigenous audiences feel provides them with the services they seek. Although these myriad community radio and television stations primarily broadcast to Indigenous audiences, they have attracted significant non-Indigenous listeners and viewers across the country. Evidence from interviews and discussions with around 200 people (including eight focus groups) who identify as audiences for Indigenous media suggests that the exceptional success of this sector is largely due to, as one interviewee succinctly put it: 'Blackfella talking to blackfella.' Analysis of this audience commentary offers strong support for the notion that Indigenous media represent essential services in communities where they are active. Six key themes have emerged from the Australia-wide data, drawn from audiences in urban and regional centres, and remote communities:

- Indigenous-produced radio and television programming, particularly talkback programmes and music requests, plays a primary role in maintaining social and community networks, languages and cultures.
- Indigenous broadcast media play a significant role in boosting community and individual self-esteem and feelings of wellbeing.
- Indigenous community radio and television are considered by audiences to be major media for education at the community level and beyond.
- Apart from word of mouth, audiences identify Indigenous media as their primary sources of news and information about issues and events relevant to their lives.
- Indigenous media play a crucial role in promoting cross-cultural dialogue and in breaking down stereotypes; and
- the Indigenous media industry, through radio and television broadcasting, has become the only reliable medium that supports Indigenous music and dance.

An important pan-Indigenous concern expressed by audiences across the country is a perceived void in national and regional leadership in the wake of the demise of the national representative body, the Aboriginal and Torres Strait Islander Commission (ATSIC) in 2005 (Pratt and Bennett 2004). For a significant number of participants in this audience study,

Indigenous media have taken up that role enabling communities across the country to be able to network – a major cultural resource. Indigenous media link individuals and groups both within and between communities. This is especially the case where sparse populations are spread over vast areas as is the case throughout remote Australia, including the northern island communities of the Torres Strait. The capacity for people to come together for meetings on a regular basis in such regions is limited – but innovative uses of media have managed to overcome this. One example is a unique system of community radio, television and UHF radio devised by PY Media to maintain traditional processes of decision-making by consensus in the Anangu-Pitjantjatjara-Yunkantjatjara (APY) lands in the central Australian desert. It allows people out in the communities the chance to know what's happening and to participate in the decision-making processes. It is common for people who are unable to get to important community meetings to call in on either telephone or radio with comments as they hear discussions being broadcast live on community radio frequencies.

It is clear from audience responses that in many remote regions, communication through Indigenous media such as the Remote Indigenous Broadcasting Services (RIBS), formerly known as the Broadcasting for Remote Aboriginal Communities Scheme (BRACS), have taken the place of regular community meetings. People in areas like the Torres Strait use radio through the RIBS (still called BRACS in many communities) network to raise and discuss issues such as erosion, disease threat, the weather and local politics. Talkback is a popular format for doing this and is considered by many to fulfil the role of public meetings. But the use of Indigenous radio and television as meeting places is not confined to remote Australia. Others from regional Australia refer to their media as 'the Murri grapevine' – 'Murri' is a term preferred by many Aboriginal people in Queensland to describe themselves. But it is about more than the simple transmission of information. As this Palm Island interviewee reminded us: 'It's all about lifting people's spirits once they know what's happening.' All of this suggests a central organizing role for Indigenous media outlets, at least from the perspectives of their audiences.

So what is it about Indigenous media that attracts audiences? We received a wide range of responses to this question, some of which we have already canvassed. But it is clear from our analysis that audiences are very happy with the relationships they have developed with their local broadcasters. We will now consider some of these specific issues in more detail.

Maintaining social networks

Audiences for Indigenous-produced media across the country talk about needing to be able to access their local radio stations, in particular, to send messages – mostly through music requests – to family and friends. On the surface, this may appear to be a straightforward practice, but audience discussions around this reveal it as an important way of maintaining contact and reinforcing kinship ties. For one North Queensland twelve-year-old boy, the way in which his local Indigenous community radio station maintains his cultural connections is straightforward (Interview, Townsville, 2006): 'I like the requests and the songs on it...They can play deadly[1] music that I want. You can send messages and they say it on the actual radio and you can give birthday calls.' While some speak about the difficulty many Indigenous people feel in picking up a telephone and making a call – even to a local Indigenous radio station – others reveal an intimate relationship with *their* local media. It highlights again the nature of the relationship local stations must develop with their audiences to overcome such barriers where they exist. However, it must be said that the overwhelming sense coming from the disparate audiences involved in our study is that there simply is *no barrier*. Such questions of access become especially important where family members are geographically separated from each other with local radio as one of the few, non-threatening communication avenues available to them. In this way, request programmes play a significant role in bringing community members closer together. As one focus group member at Umeewarra Media concluded: 'It's one way of saying that each person in the community is valued and respected.'

Thus, one of the main achievements of Indigenous radio or television services is bringing people together. An interviewee from Yuendumu in central Australia put it like this: '[PAW Radio aims] to bring people together, one people sharing one idea. Sharing, talking, culture sharing, like respect [for] one another as one people...it's all about bringing one people together.' Further north, in the Torres Strait, the power of the radio network is evident in responses from interviewees there. All acknowledge the role of radio 'because it keeps the whole community together...linking people in the Torres Strait with other Indigenous people around the country' through the National Indigenous Radio Service (NIRS). Another gave an example of radio enabling communities to keep in touch with sporting events 'because you've got family playing'. There were several examples of local media being used to ask family members attending a game to come home. In one case, a family member was spotted during a live local television broadcast and reminded of his home duties! It is doubtful if this could be achieved through anything other than Indigenous media. An emphasis on maintaining the idea of 'community' provokes expressions of 'attachment to' and 'ownership of' a station, reflected in this Townsville interviewee's conclusion: 'It is a sense of community – it's like it's ours.' Interviewees and participants describe the importance of building communities through Indigenous media because 'you can't get that sense of community anywhere else' (Interview, Laura, 2005). There are more practical reasons for Indigenous radio to focus on maintaining community connections, as this respondent to the national Indigenous talkback programme, *Talk Black*, suggests:

> It's keeping our families connected. A lot of us can't read; a lot of us can't write but we all like listening to the radio – bit of Country and Western. And it's what these programmes are doing: they are community-based; they're owned by Aboriginal people. They are controlled by Aboriginal people for Aboriginal people.

Maintaining languages and cultures

Audiences consider the maintenance of languages and cultures as a crucial role of local Indigenous media. The emphasis on language is stronger in remote Australia where English remains the second, third or even fourth language spoken in some communities. But it is important to reiterate that the role of Indigenous media in this sense is not confined to remote regions. The Aboriginal community on Palm Island, off the Queensland coast near Townsville, has had to withstand decades of mainstream media stereotyping, culminating in the Guinness Book of records describing it as 'the most violent place on earth' outside a war zone (Agence France Presse 1998). It is actually a melange of 40 different Aboriginal communities from Queensland, forcibly removed under state law from 1918 onwards – an example of the 'Stolen Generations'. As a result of almost a century of government mismanagement, the island community is confronted by many social problems including high unemployment, alcohol abuse and crime (FAIRA 1999). In 2005, a new radio station was opened on the island and training of local on-air announcers began. This response from a Palm Islander is typical of many we recorded in urbanized and fragmented Indigenous communities where traditional languages are no longer in common use, underlining the importance of maintaining cultural connections through the use of Aboriginal English, for example:

> It depends how you talk. You could talk flash like a whitefella or you could talk like a blackfella. I talk my way. I just be me...You communicate with your people and they know what you're talking about in my language; my way; blackfella way; Murri way. They can relate to that, see?

This is something that only local radio can achieve and is a major reason why it is so successful in servicing the diverse cultures that make up Indigenous Australia. In remote regions where many traditional languages and cultural activities remain active, Indigenous media have been adapted to suit community needs. Indigenous Community Television (ICTV) – before it was usurped by a new National Indigenous Television service (NITV) in 2007 – was a good example with its high level of Indigenous language content (around 80 percent). This is how one community elder explained the importance of language and cultural programmes on ICTV when we visited the community of Umuwa in the Musgrave Ranges at the northern edge of the Great Victoria Desert:

> Interviewer: What does it do for young people?
> Interviewee: They're learning.
> Interviewer: What do they learn about?
> Interviewee: Culture, and some *inma* [dances, songs]. The older people have been dancing before and they're watching and they're learning from that culture...Very important one for children learning...later they singing and some people learning singing and dancing.

Both Indigenous radio and television appear to be dealing effectively with regional linguistic differences, according to audience responses. ICTV, for example, regularly used to broadcast programmes in several different Indigenous languages – and English – and this had been largely accepted unproblematically by audiences. The Indigenous languages used by programme makers on ICTV most often had either common linguistic roots or were mutually intelligible. But even where linguistic barriers seem evident, audiences persist with viewing because it gives them insights into the subtle cultural differences that distinguish their own communities from others depicted on the screen.

Regional Indigenous television producers PY Media, PAW Media, PAKAM and Ngaanyatjarra Media, in particular, have amassed many thousands of hours of archival video – some material more than twenty years old – slowly being transferred to a digital format for better storage and access. This represents an invaluable cultural resource, recognized in part by the National Indigenous Languages Survey, which has recommended an audit of Indigenous media organizations to determine the extent of this archive (AIATSIS and FATSIL 2005: 93). Indigenous media producers routinely dip into such collections for programme material but also to fulfil requests from families who want to see images of relatives who have passed away some years before. It is commonplace for programme material with images of deceased people to be removed from air and placed in a 'not to look' box until families decide that enough time has elapsed for the images to be again viewed publicly. The management of ICTV through PY Media enabled almost instantaneous withdrawal of offensive material if something slipped through the usual cultural protocol checks.

And so programming in various remote area languages was common on ICTV, most often without accompanying English subtitles. While some ICTV viewers interviewed said they would like to be able to understand more of what was being spoken in languages other than their own, they prefer to watch programmes as they exist rather than not at all. For many, the feelings of pride that flow from seeing another Indigenous face on television overrides any potential language barrier. It is a similar response to multilingual broadcasts in Native Canadian languages by the Aboriginal People's Television Network: despite mutual unintelligibility, Native audiences across Canada's North report being able to follow programmes simply by watching and listening (Meadows 1994; Molnar and Meadows 2001). It resonates with community acceptance of Maori Television in New Zealand (Maori Television 2008: 6). In addition, audiences acknowledge the power of such local media in re-invigorating local languages and cultures, as this response from the Torres Strait suggests:

There's different languages in the Strait – Eastern Island, Meriam and Western Island – and it's important to use language because then you can retain that and, and teach it. So you not only can teach it in schools and other places, but over the radio. And people listen to it. And most of our songs are composed in language and…[the] young generation… [are] listening to the songs, learning the songs, learning the meaning of the songs and learning the language at the same time…it's important that language be spoken over the radio.

Similarly, PAW Radio (formerly Warlpiri Media), services eleven Indigenous communities in the Tanami Desert region of central Australia and as such, deals with a linguistically diverse audience (PAW 2009). This interviewee at Yuendumu describes the role of community radio: 'Radios here put on Aboriginal music, songs in language, like in Warlpiri, and they talk about the old land or community. Through that song and music and through that language, it's communicating what's happening.' Another Warlpiri listener from the same region observed: 'It's very good way to get the message across in our own languages to our own people.' Almost 1,100 kilometres north in Darwin, Radio Larrakia includes language speakers in its programming when possible by networking with the Top End Aboriginal Bush Broadcasting Association (TEABBA) which links with remote community broadcasting services scattered across the 'Top End' of Australia. One of the most experienced broadcasters in the region, 'Big' Frank Djirrimbilpilwuy, most usually speaks in language (Yolgnu) when the network switches to his programme originating from a small radio station in the Milingimbi community, 400 kilometres east of Darwin. One Darwin listener praised the station's focus on Indigenous affairs:

> It is a very unique radio station here in Darwin and as I've said earlier on, I'd say its only, the only radio station that does, hey, Aboriginal and Islander music, and links up to *Talk Black*, crossing over to the TEABBA BRACS, Wednesday and Friday mornings. And you're still getting that Aboriginal language into the greater Darwin area.

Indigenous media outlets place a high priority on setting appropriate cultural protocols for broadcasting. It is commonplace for programme material to be withdrawn for broadcast following advice that someone in a video or band has passed away, for example. Stations rely solely on advice from their audiences in such matters, another clear indicator of the existence of a strong audience-producer relationship and the trust that exists between these entities. This listener from Broome, in Western Australia, stressed the importance of respecting such protocols, explaining how communities worked around them when appropriate in this example:

> There was one bloke, from a band – he died and we didn't play the music for a while to respect the sorry business, you know. And then once…we knew it [the mourning] was over here, we went back to the family to say, it's alright to play the songs over the PAKAM and Goolarri air waves.

Boosting self-esteem and feelings of wellbeing

It is clear that Indigenous radio and television is playing a central role in boosting communities' self-image. Listeners and viewers describe it variously as 'empowerment', 'ownership' or simply, 'pride'. It is clear, too, that many believe that Indigenous media is now a mature industry in its own right, with an attraction for many young people – some as young as ten – drawing them away from negative diversions that exist in most urban, regional and remote communities (Interview, Yuendumu, 2006; Interview, Maningrida, 2006). There is no doubt that Indigenous radio and television are highly valued by their audiences but at the same time, there is frustration that a lack of recognition of their relevance and impact – reflected in minimal funding levels – offers no genuine career paths for Indigenous media workers. The advent of NITV in 2007 has offered some hope and the positive impact such services have on audiences is clear although the annual budget for this national media service is around AUD$12 million. This compares unfavourably with 2007–2008 government support for the Special Broadcasting Service (AUD$187 million) and the Australian Broadcasting Corporation (AUD$800 million).

An annual Indigenous fund- and awareness-raising competition held in the Kimberley region of Western Australia each year – Kimberley Girl – is televised by the local Aboriginal-owned media service, Goolarri Television. It is a good example of the positive impact it has on local viewers, as this Broome focus group member suggests:

> When I see that [*Kimberley Girl* on Goolarri TV] that makes me happy to see an Aboriginal role model…starring on the TV like that. And I'd like to see more role models and different things in the Aboriginal community (Focus Group, Goolarri Media, 2006).

In many Indigenous communities, locally-produced media represent often the *only* employment prospects for young people, as this listener from Port Augusta suggests:

> The good thing about the radio also is that it's opened up a whole new area for Indigenous people to get involved in, like broadcasting and journalism…We've had people from here go to Bachelor College [in the Northern Territory] and places like that to study journalism at James Cook University [Townsville] and so on. And it's good to see those people are actually broadening their horizons through…the radio station.

Community radio and television offer a way out of despair for many who have adopted substance abuse to counter the boredom and low self-esteem that flow from limited employment opportunities, dispossession and racism experienced by many Indigenous Australians. This example from Yuendumu is one of many recounted:

> We've got a young woman, for example, that has just started radio training…and she's had a really difficult couple of years through various personal circumstances. And it's simply been since she's started doing radio shows and learning how to edit radio shows that she's found her own self-confidence and that's given her enormous worth and a sense of direction.

But for the majority of audiences for Indigenous radio and television, simply 'listening' – or watching – is an empowering experience (Bickford 1996). This woman attending the Laura Cultural Festival on Cape York Peninsula exemplifies the feelings of many: 'For me, every morning, I can listen and I feel that it gives me a lot of strength...You know that they're thinking at a much deeper level than the mainstream mass culture out there.' Another, from Palm Island, put it like this:

> It makes you proud you're Indigenous when you hear your own people get up there and talk about your own cultural background, concerns of the community, voicing opinions on what could be changed, giving other Indigenous people ideas for how they can make a difference themselves.

Continuing misrepresentation of Indigenous affairs in mainstream media is widely identified by interviewees and focus group participants, fanning the fires of deep resentment at this treatment felt by many Indigenous people (Meadows 2001). Stereotyping, negative coverage, a focus on 'the bad' aspects of Indigenous affairs were all commonly raised as reasons for seeing Indigenous-produced media as offering communities an authoritative information alternative, apart from word of mouth (Meadows et al. 2007: 51). One Bumma Bippera Radio focus group participant in Cairns described it simply as 'when you listen to, like, mainstream radio, it's, like, there is a lot of negativity'. Almost 1,800 kilometres southwest in the APY Lands, an elderly local man had this to say, comparing mainstream media coverage of issues with the now defunct Indigenous Community Television service:

> I see *Anangu* [Pitjantjatjara people] on whitefellas' TV and...that's very different from ICTV...Whitefella TV, that really saddens the people – too many fights, something happening on TV and that's not good for *Anangu* people to watch.

Audiences for Indigenous community radio and television from urban, regional and remote Australia are adamant that they play a central role in boosting self-esteem, pride and happiness in the face of mainstream media coverage and perceptions of Indigenous people that often engender feelings of shame, depression, sadness and anger.

When we visited far north Queensland in 2005, it was barely eighteen months after a police station and courthouse had been burned down on Palm Island, near Townsville, with several Indigenous people arrested for taking part in an alleged 'riot'. The 'resistance' as Palm Islanders refer to it, followed yet another death in police custody of a young Aboriginal man, Mulrunji Doomadgee. Interestingly, no-one was seriously hurt in the media-dubbed 'riot'. Just one of a handful of Palm Islanders charged over the incident, Lex Wotton, was convicted and sentenced to two years' prison (Murphy 2008). All others charged were acquitted. Palm Island residents argue that their local radio service was – and remains – the only place where people can speak openly about the issue. For this community, the radio quite simply represents a space where people can hear 'Black voices, Black issues'. Almost all Indigenous people interviewed on the island described the positive feelings they get whenever they hear familiar voices on the air waves. As one put it: 'Talking in the Palm Island way, you know? I've listened to it a bit when I jumped off the plane. I heard it – hey, good eh? A good laugh and all that.'

In every one of the thirteen regions across Australia represented by interviewees and focus groups who participated in our audience study, the morale-boosting role of Indigenous radio, in particular, in re-connecting prisoners with their families was highlighted. This comment on the importance of music request programmes on Townsville's Indigenous radio station, 4K1G, is typical of many: 'It was a good message for the young boys that were in Cleveland [youth detention centre] and in Stuart [prison], so they could send out their little message to their loved ones.' Others point to the important role of Indigenous radio talkback programmes, in particular, in enabling the stereotyped portrayal of domestic violence in Indigenous communities, for example, to be challenged and discussed more openly. Although all participants who spoke about this acknowledged that it and other social issues were challenges for communities, hearing first-hand accounts and advice from those who have been through the experience is seen by many as an important way of offering a solution. However, for many, music remains one of the most powerful ways of boosting Indigenous self-esteem and pride, as this Torres Strait Islander listener explains:

> the music that comes off the radio is very important and for oldies like myself. It brings back memories and, you know, you remember the song. And your little ones, they teach you how to dance that song, you know, the dance and everything else.

Another young Indigenous woman from an audience focus group in Brisbane spoke about the impact community radio station 98.9 FM (formerly AAA Murri Country) has had on the often stereotyped Indigenous community in the nearby working-class suburb of Inala:

> I think 98.9 has done a fantastic job so far I understand that we want new up and coming artists. I remember when I was about sixteen I don't know if any of you have heard of the *Indigenous Intrudaz*? Well, I remember when those boys first started. I went to school with them and the first big break they ever had was at 98.9. And I remember driving them in and how exciting it was for them to come to this radio station and meeting all of these people. So every time I listen to 98.9, I hear voices I know from my community like *Mop and the Dropouts*, *Angus Rabbit* – people I know personally – and to hear them on a radio station, I think, it's pretty fantastic. Especially these three boys are only twenty-two and their first break was on an Indigenous radio station. Being an Indigenous person living in Inala – to our boys [to be broadcast] on an Indigenous radio station, it's fantastic.

Similar feelings of pride that stem from either hearing and/or seeing Indigenous people on local radio and/or television was strongly expressed by audiences for community radio and television across the country. A woman from the West Australian community of Beagle Bay told us: 'They [people in the community] think it's really great seeing themselves on TV, you know, and yeah, it's really deadly.' In the nearby community of Djaradjin, also in the Kimberley region, another woman echoed this feeling: 'And kids also are proud listening to stories that communities are putting out there…it's really good; good for us to enjoy.' Back in the desert community of Umuwa, this man agreed:

> It's really good [to see local Indigenous people on TV] and we see other things happening on other communities. People are really happy, too, when they see that: kids and older people telling stories and kids know what they're doing at other communities. That's really good.

The activities of the Indigenous-owned Goolarri Television in Broome attracted strong praise from all those we interviewed in the town and in the Kimberley region. One mother in the Broome focus group explained how Goolarri Television's coverage of the annual *Kimberley Girl* competition had boosted the self-esteem of her 'difficult' teenage daughter:

> And I'll tell you another thing: with [name withheld], prior to becoming *Kimberley Girl*, she was a mongrel – no brains, no nothing, you know…what we call, no *berkup*. That means no kick, you know, really wild…her attitude…to herself has lifted a hundred percent…we can't, like, sometimes shut her up and to think that this was the same [girl].

But what is it about Indigenous community broadcasting that enables it to have this kind of impact? A listener to the Indigenous community radio station in Port Augusta – Umeewarra Media – offers this suggestion: 'And when you get back in range, you switch over to Umeewarra and [you] feel a whole lot intrinsically alive and vibrant and supported and, and a part of the community, yeah.' Around 1,300 kilometres north, in the remote Northern Territory community of Yuendumu, a former community radio worker describes a different process in action with the radio production process itself playing a direct role in youth rehabilitation:

> I see a lot of people working on the radio and driving, working, mentoring programmes and they once were petrol sniffers, which is really great and they are happy – they have kids now. They look back; they've done it; they've been there, which is really great.

For many Indigenous people, simply hearing an Indigenous voice on the air waves – or seeing an Indigenous person on television – is enough to send their spirits soaring, as this comment from a woman attending the annual Laura Cultural Festival on Cape York Peninsula: 'I feel more comfortable than when I hear any white man's radio station. Absolutely more comfortable.' Another from the remote community of Yuendumu put it like this:

It's really the best thing the community can have…just making you feel that you are not alone and…all those other people around me…are excited, they're excited about what's happening in the community…That's why it's one of the best things we've got for this community…Makes you feel like community.

One North Queensland resident from Palm Island explains the importance of having 'the right voices' on the local radio station and in identifying with them:

We've got that grassroots radio happening – talking to people – just that grassroots stuff: none of that high, intellectual stuff, just the Murri way of talking and communicating. That's what I see as really important in that way so that people understand what you're talking about: you're from the same place, the same area, the same place and you know what you're talking about.

This same idea was evident in most of the regions involved in our study with an additional educational perspective suggested by interviewees from the APY Lands at Umuwa in the South Australian desert. Most of those we interviewed expressed the view that Indigenous-produced media was an integral part of the culture 'because they see the people all talking to other people and they learning and they see themselves, and they [sic] singing the right way'.

A medium for education

This role being undertaken by Indigenous radio and television was universally highlighted by participants in our audience study. The theme overlaps significantly with others we have identified, underlining the importance audiences place on the impact of media on their children and their future. Audiences identified two main elements: providing children with both a traditional and contemporary education through media; and identifying knowledge of media production skills as part of the education process. The attraction of working with media for Indigenous children is widespread with almost all accounts of media interaction involving young people. At Yuendumu, media have been part of community culture since the late 1970s when experiments with local television introduced the community to its empowering potential (Michaels 1986). Since then, PAW radio has emerged as an effective medium that draws together the three main language groups – Pintubi, Amatyerre and Warlpiri – centred in and around the Tanami Desert. One radio worker from Yuendumu described its impact:

Radio is one of the coolest things that they can do and we usually have a queue of our young people wanting to work with Warlpiri Media all out there but particularly on those multimedia projects…we have all the same issues as any other community but we also have extremely strong people, not only elders, now the young people they're taking action and they're not accepting those unacceptable ways of life.

In the Torres Strait Islands, this listener explains the importance of her local radio station to people in the region:

> …everybody listens to it. I know…a couple of higher, upper classes at Yorke Island State School, they listen to the talkback show between nine and ten as part of the…lessons because of all the issues that are up and…that's how they get people to listen to and also take part in the classroom discussions and issues.

A world away in the southern Victorian capital, Melbourne, the audience for its urban-based Indigenous radio station, 3KND (3 Kool 'N Deadly), identified educating both Indigenous and non-Indigenous people as one of its major roles, as this focus group participant explains: 'So this is where I'm learning to listen to the radio and learn about my culture and I'm trying to teach my kids to listen in and also what they are learning at school.' When members of the focus group for radio station 98.9 FM in Brisbane were asked to nominate what they thought was the station's primary role, it was unanimous:

Participant 1: Education.
Participant 2: It's an educator.
Participant 3: It's an awareness raising and…
Participant 1: It helps bring things out in the open and starts people talking – educating.
Participant 3: It's a talking point – somewhere to start, like you mentioned about a bridge.

ICTV

The advent of Indigenous Community Television (ICTV) and its slow, steady spread across remote Australia until mid-2007 had created an extraordinary level of excitement amongst audiences in remote Indigenous communities when we visited several towards the end of 2006. Wherever the community TV service was available, viewers spoke with passion and pride about the importance of seeing images of local, identifiable Indigenous people on TV – in many cases, for the first time. Although ICTV was performing many roles in the communities we visited – maintaining languages and cultures, connecting communities, promoting cross-cultural awareness, a source of news and information – audiences most commonly talked about it in terms of education: providing an environment where children, adults, both Indigenous and non-Indigenous, could learn. This was nowhere more apparent than when we visited the desert lands of the Anangu, Pitjantjatjara and Yunkantjatjara.

At that time, the population of the administrative centre, Umuwa, had swelled to several thousand, all attending the 25th anniversary celebrations of the return of Aboriginal land title. We stood by the dusty roadside with a local interpreter, canvassing people's views as they crawled by us in their four-wheel drive vehicles. One vehicle had barely stopped when an elderly woman asked: 'Are you those fellas who want to talk about our media? I want to talk to you!' Several prior meetings with council and media personnel, a request to the APY Council for permission to visit and an announcement of our arrival over the local community radio network meant that few people there would not have known about us and our objectives. She was intent on stressing the educational importance of ICTV, in particular, and was livid about rumours of its possible replacement by a new, city-based service (NITV). She apologized for 'talking strongly' and explained to us the many facets of ICTV and its influences on children and adults alike. She had a lot to say that day but this extract perhaps sums up the passion expressed by many about the importance and relevance of Indigenous-produced radio and television:

> Travelling in any way in the country, they can listen to music; they can put a TV there and make everybody happy, make everybody awake and think about the land: this is my grandmother's land; this is my *tjamu's* land, this is my *kami's* land, my grandmother's, and grandfather's, uncle's, mother's [land]. The media we started for *Anangu* children. We can't give it to anybody.

As it transpired, the rumours of the replacement of ICTV on the only available satellite television broadcast channel were well founded. And although the bush communities have been given some access to the new national service through a proposed 65-part television series, *Jukurrpa*, at the time of writing, they were working on ideas for alternative ways of distributing locally produced television programming to remote Indigenous communities across Australia. One initiative, Indigitube, is an Internet 'television station' and was due to be launched in 2009 (ICTV 2009). The crucial importance of a community-owned and run service became very clear with people time and time again reminding us that 'they got our cultures on ICTV' and that this was of interest to everyone, from the kids to the elders. ICTV had arrived in remote communities in the Kimberley region of Western Australia a few months before we visited but people there were equally enthused about the 'really deadly' new television service. They identified the importance of seeing Indigenous faces on the screen, stories from their own and other cultures, and talked about the pride they felt in knowing Indigenous people had produced it all. One avid viewer from the Kimberley community at Beagle Bay gave us her views:

> Well ICTV is a very special indigenous community television because you get stories from different places, different regions, different nationalities [from the] Aboriginal perspective. There's cultural…stories, bush medicine which, you know, you hardly ever see on, on, like for instance, SBS, GWN, GR, ABC [mainstream TV stations].

While the vast majority of interviewees and focus group participants in our study were Indigenous, non-Indigenous people without exception expressed the potential inherent in both radio and television for educating 'whitefellas' about Aboriginal and Torres Strait Islander cultures. Most non-Indigenous participants lived on Indigenous communities and voiced the same level of criticism of mainstream media misrepresentation as their Indigenous counterparts. These comments from a community store worker in the Kimberley community of Djaradjin captured the thoughts of several others:

> I reckon we should have some of those channels [like ICTV and Goolarri TV] out in the mainstream because then we get to know about what happens in communities and it's the contact, you know. When I go back out into there and I meet my friends, they've got no idea what it actually is like…how the mob live and how we all get on and how we… work together.

A primary source of news and information

Indigenous audiences see their local media, particularly radio, as the primary source of news and information about Indigenous affairs – apart from word of mouth. And leading the way on many of Australia's Indigenous radio stations are their own versions of talkback. There are several popular community-based talkback programmes on air with *Talk Black* (Bumma Bippera Radio, Cairns), *Let's Talk* (98.9FM, Brisbane) and another local programme in the Torres Strait identified as the most influential and informative. *Talk Black* is the most popular source of information for Indigenous listeners in North Queensland – along with others who tune in from Broome to Melbourne. One elderly Palm Island resident offered this view of why *Talk Black*, relayed by satellite across Australia through radio 4K1G in Townsville – and streamed on the Internet – was important in her life:

> I love the talkback. [It's] very interesting because it includes affairs that apply to our people and I'm glad that they're making [us] aware of our problems and what's going on. And good things, too, that are happening around the place – like our Debutante's Ball that's coming up.

As another Palm Island resident observed simply: 'It's good to hear our own people's voices and opinions.' This is echoed by Indigenous and non-Indigenous audiences for such programmes around the country. A Townsville listener described it like this:

> Its helpful, its informative, the issues, too – it's about us Black people having a say over the airwaves. You know, you have [mainstream] talkback programmes but it's not the same, you know. Sometimes it might be family on there, and you say, 'Hey, I know that person'.

Time and time again, audiences in the north volunteered that 'everyone tunes into *Talk Black*'. It was described variously as a 'network', 'a relay', 'a source of knowledge' with Indigenous people in control, providing cross-cultural awareness, as this telephone caller to the programme itself suggests:

> It's a great opportunity for Aboriginals to speak their mind. Whether some people believe it or not there are a lot of white people who listen to the radio station especially *Talk Black*, where we are coming from now and also 3KND here in Melbourne. So I think it's a great idea.

Similar views were voiced by interviewees in the Torres Strait, talking about their own version of talkback radio offered through local station, 4MW, on Thursday Island. This listener explains that it allows a huge variety of issues of importance to the immediate communities in the region to be raised – and by people with the knowledge and authority to discuss them:

> The talkback sort of brings up them [sic] things you know…say for example, I might say, 'Oh bala [brother], look, we have more people intruding in our waters here'. Lots of people listen because, for example, our water is important to us – this is where our livelihood is, you know, and it's part of us. So comment like that in the talkback, it's sort of inspiring that person, you know.

The Brisbane-based talkback programme on community radio 98.9 FM, *Let's Talk*, hosted by one of Australia's longest-serving Indigenous broadcasters, Tiga Bayles, came in for its fair share of praise as well:

> I would say that another reason I like tuning in, too, particularly to the *Let's Talk* show because it's a credible alternative to mainstream news…it's more balanced and you're given the truth. And as I say, it's out there – discrimination and the racism – and there's a lot of things that go on that you just don't get a balanced view [of] in mainstream media.

Listeners to Indigenous radio and viewers of Indigenous television see these media as more than alternative sources of news and information – they have become essential services for communities in which they are active. Audiences for Indigenous media we canvassed from the cities to the bush universally condemned mainstream media because of their relentless inaccurate and negative portrayal of Indigenous issues. Some argue that commercial media are 'too focused on extracting your money' and uninterested in community and family events. Others point to a persistent 'obsession' by mainstream media which seem to be 'always caning blackfellas and focusing on the negative stuff' (Focus Group, CAAMA, 2006). This is particularly the case for young people who receive coverage only when they are 'doing something wrong' – there are rarely, if ever, news stories that encourage young people or boost their confidence.

Indigenous community broadcasting audiences perceive that mainstream media are not interested in Black listeners or viewers – they are targeting non-Indigenous consumers. 'It's like indigenous people don't exist,' one focus group participant in Melbourne suggested. The importance of communities having a voice is nowhere more evident than in the 2004 'resistance' which led to the burning down of police and court buildings on Palm Island. Indigenous people had access to their own radio station at that time – 4K1G in Townsville – which encouraged open on-air debate, networking it around the country and ignoring a threat of legal action from the Queensland Police Union. This Palm Island man recalls the moment:

> It was a case of getting the facts right and that was important for our mob. Last year [2004], we had every man and his dog against Palm Island at that particular time we had the police union against Palm, we had the Premier talking against Palm, we had the Minister for Aboriginal Affairs talking against Palm, so the mainstream media were getting *their* story rather than the community's story. The only tool for the community to use was 4K1G to get that message back out there that saying that things are not what they're made out to be these are the facts and these are the facts coming from the people.

Audiences are well aware of the tightrope that Indigenous radio and television stations must walk in dealing with sensitive community matters such as domestic violence and child abuse. And their own media occasionally came in for criticism during our study, although this was usually related to programme presenters, formats or reporting style. Interviewees in the APY Lands and focus group participants in Alice Springs were critical of Imparja Television's approach to covering some sensitive issues in Indigenous communities with CAAMA radio listeners suggesting Imparja was 'taming down' negative local news stories, rather than covering them more thoroughly by providing context. They argue that it is crucial that communities hear about such issues:

> It's one of the only ways that people in remote communities find out, other than word of mouth, about what's happening in the rest of their community…CAAMA [radio] will report the negative but it will look at the problem and how it can be solved and what should be done.

Indigenous radio stations, particularly in northern Australia, play a critical role in alerting coastal communities of cyclone and tsunami threats. James Cook University scientist Douglas Goudie found that the most effective way of conveying warnings was by using remote Indigenous radio and combining 'the techno weather reading with more traditional weather-reading in a way that would respect both ways of looking at weather' (Goudie 2005). When Category 5 cyclone Ingrid in early 2005 swept across the north, Indigenous radio stepped to centre stage, as Goudie (2005) recounts:

During that time, day and night, 4K1G and all their affiliates through BRACS gave very good how-to information on what to do if you are in the area at any time threatened – get to higher ground, make sure you have water, torch and the rest of it, which most people already know, but they were very attentive to not over-dramatise it, just giving good clear messages about where it was and maximise safety. So much so I went back to the Bureau of Meteorology in Canberra and said they should get the first formal award in the world from the weather bureau to any media outlet as a reward in appreciation of their accurate, timely and safety-oriented coverage of that event.

On a day-to-day basis, Indigenous radio is the only provider of news and information that directly affects the lives of Indigenous Australians – information about community events, meetings, deaths, funerals, tombstone openings, local sporting results and coverage and, as one participant who called into *Talk Black* to air his views concluded: 'Bumma Bippera's broadcast of the Laura festival; rugby league in the cape; the memorial service for old fella McGuiness [a respected local Indigenous identity]; the tribute concert for the Mills' sisters'. All of this is available *only* on Indigenous radio. It is information of central importance to the daily lives of Indigenous people across Australia. Audiences are in little doubt that mainstream media have failed to provide such services whereas Indigenous media, focused on its Indigenous audience– 'the Murris around here' (Focus Group, BBM, 2005) – is clearly meeting this need.

Promoting cross-cultural dialogue

Several prior studies of the Indigenous media sector have identified its dual role as providing a primary level of service to Indigenous communities as well as representing a cultural bridge between Indigenous and non-Indigenous audiences. Audiences strongly believe that Indigenous media are playing a crucial role in educating the broader Australian community. Many believe, too, that it should be supported and encouraged to play an even more central role in promoting greater cross-cultural awareness and understanding. A significant number, albeit a minority, of focus group participants for this study were non-Indigenous, revealing an existing strong audience for Indigenous media programming amongst the non-Indigenous population. And it was largely from this cohort that the strongest statements about the role of Indigenous media came. Focus group participants from Umeewarra Media in Port Augusta identified it as 'a very racist town' but acknowledged the role being played by local Indigenous radio station Umeewarra Media in 'breaking down some of these barriers'. Indigenous radio has become part of the mediascape in many regional towns and is clearly fulfilling a role in providing all listeners with insights into Indigenous society and issues, absent from mainstream media agendas. This CAAMA radio listener sums it up:

> Sometimes I think that it's only Aboriginal people who are listening but you walk into a business and it's coming out of the speakers in the shop and there's a lot of non-Aboriginal people listening to it and I think that they like the station and are probably interested in Aboriginal issues.

For example, a human services worker in Brisbane is a regular listener to local Indigenous station 98.9FM, primarily because it gives her an insight into local community issues as well as hearing positive stories. In the same focus group, another listener highlighted the importance of station manager Tiga Bayles' regular talkback-interview programme, *Let's Talk*, in providing alternative views of Indigenous Australia than those that predominate in the mainstream:

> I think Tiga's show does a lot to educate the community. We're always going to have people who are going to say, 'What a load of garbage' but it's there and it's a start, and it's a good start and they're bringing the focus on people's way of life.

A crucial medium for music and dance

There is little doubt that without the Indigenous media industry, there would be an almost total absence of Indigenous music on the Australian airwaves. In 2008, blind Gumatj singer Geoffrey Gurrumul Yunupingu won two Australian Record Industry Association (ARIA) Awards – Best Independent and Best World Music Release. For most Australians, he is a 'new' artist – but he has been known to Indigenous Australia, particularly to communities in the Top End, for decades as a member of the internationally successful group, *Yothu Yindi*, and more recently, as lead singer in the hugely popular *Saltwater Band*. It seems that every Indigenous community in the country – no matter how small – has a band or two or three or more somewhere with many having recorded their own CDs. The Indigenous community radio airwaves sing with this music with its widespread appeal. 'It's deadly when they sing in language, eh? It makes your hair stand, eh?' one Palm Island listener explained. The range of musical styles being adapted is extraordinary – country, rock, reggae, ska, hip hop, gospel, alongside traditional forms both on the mainland and in the Torres Strait. CAAMA radio announcer and musician Warren H. Williams (2005) is in no doubt about the importance of Indigenous media:

> I think CAAMA was one of the first to ever have a radio station and a recording studio all in one. So as soon as they recorded that stuff and then put it straight on air, you know – can't get any better than that…most of the BRACS' broadcasters play their own community's music which is very good.

Indigenous music and its widespread appeal across the country on Indigenous media outlets was a common topic in all focus group discussions. It is seen as a key element in establishing and maintaining Indigenous identity, languages and cultures. From the group of teenagers in Townsville who spoke passionately about their love of Indigenous music on their local radio station (4K1G), to the elderly residents on Palm Island and in the Torres Strait, nostalgic about hearing their favourite 'golden oldies' – or songs about 'the pearling days' – Indigenous audiences clearly feel their local radio stations are performing a role that no others can achieve. There is clear enthusiasm for community radio that supports local artists, typified by this listener to Umeewarra Media in South Australia:

> Black artists out of the community, can be…heard and it's also the fact that it, it really supports indigenous artists you know…So it's about local artists from the local area that are singing about things that impact on local people and you wouldn't get that through any other radio station.

Audiences, particularly in remote regions, emphasized the importance of traditional dance as an inherent part of local cultures with community television – particularly ICTV – playing a critical role in both maintenance and education. This comment from a non-Indigenous man who had lived on the APY Lands for decades exemplifies the concerns expressed in the remote communities visited:

> The filming of *inma* [traditional dance] and song and all of that is really important for future generations. Every time someone dies here we lose a library. We lose an enormous amount of information and under the pressures of the outside world that's increasingly at risk.

Conclusion

Audiences for Indigenous radio and television see these media as essential services in communities where they are active. The intimate relationship between Indigenous media producers and their audiences is clear from the commentary offered by listeners and viewers across a wide variety of geographical and cultural settings. It is about giving voices to communities who have something to say as a response to their almost total exclusion from the processes of the mainstream public sphere. Indigenous issues have featured prominently in mainstream news headlines almost since the birth of news media in Australia – but seldom, if ever, have Indigenous people had control of the treatment, form or content of these stories. Indigenous community radio and television have afforded them this power and audiences are clearly participating in the process with passion. For most, these are the only spaces where Indigenous voices on a wide variety of issues that concern Aboriginal and Torres Strait Islanders can be heard without having regard to the constraints of non-Indigenous gatekeepers.

Indigenous community broadcasting provides its audiences with a primary level of service across many areas – social cohesion, maintenance of languages and cultures, boosting self-esteem, education, a source of news and information, promoting cross-cultural dialogue and supporting music and dance. Drawing from all of these, Indigenous media also acts – most often quite deliberately – as a cultural bridge between the parallel universes of Indigenous and non-Indigenous society. But perhaps the most significant element to emerge from the multifarious audience responses on which we have draw here is the notion of a collapse of a barrier between media producers and their audiences. The various ways in which listeners and viewers describe relationships with their media suggest this as a defining characteristic of Indigenous radio and television in Australia. As one non-Indigenous community media worker from the central Australian community of Yuendumu concludes: 'The audiences are the producers.' This is an issue we will take up in more detail in later chapters.

Note

1. 'Deadly' is a term used by Indigenous people across Australia to describe something that is positive and good.

Chapter 5

Audiences for Ethnic Community Radio

It is people's everyday life, everyday awareness and the small things that people hold on to that I find fascinating...For example, how as a foreigner you are constantly prevented from having a sense of genuine belonging, in this instance in Australia. It has a lot to do with the indifference of the dominant culture, and the dominant can't do very much about it either because they live in their own culture, which affords them a certain cultural unselfconsciousness. They have the privilege of not having to question their own identities, ethnicities and cultural specificities (Ang 1999).

Australian cultural theorist Ien Ang – of Chinese ethnicity, born in Indonesia and now living in Australia – has expressed the questions of identity and 'belonging' that arise for so many, if not all, migrants to a new country. Where Indigenous communities can and should feel an even greater ownership and 'belonging' to this land than the mainstream (European) culture, ethnic communities sometimes express a sense of conflict between their identification with their home country; and their need (and desire) to also identify with their new country. This component of our study sought to examine these issues and discover what it is that community broadcasting can offer ethnic audiences, in terms not only of identity and belonging, but also cultural maintenance, education and social diversity. Recent research in the United States has found that 45 percent of all African American, Hispanic, Asian American, Native American and Arab American adults now prefer ethnic television, radio or newspapers to mainstream media sources (Deuze 2006). It is within this context that we embarked on this component of the study – to determine what exactly ethnic audiences value about *their* own programming on Australian community radio.

In analysing the data from our focus groups with audience members and interviews conducted with programme producers and contributors, we were mindful of the special role that community media can play for ethnic communities. The notion of 'giving the voiceless a voice', while much-used, remains pertinent and is relevant on two levels – ethnic community media provide a voice for their communities to communicate their own thoughts, feelings, politics, etc. to the dominant culture; but most importantly to provide a voice to communicate en-masse with each other, to create 'important social hubs and promote inter-cultural dialogue' (Peissl and Tremetzberger 2008: 7).

Programmes produced out of the migrant experience necessarily reflect elements that are both local and global as Moylan (2009: 123) argues in her analysis of 'transnational spoken accents' on Dublin community radio stations. She concludes (2009: 124) that an ongoing demand for migrant-produced programs in Ireland will enable a bridging of the gap 'between publics' – the mainstream public sphere and the multiple, overlapping counterpublics of Irish migrant communities. This strongly suggests a process of social cohesion, a theme taken up by a Peter Lewis-led study for the Council of Europe. The report concluded community radio played a critical role in providing social cohesion generally, and particularly for 'minority ethnic communities and refugee and migrant communities' (Lewis 2008: 7).

Our own research substantiates many of the assumptions that community media scholars have made previously about the role of community broadcasting for ethnic audiences. And ethnic community audience responses mirror, in part, those from Indigenous media audiences. This is particularly evident in relation to language and cultural programming and its acknowledged importance in the maintenance of cultures and identity. The evidence, too, reinforces common threads which link all elements of the community radio and television sector – themes such as provision of local (or community-specific) news, maintenance of 'community' and 'hearing our own voices'. Key themes emerging from ethnic community audiences include:

- programmes and/or stations contribute to the maintenance of cultures and languages;
- audiences are able to maintain or create community connections and networks as a result of programmes;
- specialist music helps to maintain language and culture while also reminding people of home and creating a sense of belonging;
- provision of community news enables audiences to communicate with friends and family, and to find out local community gossip and community events; and
- provision of news and information from overseas is a notable, but less important function for ethnic community radio audiences – while they want to hear news from their home countries, it is more important for them to be able to access Australian and community news *in their own languages*. This enables access to community services and support networks that otherwise remain unknown. It also enables newer migrants to participate more fully in Australian society and interact with co-workers, neighbours, etc. about issues in their town or state.

The findings indicate that while metropolitan and regional stations are performing an important social, cultural and informational role for 'generalist' audiences (i.e. 'mainstream' audiences often a part of the dominant culture/s), ethnic language programming appears to be fulfilling an essential role for many ethnic communities that simply cannot access the critical information they require from any other source. Our results indicate that it is providing an essential service for new migrants. But it is doing far more than this – when a community becomes more established in Australia, ethnic language programmes act as an important link to other members of the same community in their local area through maintenance of languages and links to home which other information and media sources cannot provide. An important example of this process is the provision of ethnic music. When it is not played anywhere else, it creates a sense of 'home', wellbeing and comfort that audiences cannot receive from other forms of entertainment. It assists to create a sense that, while the cultures of ethnic audiences may differ from the dominant mores of their new home, they are still able to 'belong'.

Other important topics of discussion raised by ethnic audiences which appear a little less regularly than the five major themes identified above, include the following:

- station accessibility;
- provision of community announcements (government information, visa information, etc.); and
- news and information from Australia (national and state news, as opposed to the 'community news' theme identified above).

While these themes are important, our discussion in this book is limited to evidence supporting the five major themes identified – further work by the research team on specific aspects of ethnic community broadcasting will expand on these latter three issues.

The five major identified themes provide some guidance. Three of the five themes – maintaining community connections, music programming and provision of community news – are consistent with the attitudes of generalist community radio audiences living in metropolitan and regional areas of Australia. So ethnic audiences share many priorities with them. Ethnic community audiences' identification of the ability for community radio to create/maintain community networks, to support their own music programming and to maintain cultures and languages also creates strong connections between ethnic and Indigenous audiences, as these three themes are common to both cohorts. In these three areas, ethnic and Indigenous audiences have a strong common interest. The fifth theme – provision of news and information from overseas – can be considered unique to the ethnic radio sector and it is no surprise that this is judged by audiences to be one of the most important functions of community radio. It is important to note that there is some difference in the importance of the various functions between 'emerging' communities – that is, new ethnic groups in Australia such as the Sudanese, and some Middle Eastern representatives – and 'established' communities such as Italian, Greek, Chinese and Vietnamese who represent the bulk of post-war migrants. We present our findings on the ethnic community audiences as a whole, but will occasionally make reference to the fact that particular findings related more to 'emerging' or 'established' communities.

Maintaining languages and cultures

Audience focus group discussions centred around 'reasons for listening' to ethnic programming very often turned to a simple observation – based on the notion that it was 'comforting' to hear one's own native language spoken on the radio. Even though many of the focus group participants speak fluent English, the need to hear their own language and to engage with their own culture is paramount. The comments relating to this section are also reflected in another category of responses which we have called 'homesick and longing for home', suggesting a desire – not necessarily to hear news from the home country – but to simply hear the language. One young person who listened to a Chinese-language programme recalled: 'Well in my case, it's just like listening and speaking and thinking English for so long, I just like kind of want to hear my first language for a moment, I feel like, "oh" [relieved sigh], just like that [when I hear it].'

A Sudanese participant, representing one of the emerging community radio programmes which broadcasts for just one hour per week, found the fact that his native language is being used on the radio makes him more interested in the content:

> First of all it's because it's in my language and it concerns me. Yeah, also it encourages me and it actually attracts me to listen to it because it is, it is in my own language. It also reminds me of my own country and the same kind of songs and it informs me of certain people and different issues that I love to keep abreast with.

A second participant from the Sudanese focus group further explained: 'Yeah, it preserves the culture and the national origins and it keeps people, makes it easier for people to, to settle knowing that they are not really total strangers.' A focus group participant who had arrived from Turkey just twelve months previously, with limited English, found the religious and particularly Ramadan programming provided on ethnic radio to be extremely important to his settlement experience. He further commented on the positive feelings that arose upon hearing his own language after his arrival in Australia: '…we came to a country where we didn't know the language or the religion but to be able to hear our own language on these radios, even for a short time, it's quite, it's quite good, we're happy.' A Filipino/Tagalog programme presenter explained some of the feedback she received from audience members upon hearing their own language on Darwin radio:

> it's very brain draining but it is very nice because, at one stage somebody has texted me and this is from the boat, from an international boat that docked at the wharf and they said to me that, 'Oh, it is very nice to hear your voice on the radio, speaking our own lingo'.

Participants in the Tongan focus group, which was run entirely in English because of the strong English proficiency of participants, also found this notion of language and cultural maintenance very important. In fact, the Tongan discussions were indicative of many other comments within the 'language' theme which highlighted the importance of hearing their own language for a variety of reasons – essentially because it was comforting, the educational value of being able to learn more about their own language, being reminded of words that have been forgotten and using language programming to help children and grandchildren pick up the finer elements of the various languages. An exchange during the Tongan focus group discussion illustrated this:

Participant 1: Most of us don't use language at home and listening to the radio makes us feel more like we are at home (in Tonga).
Participant 2: And there is a sense of pride there too, hearing you own language go over the radio, it really helps there too.
Participant 3: The programme is good for language retention and it helps you learn new words, I always learn a new word or two when I listen to the radio programme.
Participant 4: It is something to do. You get to listen to the radio and you feel at home listening to your own language. It also helps me to practice my language.

An exchange during the Chinese youth focus group discussion emphasizes the importance of language programming to young people who may be fluent in English but who still wish to practice their native tongue – or perhaps the language of their parents – in order to maintain and improve their language skills:

Mediator: What would you do if this programme didn't exist? What would that mean?
Participant 1: If it didn't exist, I wouldn't know all of them [the other audience members] right now, maybe only Alice and Lena.
Participant 2: Yeah we all know each other [through the programme]...
Participant 1: And my Chinese would probably be a lot worse.
Participant 2: A lot worse or a little worse?
Participant 1: A lot worse.
Participant 2: No way.
Participant 1: It can actually get a lot worse, you know!

The Turkish focus group further expanded on the notion of the importance of language programming and it was a relatively consistent comment that audience members – particularly older audience members – wanted to hear voices on the radio that spoke their mother tongue 'well'. This, they argue, is important for their own language maintenance as well as for benefiting their children, who they often feel are speaking a 'tainted' version of their native language due to their increasing proficiency in English. This comment is representative of other participants from the Greek Seniors, Tongan and Serbian focus groups who emphasize the importance of hearing 'well-spoken' languages on air:

We are getting so much enjoyment out of this radio, but there is also the side that needs, that needs to be bettered as well, for example...the Turkish language must be really, really good. When Turkish children listen to this radio, they need to, they need to learn the language properly and also for bilingual people, it's very important.

Language maintenance and even revival, then, is considered by ethnic audiences to be one of the most important contributions community radio has made and continues to make.

Maintaining community connections and networks

There are a number of comments or discussion themes arising from the ethnic programming focus groups which fall within the general category of 'maintaining community connections and networks'. The desire for local community news, for example, is closely related to the theme of maintaining community networks but because we are able to sufficiently distinguish them, they will be discussed separately.

This discussion deals specifically with the role of ethnic programmes and stations in 'creating' or 'maintaining' community spirit, social life and connections between members of the same community. Interestingly, this is being done in a number of different ways by radio programmes. Some audience members feel the provision of a music request and talkback show is an important contributor to the maintenance of community networks, while others identify the establishment of a programme 'fan club', or regular organization of community gatherings, as evidence that a radio programme is assisting in the maintenance of community connections and networks.

The Sudanese focus group discussed the importance of its weekly radio programme in creating community connections and the findings indicate this is perhaps more important to emerging communities. Established communities such as the Greeks and Serbians seem to have multiple avenues through which to be in touch with community members – regular church gatherings, cultural events, social clubs and so on – in which radio programmes are not necessarily directly involved. For emerging communities, however, these organized social groups are non-existent and it is in these cases that radio provides a more important source of 'community glue'. This comment from a participant in the Sudanese focus group discussion is typical of many around this topic:

> The radio broadcasting is the only thing that also connects me to other members of the community and I'm unable to do that within just this one hour. The other thing and again it's the time when it's broadcast because whether it's girls, boys, men, women, housewives, they either go to school, or go to work or go even, even housewives are studying languages, and the only time when they come back home is after this broadcasting time and this is their only means whereby they can get the information.

Another Sudanese focus group participant further demonstrated that radio is often the only source of information for this emerging community, which has yet to make solid connections between new arrivals and those already established here:

Yeah, that's what it's considered, a connecting means for information…when you turn the station on, you can hear names of some people that are around that you are not aware that they're even here and this gets you, starting to search and find where they are and by talking between the listener and the announcer. Also it's, it's a means of contacting certain people or anyone for that matter, especially if there is an occasion that you want to send a greetings or a congratulations, there's a wedding of some people, or presenting them as song and saying presented to such and such in the names and song and of course this is something very interesting. Also, recently the Horn of Africa had some big celebrations for the community and in it there were quite a lot of different, not just issues, but different things that were happening and the radio was able to basically take all that and transmit it to the community at large and this was something very exciting for them…this of course was a medium for them that otherwise they would not have been able to bring it to everyone that maybe didn't know about it.

The Tongan community in Adelaide feels a little isolated from other larger Tongan communities on the eastern seaboard, and suggests that for this reason, radio performs a more important function as a source of community networking:

You find Tongans in groups in the same areas in Sydney, Melbourne and Brisbane but we are spread out in Adelaide and there are only a few places and times that we get together and we do that by listening to the radio.

Significantly, focus group members across this sub-sector identify not only the importance of connecting with their own community through the radio station, but also with the broader Australian community. Several participants in the Turkish focus group felt this is one of the key roles of the programme, which at the time broadcast only one hour per week:

The radio, this radio station is not separating us from Australia, as our friend said before, it's integrating us to Australia. It's very important. Our children are growing up Australians anyway, maybe they're having difficulty adapting culturally, but through the radio, they will be able to get some help or adapt anyway. And also we see our differences as richness, in Turkey too, where we come from different backgrounds…we're living the same thing here too and we're happy about that. Everyone's got their own different folklore and songs and everything else so we have that here too and we're happy with that.

Participants in the Vietnamese focus group were particularly vocal on this theme, as their programme seems to provide a unique mix of requests, talkback, oral history, counselling and even live karaoke. The overwhelming impression is of the importance of the programme in introducing community members to each other, keeping listeners up to date with what other community members are doing and informing listeners about community events.

Significantly, it is the humour and entertainment value of the programme which seems to draw listeners together:

> Participant 1: I like this station because it is a very open programme. We can call in and you know, and share our feelings with others and we can recognize their voice but we don't know who [they are] but we can call in and talk and share our feelings and it makes us feel good about that. After a long day at work we look forward to tuning into this programme and we can talk to all the listeners and we hope that the programme can have longer time because the time we feel is not enough, the broadcasting time. We highly appreciate the service of this radio station. It provides a great service to our community so I always recommend this station to all the people I know.
> Participant 2: …this community radio programme is mainly for entertainment, and it's like a bridge to connect the listeners to one another.
> Participant 1: It's, this community programme is a, mainly to do with entertainment and you know, to connect people in the community to one another.

The Vietnamese focus group gave examples of community members calling up during crisis times for the family – and receiving advice either from the programme presenter on air – or from other community members who then called up the station to offer advice. They often recognize the voices of people who call in to the station regularly while out shopping or in the street, even though they do not know that person by sight. Another listener uses the programme as a kind of dating service, and if he 'thought the caller was a good singer or a good talker', he leaves his number with the station and asks that caller to get in contact with him. Several of the focus group members had met up in this way.

The Chinese youth programme at radio station 4EB in Brisbane led to the establishment of a fan club for the program and the focus group we conducted there was primarily comprised of club members. They organize social gatherings, barbeques, quiz nights and regularly speak to each other during and after the programme through MSN and other Internet sources to discuss on-air content. All members of this focus group agree they have been introduced to a range of like-minded young Chinese people through the programme and the fan club.

Closely related to the themes of language preservation and creation or maintenance of community networks is regular mention of music programming as one of the key reasons ethnic audiences listen to community radio. Music is, of course, a real avenue for language and cultural maintenance as explored in the first theme. But because it was regularly raised as an issue by focus group participants, we have considered it a separate theme. The emergence of ethic music as one of the key reasons why people listen is a further demonstration of the importance of ethnic programming in maintaining cultures and languages.

Music programming

Like metropolitan, regional and Indigenous audiences, music programming emerged as one of the key reasons why ethnic audiences tune in to community radio. While music content is more important for some ethnic radio programmes than others, there is a widespread view from audiences that 'music from home' is one of the key reasons they listen to community radio. For the older generation, exposing their children and grandchildren to traditional music is an important function of ethnic radio which reinforces that audiences are not just listening to 'music from home' for entertainment or familiarity, but as a means to further maintain their cultures and languages. There is also a sense that members from outside particular groups enjoy the music even though they might not understand what is being said or sung – and so music is seen as a way to bridge cultural gaps between ethnic communities and mainstream Australia. The love of music programming is an integral part of these audiences' desires to hear their first languages:

> I just feel that looking forward to listen to broadcast in my language every Wednesday, every time I come home from work, I am looking forward to listen to the broadcasting in Indonesian. Yeah, not just the music, the Dangu music. And because the, also the broadcast keeps me up to date with what's happening in the community, even though the music is probably, have more priority. I feel happy (Indonesian Focus Group, Darwin, 2006).

Another Indonesian participant called home to Indonesia to let his family hear the music he was able to enjoy in Darwin:

> When I listen to radio, if I talk to my father on the telephone I will put the telephone close to the radio so he could hear the standard of [Indonesian] music, he will be surprised to hear the standard of music in Australia.

The Tongan focus group in Adelaide reiterated the importance of music to the popularity of its programme, primarily because it was music they cannot get from any other source:

> Participant 1: For me, it is the music. I want to listen to Tongan music.
> Participant 2: If the time devoted to the programme was expanded, it would be good to have more music.
> Participant 3: The main thing for me is the music because some of us don't have access to Tongan music.
> Participant 1: Commercial radio stations are not so into Tongan music.

The Turkish focus group, which provided a great deal of interesting conversation and extended comments for the project, identified the centrality of music to cultural maintenance. Language, cultural events such as religious occasions and music are consistently identified by focus groups as important services provided by ethnic community radio that are central to the celebration and maintenance of traditional culture:

> I just want to add something. Turkish folklore is very strong and…culture is very, very strong. Within this folklore, the music, the songs, they are written from the heart, when someone's died or come through or…through love, the songs are written that way so we are able to listen to those songs, cultural songs through the radio (Turkish Focus Group, Melbourne, 2006).

The music programming provided by the Vietnamese youth programme on Melbourne's progressive community radio station 3CR also received a positive response from focus group participants, although in the case of the Vietnamese community it seems the music programming is more interactive than with other groups we examined in this study. Rather than just listening to and enjoying the music, participants call in to the station and sing their favourite songs on air or play musical instruments, live, for listeners:

> Participant 1: Yeah, elderly people like myself like the music programme. And we all take part in that, I sing, she sings, he sings.
> Mediator: Karaoke on radio?
> Participant 1: Yeah.
> Participant 2: We can play guitar.
> Mediator: Oh great!
> Participant 2: Play guitar and sing karaoke sometimes.

Within this theme, which demonstrates the importance of music to ethnic audiences, many focus group participants pointed out the bridging role that music actively plays between the ethnic community cultures and mainstream Australia. Several reported listening to their own language programme at their workplaces with co-workers 'always happy' to hear the music and talk even if they often cannot understand spoken word content. One Serbian focus group member explained:

> Oh, I can tell you, I work at the hospital in the evening [and] when I can I turn on the radio and then I said to the nurses, 'come on this my music'. A few times I took the CDs of the bands [in to work]…

And the Turkish focus group:

> I talk to people who plays Turkish [music] but they are Australians and when I ask them, what's the difference between Turkish music you know, in Australia, you know the Western music, he said you can't compare because Western music just one, two, three, four, but Turkish music five beats…Australian culture started to discover Turkish

music…I was in the city, about two months ago, when these people played Turkish music, all Australians, more than 80 percent of audiences were Australians, they danced with the Turkish music…it was Turkish music so this kind of things connects the Australian culture towards our culture…

This was supported by some comments from generalist metropolitan and regional community radio focus groups. While some in the metropolitan and regional groups say they switch off when ethnic language programmes start, others welcome it as part of the diversity of programming they enjoy (Focus Group, 3CR Melbourne, 2005):

Participant 1: And that's what you love about it.
Participant 2: The diversity, the diversity.
Participant 1: Switch it on.
Participant 2: Yeah.
Participant 1: And not understand what's being said.
Participant 2: Absolutely.
Participant 1: And you might even just listen to it because you like the music.
Participant 2: Yes.
Participant 1: I quite often do that.

And from the music-loving audiences of Canberra's community radio station, ARTSOUND:

What I like most is the amount of information some of the presenters have, the knowledge they have about the music they present and it's, the music is so different from what you hear everywhere else, you don't find anywhere else. Because I didn't realize how much there was out there until I started to listening to Artsound. Especially the South American and what's the music, African music, it's just, so much of it, really brilliant.

The importance placed on music programming by a majority of ethnic focus group participants suggests to us that music is one of the key reasons why they listen – and this applies to both ethnic and non-ethnic audiences. For ethnic audiences, hearing music is an integral part of the process of maintaining cultures and languages. It is also something familiar which reminds them of home. Many participants feel there are many 'non-ethnic' Australians who tune in to the ethnic music broadcasts just for the pure appreciation of the music.

It is this regular mention of music and the importance of request shows on ethnic community radio that leads us to suggest that the large number of community radio listeners identified in the quantitative McNair Ingenuity survey who nominated 'specialist music and information programming' as their main reason for listening may indeed have been referring to specialist ethnic or world music programming – not just the usual jazz, fine music or country music 'specialist' formats that exist. The Community Broadcasting

Database Surveys (Australian Communications and Media Authority 2005; CB Online 2006) conclude that music programming is generally less important to the ethnic broadcasting sector than to the generalist sector, with a higher proportion of spoken-word content run on ethnic radio programmes. This is clearly the case, and is probably primarily due to community media sector funding arrangements which requires programmes to provide at least 50 percent language content before a programme can receive specialist funding. These focus group results bear out the importance of spoken-word programming, which will be dealt with in the next section. But they also suggest that music programming is not just a source of entertainment. For many people, it is a way of maintaining cultures and languages and for some is clearly as important as spoken-word programming in terms of learning and/or maintaining languages. Put simply, music is considered by ethnic community radio audiences to be a central component of creating and maintaining cultural and community connections.

Provision of community news

Closely related to the earlier theme of 'maintaining community connections', the provision of local community news is one of the key reasons why ethnic audiences tune in to local volunteer-run radio. This finding is also consistent with results from both the metropolitan/regional generalist stations and the Indigenous media fieldwork which concludes that provision of local news and information is one of the key functions of community broadcasting. Within this general definition of 'community news', we have primarily considered news about local ethnic communities. However, many focus group participants mentioned the importance of finding out about what was going on *in their local area generally,* particularly if they were new arrivals to Australia. We had expected most focus group participants to nominate 'news from home/overseas' as one of the key functions of their chosen radio programme so it was something of a surprise to discover that they were more concerned about accessing information about their own communities here – and the broader community surrounding them – provided it was in their own languages.

Vietnamese focus group participants – all from Melbourne – who generally love their music content, also greatly appreciate the high levels of spoken-word content on their programme. One older woman reported calling in for counselling and for someone to talk to. Another explained that community members call in to talk about trouble they were having with their families. Essentially, though, they are more interested in what is happening in the Melbourne Vietnamese community than issues outside Australia:

Participant 1: We talk about you know, that drug dealer, the one that was caught in Singapore[1] that was hanged and sometimes we talk about communists and communism.

Participant 2: And sometimes we talk about other things but on the whole we talk more about the issues here in the Vietnamese community here rather than issues outside the community.
Participant 1: Yeah.
Participant 2: Anything that affects us right in Melbourne, yeah.

Clearly, this 'community news' theme and discussion was dominated by audiences' desires to find out what is essentially community gossip (e.g. 'who's married their daughter off' [Greek Seniors' Focus Group, Brisbane, 2006]), funerals and achievements of local community members. Such programmes are also a source of information about community events. The Tongan focus group, which identified that they are essentially an oral culture whose people rely heavily on face-to-face contact and telephone conversations, find the radio particularly useful for disseminating information about community events and gatherings:

Participant 1: It is a really effective communication tool. Everyone knows what is going on and where you should be.
Participant 2: It is the last confirmation for us. Hearing things on the programme reminds us that they are on.
Participant 1: Really, it is like the final confirmation to cement plans and that is a more effective way of doing it (letting us know about events), than phoning people or emailing them.
Participant 2: You hear that radio every Friday and you know what is going on for the weekend.

The Serbian community also discussed the use of their programme as a very localized source of information about the Albury-Wodonga Serbian population:

Mediator: OK, so just to follow up on that, some of the communities that we've spoken to have said that their language programme enables them to keep up with what's going on in the community and to find out what's happening with individual families, you know...
Participant 1: Yeah, that is true, true.
Mediator: Do you find out those sorts of things from your programme?
Participant 2: Yep, absolutely, yes.
Participant 1: Only thing, we don't announce death.
Participant 2: Well we should do that too.
Participant 3: It's much less local Australian news because everybody can see it on the television and out from the community, it's mainly the, the happy things.
Participant 1: Happy things and social events, like when the minister, the priest comes around and there's the church service...

The Greek community, which enjoys a number of weekly programme on Radio 4EB in Brisbane, similarly reiterated:

> In local news, in our local news, we find out who's died, who's in hospital, what's happening to people we're interested with…we hear about funerals that we might have missed, we hear about birthdays, people's birthdays, you know someone, they have a habit of ringing up and saying, 'play this record for my friend because it's their name day or their birthday' or whatever. So that way I find out about who's celebrating what and the, various functions that are on, whether I can attend or not, as the other lady said.

Established communities such as the Tongan, Serbian and Greek communities seem more likely to use their radio programmes for this type of community news, announcement of events, etc. than they are to use it as a source of local Australian news in their own language. This is because they generally feel confident about accessing news about Brisbane, Queensland, Australia and so on from the English-language media – and so their programmes have taken on a more localized/community component. This is not the case for emerging communities, such as the Sudanese and some new Turkish migrants, who rely on programming for Australian news, presented in their own languages, and more essential information about visa processes, employment and so on.

A Sudanese focus group participant reiterated the importance of not just hearing news from the home country, but being able to easily access local and national news from Australia through Sudanese-language programming:

> Because you don't have much time here to meet with all your friends…and especially when you're driving, you turn the station on and it attracts you, you know just pulls you towards it because you're anxious to hear what's going on, something in your own language and it keeps you occupied and abreast of what's happening. And again it talks about issues that are also happening in the country itself, not just overseas.

A member of the Turkish focus group further clarified the importance of ethnic language programming in providing access to essential government-related benefits – administered through the Centrelink agency – and information:

> As we're living here, we're able to hear what our responsibilities are and also our rights are here, like for example, when you hear information about Centrelink, or about taxation office, traffic infringement notices to be aware of those and what to do and what not to do. Legal, family matters, divorces, domestic violence, those kinds of things, to get those information in Turkish. To understand these matters wrongly or understand them a little bit does not, will not help you.

One of the Greek Seniors' focus group participants explained the importance of receiving local community news – in Greek – from community radio because of the difficulties in accessing that type of news from Australian sources which are too difficult to understand:

> In my case, I was very happy because it's true Greeks are very interested in news, they are very news conscious. Whether it's local or Greece or the world at large, at last people would be informed because you know a lot of them say, migration is, you're deaf and dumb. So, suddenly you're getting your communication skills back.

Many of the focus group participants commented on the role of Special Broadcasting Service (SBS) language broadcasting in the discussions, and this material will be dealt with shortly. However, it is important to mention here that the ethnic community members draw an interesting distinction between the role of language programming on the government-funded SBS and that provided by their local, largely volunteer ethnic community broadcaster. A member of the Greek Seniors' focus group explained that while SBS is considered a source of information for Greek Australians and about news from the home country, it cannot provide the immediate and local news that Brisbane's ethnic community radio station 4EB, for example, provides to listeners, specifically about the Brisbane Greek community. Local Greek programming is more accessible, and in many ways, more relevant to their day-to-day life, than the Greek-language programming on SBS Radio (albeit the latter was very highly valued).

These findings highlight the importance of local community information and are consistent with the quantitative results from the McNair Ingenuity studies (2004; 2006; 2008), which reported that 'local news and information' was one of the primary 'reasons for listening' cited by community radio audiences. Similarly, data collected by the Centrelink agency provides further support for these findings, revealing that radio broadcasts in a community's first language are the *second most-preferred method* for ethnic communities to obtain information about government services. They are a more preferred method than newspapers in their own languages, and came in second behind translated brochures and fact sheets easily accessible from Centrelink offices (Centrelink 2003: 5).

Provision of news and information from overseas

While local community news content slightly 'out-rated' in popularity this final theme of provision of news and information from overseas, these two categories are clearly related to community members' needs to not only be informed about events and happenings in their Australian community, but also their desire to maintain a link with their home countries. This theme is closely related to another series of comments we have considered within the framework, 'homesick and longing for home', and both reflect a desire by participants to hear familiar terminology, familiar towns and place names, and to keep up with the politics of their home country. It also enables community members to hear news that may affect family members who remain in their countries of origin. The importance of news from overseas is borne out by the quantitative data from community broadcasting industry surveys (Australian Communications and Media Authority 2005; CB Online 2006), which demonstrate that ethnic stations use three times as much international satellite content as their generalist station colleagues. These two themes are also generally reflective of a broad range of comments from ethnic radio audiences which suggest the heightened importance of news and information programming. Indeed, many comment that news, followed by traditional music, is their primary reason for tuning in. Participants from the Tongan focus group in Adelaide explained:

> Participant 1: Even the general news for people like us who have been raised here (in Australia) is good because we learn news about what is going on in Tonga.
> Participant 2: Not everyone has the Internet to access news from home (Tonga) and listen to what is going on in Tonga and Tongan communities around the world, especially in American, New Zealand and Australian Tongan communities.

A young woman in Year 11 who attended the Turkish focus group was born in Australia but still considers it important to keep up with news from Turkey:

> It's also given me a chance to, like, most of my friends they don't usually tend to, like, follow the issues that are going in Turkey and this is easy for me to, by automatically listening to the Turkish radio to actually go to school the next day and actually explain the problems that are happening in our own country so it actually gives me an advantage in that way.

There was also a sense that the only time their home country was mentioned by mainstream Australian media was when there was a war, major disaster or an event involving 'Australians' – but what they really desire is general, 'ordinary' day-to-day news from their country. A Sudanese participant explained:

> Another thing as far as the importance of the station for me, almost all the information that we get, for example on Sudan through the other media, like television and so on, the news, it's basically when something is happening, something big with a foreign major disaster or something, they bring in and they concentrate on that particular area but they don't talk about the street life, about daily life in general, how is it happening there, that's not giving them any information from any of the other media.

Several focus group participants mentioned the importance of receiving news from home, but where possible, suggested the international news component be produced locally to ensure old tensions and arguments occurring in the home country are not continually reiterated in the ethnic media here. A Sudanese focus group participant again offered this comment:

> The role [of the programme] is very sensitive of the station because it's probably the only medium that joins north and south because we come from a war-torn country and it's always between the north and the south and…the radio is the medium that joins them together peacefully and they become one [here in Australia] and that is very important.

The National Ethnic Multicultural Broadcasters' Council (NEMBC) has recommended to a Australian Parliament's House of Representatives Standing Committee inquiry into community broadcasting that locally produced news services for ethnic communities are an essential part of smoothing the migrant settlement experience, and promoting cohesion among ethnic communities in Australia:

> News services provided by ethnic community broadcasters mediate against the sometimes undesirable influence of foreign news services. The latter are generally produced to serve the national interests of the country from which they emanate. As such they are often hostile to the tenets of multiculturalism. Locally generated ethnic news services are broadcast in an Australian context giving the immediacy and localism that it implies (National Ethnic and Multicultural Broadcasters' Council 2006: 16).

Harking back to a previous comment about the role of SBS radio, it is quite possible that many people in ethnic communities rely on SBS for their general news from home but are, in fact, relying on local ethnic language programming for more localized and specific information, music and cultural content. SBS radio began in 1975 with television following in 1979–1980. SBS is most commonly mentioned by older focus group participants who identify it as a major source of news and current affairs for them, not just about their own country but about other nations around the world. Limited television news programming in language on SBS is also identified as a major source of international news for some, although there are also some complaints that SBS is dominated by certain ethnic groups and does not provide news relevant to all significant communities:

> Participant 1: Sunday morning I wake up and I want to put it [on] SBS. From six o'clock to twelve o'clock, every different nation, country.
> Participant 2: Every country.
> Participant 1: Foreign languages only not Serbian, never.
> Participant 2: Yeah, never.

Participant 1: Then, now, even Centrelink, I go over there, I find it, all other people, languages, didn't find the Serbian…A few years ago Red Star was a [Serbian soccer team] champion, like a champion on the belt, they'd beaten Japan and one South American team. Never been in any Australian newspaper around Australia, on the TV or broadcasting.
Participant 2: Anywhere.
Participant 1: Nowhere and we hardly even could find out that Red Star beat that South American team.
Participant 2: Yep.
Participant 1: And they're world champions.
Participant 2: Three nil.
Participant 1: And they, so many Serbs around the world…if they win, they don't mention it, if they lose, they don't mention it…

Despite this exchange, focus groups participants generally agree that they do obtain news about their home country from SBS radio in language, or from their ethnic community radio programme. As discussed previously, though, community radio ethnic programmes seem slightly more likely to be valued as a source of local community news or news about settlement in Australia, than as a source of 'news from home'.

While the five key themes identified above represent the most commonly cited value of community broadcasting for ethnic audiences, comments made by audiences about the role of community radio in promoting what we might call social wellbeing and social cohesion (Lewis 2008) are significant. It suggests that community radio might be considered a useful avenue for government and community services to access as a means of improving the emotional and social wellbeing of many ethnic community members, particularly recent immigrants.

Community radio and social cohesion

For ethnic communities, the joy of hearing a familiar voice or music on radio was a common example cited for making audiences 'feel better'. One Macedonian listener described the transition from feeling depressed on arrival here to one of joy: 'I was happiest when I heard the Macedonian radio and [then] Australia was very nice.' Others talked about the camaraderie that stems from being aware of a supportive cohort and having easy access to it. It is clear that ethnic community radio, like Indigenous broadcasting, is creating a 'sense of belonging' among audiences across Australia. Clearly, this is having a positive impact on individuals in terms of their perceptions of wellbeing. Most ethnic language programmes are broadcast on generalist community stations thus 'including' a far wider audience than would be the case if they were broadcast on a sequestered frequency. As many of our interviewees and focus group participants volunteered, this tends to bring cultural communities together –

immigrant communities, in particular, suggested that it gave them an opportunity to alert the broader Australian community that 'we are here'. Others acknowledged the importance of access for otherwise marginalized groups. This exchange from the 3CR focus group in Melbourne is instructive:

Participant 1: Well when you think about it, like, the groups like the Palestinians don't have a voice in the mainstream at all.
Participant 2: They're at least given the chance to articulate their views.
Participant 1: That's right.

Although some participants acknowledge their lack of comprehension of various community languages involved, they nevertheless persevere with listening because it reminds them of Australia's multicultural nature. And listening to music is identified as being able to transcend virtually all cultural barriers.

The process of inclusion is also manifested in the way that several of the ethnic and Indigenous radio presenters had become well-known celebrities within their own communities. The enthusiasm with which focus group participants and interviewees spoke about such figures – for example, a presenter for a Vietnamese youth programme and a local talkback host on Indigenous radio in North Queensland – suggests these programmes provide an anchor for such communities. A similar process is evident in the relationships between community organizations – for example, the Asylum Seekers Resource Centre in Melbourne – and their local radio stations. The broadcast of diverse ethnicities or Indigenous cultures – either by generalist stations or via exclusive Indigenous or ethnic stations – communicates the presence of diversity to the broader community. All of this engenders a sense of belonging and, we suggest, is highly likely to lead to increasing levels of individual wellbeing.

The deep emotional impact of the settlement experience on immigrants to Australia was a major issue evident in all ten focus groups conducted with ethnic community radio audiences. As one Sudanese interviewee commented, 'When you come to Australia, there are a lot of things very, very difficult for you, you know.' Another summed up the process of arriving here with little or no English literacy, only to discover a local radio programme using a recognizable language as an epiphany (Turkish Focus Group, 2006): 'A lot of them [migrants] say, migration is, you're deaf and dumb. So, suddenly you're getting your communication skills back.' Another said simply (Macedonian Focus Group, 2006): 'When I came to Australia here, I felt like I was on Mars. I wasn't aware there was [sic] that many Macedonians.'

But, as this Macedonian focus group participant explains, social exclusion is not confined to one linguistic community and those whose first language is English:

So you're isolated linguistically and socially. And quite often the, other language groups isolate other language groups because then you go to the assistance of others and someone has to stand up and protect your own patch.

Feelings of isolation, homesickness and loneliness loom large in the settlement experience, according to the commentary from ethnic community media audiences. And it is to counter this that many groups have turned to community radio in Australia to offer an alternative, as this Tongan listener in Adelaide explains: 'We started the programme because of the isolation the women were feeling.' More than 2,500 kilometres north, members of the Filipino community in Darwin explained how 'discovering' a Tugalog language programme on a local community radio station changed their attitudes about being in a foreign land. Hearing news from home, along with information about local support services and music – in a familiar language – helped many to overcome feelings of isolation and depression, commonly described simply as 'homesickness'.

Australia's growing Chinese community, too, revealed feelings of social isolation, especially for newly arrived immigrants or older members of the community whose English literacy was either poor or non-existent. Members of a Chinese youth focus group explain it variously like this (Chinese Focus Group, 2006):

> You feel comfortable to talk to people you actually know. You can actually, like, post it up and they can actually help you…they help give, like, advices [sic] and stuff…Well it's basically a connection of all the audience.
>
> A lot of Chinese people have their cultural lives at home. We provide a constant media to give information and in a dynamic way for Chinese. So it's a different approach to bringing the culture back. By providing a weekly programme it constantly draws them back.
>
> You have to listen, because listening to your own lingo, it compensates your homesickness and then, you know, it, it gives a smile on your face.

This feeling of wellbeing flowing from familiarity became a common theme emerging from ethnic language focus groups and interviews. One summarized it this way: 'The Macedonian people are very happy because they're being informed, not being isolated.' Another from the Greek Seniors' focus group focused on the social networking aspect: 'I guess companionship is part of it, not feeling isolated, connecting even from home.'

Although audiences are overwhelmingly supportive of the role of community radio, in particular, in bringing people together, it has not been an easy path for several ethnic communities. Members of the Sudanese community in Melbourne, for example, explain how starting a local programme in Australia – their adopted new homeland – has enabled the political division between North and South Sudan to 'remain in Sudan' because of a neutral stance being adopted by presenters of and participants in the Sudanese programme on Melbourne community radio. But for this volunteer producing Macedonian community radio programmes, the horrors of a homeland war returned in various ways to haunt her:

> During that horrible war, knowing in that war-torn country [things] used to be really awful and hurtful, I used to have a good cry – half an hour, one hour before I go to programme, because it was awful. I was trying to concentrate and think, 'How am I going to handle this?'

Despite trying to deal with the realities of family and friends being threatened, the politics of persecution followed her to Australia:

> And they used to threaten me; they used to call me, oh yes, they used to tell me, you know, when you come out, there is a bomb under your car and everything. And I used to…listen and say, 'Thank you very much, is there anything else?'…So the nights I… would put the…receiver [down] and they would call back again and again…But after that, the shiver goes through my spine – oh my god, should I call the police? What should I do, you know?

While this may not be a common story, it is not the only case we came across where volunteers working for the betterment of their own communities fell foul of internal political differences. It offers another sobering insight into the enormous emotional strain experienced by some ethnic community radio producers. The support network community radio stations offer people like this volunteer presenter provide a barrier, of sorts, against such attacks. As suggested by the overwhelming commentary from community broadcasting audiences, both production *and* reception are empowering processes. Moreover these experiences remind us, as researchers, to be mindful of the differences and divisions within ethnic communities and to avoid assumptions of homogeneity.

Conclusion

The results from this series of ten focus group discussions with ethnic audiences from a range of communities around Australia indicate that audiences are overwhelmingly supportive of the information and entertainment service provided by their programmes. They are grateful to both the stations and the individual presenters and producers for the offerings they make to the community, and to issues they consider as essential to their community life – maintenance of cultures and languages, enjoyment of traditional music, creation and maintenance of community networks, provision of local community news and essential 'settlement' information and provision of news from home to help with feelings of anxiety and homesickness. In addition, not only the 'news from home', but also the simple broadcasting of familiar language and music helps to relieve feelings of anxiety, promoting feelings of wellbeing. The additional community connections created by ethnic community radio programming could indeed be considered an important tool in the creation of social cohesion within the ethnic and broader community.

The importance of all types of news programming to ethnic communities is particularly important to consider. The provision of news serves multiple purposes – informing people about local community events and gossip, as well as providing important information for new migrants and older people with poor English skills about legal issues, visas and Australian cultural practices, amongst other things. The role of music in the lives of all the community radio listeners is strong, with many ethnic focus group participants speaking passionately about the impact that traditional music programming has on their general feelings of wellbeing and happiness. Music programming is essential to their enjoyment of ethnic radio, and is integrally connected to maintenance of cultures and languages. Indeed, 'hearing your own language' was the most commonly expressed reason for listening to ethnic community radio and the further experience of 'hearing music in your own language' only serves to underline the importance of such programmes. Music is used for entertainment, to improve and maintain language skills, to communicate with other community members through request programmes and to reignite memories of home.

This suggests that while ethnic audiences are extremely supportive of and interested in spoken-word language programming – particularly news content – any regulatory requirements (which currently exist in Australia) to fund only ethnic programming that includes a large spoken-word component should be reconsidered. Ethnic audiences have clearly indicated that music is not only just a form of entertainment, but also fills a central cultural and language maintenance role. While some balance between spoken-word language programming and music programming is certainly needed, audiences seem to place equal cultural value on both.

We have so far presented a range of information based on findings from Indigenous and ethnic community broadcasting audiences. It is important, however, to put these findings into the general context of 'what it is' community broadcasting does, and should do. The next chapter takes up this issue and suggests a model for evaluating the broader functions of community broadcasting.

Note

1. In December 2005 Vietnamese-born Australian citizen Nguyen Tuong Van was hanged in Singapore for the importation of 400 grams of heroin. He was twenty-five years old and had been on death row for almost two years. His trial and subsequent death received considerable media coverage in Australia.

Chapter 6

Breaking down the Barriers

There is more than a verbal tie between the words common, community, and communication. Try the experiment of communicating, with fullness and accuracy, some experience to another, especially if it be somewhat complicated, and you will find your own attitude toward your experience changing (John Dewey 1859–1952).

The community broadcasting sector in Australia is perhaps unique internationally in that it incorporates a vast range of popular cultures. The generalist sector represents views ranging from the extreme political left to the far Christian right with the majority of stations identifying with middle of the road politics (Forde 2001). Equally, Indigenous and ethnic community broadcasting sectors present diverse views on issues such as identity and belonging. In these ways, the Australian experience with community broadcasting as a whole does not fit easily into definitions drawn from particular social, political and cultural arenas because all are represented and often compete for space. Listeners become resources for the development of multiple and complex media and cultural literacies through participation on a localized and personalized scale. From a pragmatic perspective, the key to the success of community broadcasting for Indigenous and ethnic communities in particular is functionality – where local communities identify concrete, functional outcomes as a result of their involvement with stations at any level, then their participation will continue, even if that participation amounts to 'merely listening' (Bickford 1996). In these ways, the Australian community broadcasting sector plays an important role in encouraging dialogue between the diverse cultural arenas we have considered at length in this book – a process which is integral to sustaining communities' social structure.

In making our arguments around 'community media', we acknowledge the complexity of the term 'community' and thus invoke a broad working definition. We define 'community' as a group with common interests and shared concerns, which is characterized by a sense of belonging for its members (Day 2006; Little 2002: 3).

The chosen methodology for our investigations of the community broadcasting sector thus far – grounded theory – has meant that the ideas we propose originate in the sector itself. These are the thoughts, comments and observations of those who participate at various levels in the everyday practices of what we call – perhaps sometimes offhandedly – 'community broadcasting'. We suggest that this approach, particularly in terms of an engagement with audiences, has given us an insight into the processes that 'make' community broadcasting cultures. Until now, the voices of participants – audiences – have been largely absent from such analyses. A need to try to fill this theoretical void was one of the driving forces behind this book. Our study of audiences confirms that for many marginalized groups in Australia, community-produced radio and television represents a primary level of service. This is most evident in Indigenous and ethnic communities. The community broadcasting sector as a whole represents a valuable cultural resource that contributes to Australia's rich and diverse cultural heritage through its commitment to maintaining, representing and reproducing local cultures and, in the case of some Indigenous and ethnic communities, local languages. It was the basis on which community radio was established in Australia more than 35 years ago and our subsequent investigations reveal that this philosophy persists. Despite a significant growth in 'radio regionalism' during that period – a tendency for commercial radio stations, in particular, to deliver programming to far-flung areas from a central hub – the sector continues to define itself in terms of its commitment to local audiences. No other media sector operating in the public sphere in Australia has the capacity to do this. With the additional benefit of both qualitative and quantitative audience data – the missing link in the research process – we can take another step towards theorizing the sector and its processes.

Our earlier study (Forde et al. 2002) showed that many community radio workers asserted their commitment to contesting mainstream and dominant representations of Australian culture by consistently identifying the local roles they perform as being instrumental to their sense of identity. This perception of community radio highlights the empowering processes facilitated by local access and participation and the relationships that exist within stations and through their many and varied connections with local community groups – and audiences. We suggest that the very nature of their engagement with audiences is a defining characteristic of the sector as a whole, echoing Hochheimer's reminder that such broadcasting processes should be seen as a response to 'an existing will to communicate' rather than a technology that somehow organizes people (1999: 451). In other words, a foundation for organization is a prerequisite. Howley (2005: 2) also asserts the need for community media to emerge from communities who are dissatisfied with the form and content of mainstream media, referring to the 'felt need of local populations to create media systems that are relevant to their everyday lives'. And it is not all altruistic 'sharing and caring' which characterizes the establishment and operation of a community media outlet. There is a process of management and control which occurs and this is necessary to ensure a station's identity but may result in the exclusion of some groups from the processes involved. A community media outlet can thus be seen as a microcosm of broader power relations in the community and certainly not immune to conflict and controversy (van Vuuren 2006). Despite this possibility, on a continuum of potential to empower, community media fare much better than other media. The baseline requirement to 'qualify' as a form of community media is the presence of participatory links with local communities. The nature of the relationships involved – particularly between audiences and producers – is at the core of this assertion.

Theorizing community media

Media theory is mostly an attempt to conceptualize the power relations between broader societal structures, the media and their audiences. Approaches to the question of how media might impact on their audiences and society are ubiquitous – as are questions surrounding the role of the media in the lives of audiences and as a broader institution alongside other cultural institutions such as the family, the church and the judiciary. Trends in communication and media theory can be likened to a pendulum which swings between a focus on the broader societal or structural impacts of media to a renewed interest in audience-based research – with various text-based approaches in between. Grossberg (1989) described this pendulum as a persistent attempt to put the 'Humpty Dumpty' of communication back together again, arguing that dominant research trends had neglected a crucial aspect in attempting to conceptualize the role of the media and the inherent processes of communication. And his observation persists. Indeed, it is likely to do so indefinitely as the media have such a significant influence over the systems of making meaning which govern our everyday lives.

Theories surrounding community media and their relationships with audiences and society have followed a similar trajectory with different researchers focusing on various aspects of the production and consumption process. This is perhaps most evident in academic debate surrounding the 'naming' of community radio with some theorists focusing on it as an 'alternative' to mainstream media, defining it in terms of its relationship to other media structures and favouring production processes (for example, Atton 2002). Others emphasize the activity of producers and audiences in the term, 'citizen's media', favouring consumption processes (Rodriguez 2002). In our analysis of community media, we oscillate between community media as 'alternative media'; a focus upon the production of community media texts and their impacts upon global and local cultural production; and in this book, their reception by audiences. And while we are not the first to suggest a diverse theoretical approach, we are arguably in the vanguard in not only including audience perspectives, but also privileging them in the process of theory-building (see also Howley 2005; Carpentier et al. 2003). In the Australian context at least, we are able to combine our knowledge of the community media sector to produce insights into all of these processes – from production to consumption. This practice of combining production, text and audience perspectives provides a comprehensive picture of the ways in which culture and the media operate in everyday life (Kellner and Durham 2006: xii). To borrow from public policy vernacular, this approach might be termed a 'whole of communication' approach. In many ways then, theorizing community media has followed established media theory trajectories by questioning the relations between broad social structures, the media and their audiences. What is the relationship between community media and other media institutions? Or other societal institutions such as local churches or the police service? What are the 'texts' of community media and who do they represent? How are these texts consumed by audiences?

Rumbling beneath these questions is a need to assess the nature of the power relations involved. There is power in the production and consumption of community media texts which takes many forms. Consider the production processes that enable everyday people and communities to produce their own cultural texts. Consider the power of audiences to reject globalized, commodified forms of cultural production in favour of discrete, local community-based models. In previous papers, we have asserted that the key term which encapsulates the role of community media in society both as a cultural text and as a site of audience consumption is 'empowerment' (Meadows et al. 2007). We will discuss this concept later in this chapter but it is necessary to emphasize its overall relevance not only to community media but also to media theory generally – and to simultaneously distinguish the operations of most Australian community media outlets from other media. Empowerment in the community media sector is enabled by a single characteristic which defines community media: it is the dissolution of the boundary between producers and audiences which makes possible the empowerment of citizens and their communities. This absence of a defined audience-producer boundary highlights the potential of these media to empower citizens and their communities both at the level of the local – for example, in loungerooms and community centres – and as a crucial element of the broader democratic process.

Power relations between various societal structures, community media and their audiences are different to those that are re/produced by other media. This may be the reason why mainstream media theory has failed to engage with community media. Indeed, three of the leading texts on media theory, McQuail's (2005) *Mass Communication Theory*, Durham and Kellner's (2006) *Media and Cultural Studies Key Works* and Curran and Gurevitch's (2005) *Mass Media and Society*, make no significant reference to community media. This is a significant oversight given the ways in which community media seem able to fulfil the emancipatory potential which seems so elusive to other media. While community media are by no means perfect, our experience of them has revealed a clear and consistent 'fissure' in the usual one-way flow (or at least uneven flow) in the power relations that largely define media producers and their audiences. The processes which have led to the dismantling of the audience-producer barrier represent a quiet revolution which seems to have been largely ignored by many contemporary media theorists.

It is the activity of audiences in the processes of both production and reception which defines and distinguishes the community media experience. This means that traditional accounts of the media require some reconfiguration to accommodate community media. Primarily, the assumption that the 'official' production of media texts is located within the 'professional' ranks of media organizations is challenged by the existence and persistence of community media. While mainstream media claim audience participation through various forms of interaction – blogs, readers' feedback groups, letters to the editor, talkback, etc. – the political economy of these organizations and the way in which expertise is necessarily organized thwarts attempts at meaningful involvement by citizens and their communities in the production of cultural texts. Mainstream media are, by design, unable to offer such opportunities simply because they seek to sell audiences to advertisers with 'professionals' responsible for their 'high quality' programme production. Almost by definition then, these media must maintain the distinction between audiences and producers. This is not a criticism of mainstream media outlets – their intent and focus is different from community media on a number of levels. It is, however, a critical difference in the way these media forms set about re/producing culture and engaging audiences – and it is the key to understanding their actual and potential prospects for empowering citizens.

The weakening of the audience-producer boundary signals a small fissure in power relations surrounding the media and their audiences. It is precisely at this moment that social change is evident for audiences, citizens and communities, reflected in the phenomenal growth of community media outlets in Australia and beyond and certainly, in the expansion of Internet-based news blogs and initiatives such as Indymedia. All are contributing to a general demystification of media production process. This 'democratization of communication' is all the more important to those communities who in their local and/or global contexts already experience a significant degree of social disadvantage. Thus the potential for community media to empower these people, already on the margins, is enhanced. Consider forms such as the 'lamp post' radio in the *Favela* in Brazil, offering local audiences an alternative and community orientation albeit operating within a quasi-commercial environment. Its low-level commercial orientation does not make it any less community – or less empowering for the range of slum-dwellers who support it (Medrado 2008). This is the case, too, for ethnic and Indigenous audiences in Australia and other marginalized communities. In our society where the media perform a central role in the production and maintenance of cultures – through the broadcast of music, news and information, representations of identity and generally, a community's 'whole way of life' – participation by community members in media processes is an acknowledged site of empowerment. This does not discount the elusive and contingent nature of these media (Carpentier et al. 2003), rather it proposes a way of thinking about them – Indigenous and ethnic broadcasting in particular – by incorporating the organic processes that bind producers and audiences through a matrix of empowerment. A lack of qualitative audience studies globally may initially limit the application of such an idea but we suggest it is one worth pursuing in other domains.

Culture, community public spheres and the potential to empower

The disruption to the traditional relations between media and their audiences heralded by the establishment and expansion of community media is deeply imbued with ideas of power and knowledge – the power to produce 'knowledges' which are an expression of those involved in the processes of programme production. This idea resonates with Foucault's positive conception of power (1977: 194):

[W]e must cease once and for all to describe the effects of power in negative terms: it 'excludes', it 'represses', it 'censors', it 'abstracts', it 'masks', it 'conceals'. In fact, power produces; it produces reality; it produces domains of objects and rituals of truth.

The 'felt need' (Howley 2005) to establish their own media empowers communities to produce their own realities – to re/produce and maintain the meaning systems, the cultures which are important to them. This occurs alongside but is not directed by mainstream media and their representation of cultures. But what is culture? The concept has been variously defined but Colin Mercer perhaps captures the essence of its meaning when he asserts (1989: 17): 'Culture is "in" the body, "in" repertoires of conduct, "in" techniques of self-management.' This focus on the location of culture within the 'subject' underpins Williams' notion of culture as 'a constitutive social process, creating specific and different "ways of life"' (1977: 19). Stuart Hall (1982: 77) extends this line of thinking by describing culture as 'the lived practices which characterise a particular society, class or group at a particular historical period'. At the same time, it includes 'the practical ideologies which enable a society, group or class to experience, define, interpret and "make sense" of its conditions of existence at a particular historical period'. Importantly, culture here is defined in relation to the 'concrete' forms of life (Hall 1982: 8):

> the actual ways of life which become distinctive to a group or class in a particular period; the common-sense ideas which actually inform their practical collective social life; the beliefs and ideas which are concretely active in the practical moral choices which are made; the images, representations which are 'in use', collectively, at a particular period, to 'make sense' of existence.

Mainstream media – and, we argue, community media – play a pivotal role in these processes through the publication of beliefs, ideas and assumptions about the world. This is manifested in various ways such as music, news and information. But media are not the only sites where culture is communicated. It occurs between individuals, within and between diverse groups and communities – this is the extent of 'culture' which, in our present era, relates to the media but is also 'threaded through all social practices and is the sum of their relationship' (Hall 1980: 60). Culture concerns our everyday frameworks for understanding and communicating our experiences of the world and importantly our place (or identity) within it. Community media enable the dissemination and affirmation of an extraordinarily diverse range of 'everyday' cultures which serve to assure a place for millions of Australians within their local communities of interest and thus, the public sphere. By enlisting media technologies to suit their own purposes, Indigenous and ethnic communities use the community broadcasting sector as a cultural resource that facilitates cultural citizenship. Producing community media becomes a process of cultural empowerment.

It is important to remember that content production is not necessarily the prime purpose of these ventures (Tomaselli and Prinsloo 1990: 156; Forde et al. 2002; Meadows et al. 2007). A growing body of evidence suggests that the ways in which Indigenous and ethnic community broadcasting facilitates the process of community organization is more important than media production alone. Community broadcasting in Australia, in general, plays an important cultural role by 'imagining' the notions of culture and citizenship through shared meanings, values and ideals. Put simply, it is a process of 'making sense' of the world and our places in it. This is more apparent – and unquestionably more important – for minority media audiences. In this way, community media play an important cultural role by encouraging dialogue between diverse 'public arenas' – a process which is integral to the creation and maintenance of community social structures. This is clearly evident in successful Indigenous media enterprises where production practices and organization, by definition, have strong links to traditional community frameworks (Morris and Meadows 2000; Meadows 2005). The same assertion can be made for ethnic community radio and in particular, their local diasporic experiences (Shi 2005; Forde 2005).

These notions of community cultural production revolve around the ideas of the public sphere and democracy, drawing on Habermas's notion of the public sphere but extending it in several ways. Studies that have looked at Indigenous media production have theorized it in terms of a reconceptualization of the broad public sphere (Avison and Meadows 2000; Molnar and Meadows 2001). Forde (1997; 1998) reached a similar conclusion in her analysis of the independent press sector in Australia, arguing that it extends contemporary ideas of the public sphere and democracy. As we have argued elsewhere (Forde et al. 2002; 2003), rather than adopting the idea of a single, all-encompassing public sphere, it may be more appropriate to think of media operating in terms of a series of parallel and overlapping 'public arenas' (Fraser 1999: 126). These are spaces which engage participants with similar cultural backgrounds and beliefs – 'communities of interest'. Such entities articulate their own discursive styles and formulate their own positions on issues that can then be brought into the broader public sphere where they are able to interact 'across lines of cultural diversity' (Fraser 1999: 126). What we might term 'community public spheres' are discrete formations or spaces that develop in a unique context and are the product of contestation – and sometimes, alliance – with the broader public sphere. As Atton (2002: 153) has suggested in relation to alternative media, it is a process enabling empowering narratives of resistance for participants, largely because they are produced by participants. This is possible because, as Fraser (1999: 127) concludes, 'the unbounded character and publicist orientation of publics allows people to participate in more than one public, and it allows memberships of different publics to overlap'. Where our concept of 'community public spheres' may differ from Atton's theorization of alternative media is in that not all community stations see themselves as necessarily resisting anything. Indeed, not all community broadcasting stations would be defined, or would *like* to be defined, as alternative. Downing, too, supports these ideas in his theorization of 'radical' media, acknowledging (2001: 3) that popular cultures 'are not automatically oppositional or constructive' and defines radical alternative media as constituting ' the most active form of the active audience' expressing 'oppositional strands, overt and covert, within popular cultures'. In fact, some forms of community media may aspire to mainstream status in terms of both programming and philosophy – but they continue to work within the discursive arena of the local community.

In summary then, the dissolution or weakening of the audience-producer boundary enables communities to produce and articulate their own cultures through participation in community media outlets. This process creates a 'community public sphere' where the production and reception of cultural texts affirms and validates the existence of a multitude of different ways of life. In the process, it exposes other cultures to beliefs, ideas and assumptions both different from and similar to their own. Community media production thus maintains and sustains communities by promoting social cohesion and social structures at the local level.

Empowerment

The concept of empowerment encapsulates most, if not all, of the sector's operations, functions and services. It is enabled by the dissolution of boundaries between audiences and producers. Grossberg (1987: 95) defines 'empowerment' as 'the enablement of particular practices, that is…the conditions of possibility that enable a particular practice or statement to exist in a specific social context and to enable people to live their lives in different ways'. Indigenous and ethnic community broadcasting empower producers and audiences to 'live their lives' through the media 'in different ways'. This occurs by enabling the affirmation of cultural identities and at the same time, offering ways of 'resisting cultural hegemony' through the dissemination of alternative ideas and assumptions that align more closely with audiences' needs (White 2004: 10). This is also 'an inherently interpersonal process in which individuals collectively define and activate strategies to gain access to knowledge and power' (Summerson Carr 2003: 18). Put simply, the process of empowerment occurs at the level of the individual and their communities but also impacts on broader structures – such as 'the media' – and broader processes – such as the pursuit of 'democracy' through participation in the public sphere.

Comparatively, mainstream media maintain a powerful position in terms of their capacity to produce cultural texts and to disseminate them to a broad audience. A steady increase in the numbers of Australians shifting allegiance from commercial to community radio, in particular, is evidence of change occurring at the margins. In this book, we have taken the opportunity to focus on this 'fissure' to celebrate the power of local citizens to challenge the dominant ideologies characteristic of mainstream media:

> Most cultural criticism focuses on culture's critical relation (negativity) to the dominant positions and ideologies. Politics becomes defined as resistance to or emancipation from an assumed reality; politics is measured by difference. But empowerment can also be positive; celebration, however much it ignores relations of domination, can be enabling. Opposition may be constituted by living, even momentarily, within alternative practices,

structures, and spaces, even though they may take no notice of their relationship to existing systems of power (Grossberg 1988: 170).

Audiences for Indigenous and ethnic community broadcasting articulate this 'enabling celebration' of inhabiting alternative 'practices, structures and spaces'. The fissure in dominant power relations instigated by these media is empowering for communities who, prior to the establishment of community broadcasting stations and programmes, were relatively powerless in their interactions with mainstream Australia. This has also empowered individuals and communities, as well as having broader societal impacts in relation to democracy and citizenship. It is a fissure which begins at the level of the local but increasingly is having a global impact.

We have identified three elements in the process of empowerment which in practice intersect, but are worthy of individual attention in any exercise that sets out to explore media and their potential effects. We have thus considered the potential for empowerment at the levels of 'community', 'media' and 'society' in an attempt to explore the processes involved in the creation and consumption of community media. This approach draws upon McQuail's (2005) approach to mass communication whereby media, societal and cultural analyses take their places alongside material forces and conditions – each providing insight into the processes of community broadcasting and in this case, ethnic and Indigenous communities. This corresponds to Kellner and Durham's (2006) need for a 'multiperspectivist approach' which is able to account for, in this instance, the breadth of community media, their sites of challenge and their potential to instigate social change.

Empowerment: community

We have outlined in detail how Indigenous and ethnic community broadcasting empowers audiences to participate in and shape their communities in a variety of different ways – 'listening', requesting songs, taking part in live on-air discussions, hearing news and information of specific relevance, using community media to educate and to break down cultural barriers. In communities which experience a significant degree of social disadvantage, these media represent critical services and for many, it is about survival. The significant contribution Indigenous and ethnic community radio and television is making to countering the potentially damaging effects of mental illness is a case in point. Audiences acknowledge that these media are helping not only to stem feelings of depression, sadness and anger, but also to build feelings of pride, self-esteem and happiness by enlisting existing community and external knowledge and experiences. This is empowerment in action and if it encourages such at-risk individuals and communities to survive, it is an example of community media at its most constructive (Meadows and Foxwell 2009).

Community broadcasting for disadvantaged citizens incorporates the everyday but is critical for the survival of communities and individuals within them. For example, in remote

Australia, Indigenous community radio and television performs a vital service in not only maintaining social and cultural networks, but also providing critical information on health, community services and links between prisoners and their families, for example. Local control of these media ensures that topics that are considered relevant for the community can be discussed by members of that community, thus empowering all of those involved – from audiences to producers. Indigenous and ethnic communities are at least able to challenge continuing experiences of misrepresentation, disadvantage, stigma or even repression. This process strengthens internal community identities and enables the projection of these to the outside world, enabling the possibility for social change and development (Carpentier et al. 2003: 55–56; Bailey et al. 2008). The leakage that occurs at the intersections and overlap of community public spheres with the broader public sphere is the catalyst with the potential to activate this process.

Analysis of the complexity of 'local talk' narratives compared with the narrow frames of mainstream mediated discourse in the formation of public opinion identifies a process through which members of communities – however they are defined – might engage. This process draws our attention to the importance of 'local talk' as 'a powerful resource for understanding public opinion' (McCallum 2007: 27). In her examination of the ways people talked about Indigenous issues in their everyday conversations, for example, McCallum identified 'multiple and contested discourses' at play in local discussion of their meaning. Drawing on these ideas, the nature of community broadcasting – by virtue of its ability to connect local communities of interest – places it in an ideal position to facilitate the more complex 'local talk' narratives that operate at community level. This plays a significant role in creating public consciousness by offering alternatives to mainstream ideas and assumptions that are constructed within the 'narrow frames of mediated discourse'. This offers one explanation for the processes that define the audience-producer relationship in Indigenous and ethnic community broadcasting. As part of the process of enabling such 'local talk', community radio and television perform a pivotal role in representing diverse cultural interests as well as bringing like-minded individuals and groups together – in many cases, simply by listening (Bickford 1996).

Empowerment: media

In a practical sense, community radio and television empower communities or groups by enabling dissemination of their ideas to a much larger audience. Enlisting this role, community media challenge the status quo by providing a space where citizens can encounter, debate or experience alternative viewpoints and lifestyles. This is in stark contrast to the mainstream where voices of the elite have the power to set agendas in ways which affirm a position of dominance and overall, a preferred 'whole way of life'. Community media enable the representation of other ideas and assumptions and this is perhaps their strongest contribution to 'communicative democracy'. The gradual encroachment of community broadcasting into mainstream Australia is pivotal in affirming for audiences a sense of difference and, by extension, belonging, in the communities which have enlisted it as a cultural resource. Rodriguez (2001: 154) reminds us:

> Citizens' media do not have to compete for global markets; they do not have to reach all audiences; they do have to 'talk to everyone' and therefore, local dialects, local issues, and local codifications of social reality find their way into citizens' media programming... citizens' media are in a privileged position to delve into, to explore, and to articulate (differences between subordinate groups) – unlike mainstream media which tend to generalize and smooth away such differences.

Mainstream media's failure to fulfil their true democratic function is the 'rational result' of their operations (McChesney 2003: 299). In their goal to attract the largest possible audience, driven by commercial and political motivations, mainstream media regularly neglect small, minority, disenfranchised, disempowered, local, specialist groups. Considered together, these groups represent a large mass and in Australia – as in other places around the world – they are able to be serviced by community radio and television which are by nature and mandate more structurally able to meet the needs of this cohort.

Community radio and television empower disempowered, disenfranchised and disadvantaged groups in Australian society, enabling representations of their ways of life, priorities and agendas. This is particularly pertinent to Indigenous and ethnic communities and relevant – albeit less obvious – in other communities of interest including prisoners, gays and lesbians, print-handicapped and vision impaired, youth, seniors and so on. Indigenous and ethnic community media, in particular, enable citizens, regardless of social demographics, to interrupt the established dominance of mainstream media and society, by inserting their own content, style and cultural perspectives into community public spheres. These, in turn, interact with the broader public sphere where ideas from an increasingly diminishing range of perspectives compete for public attention.

Empowerment: society

Citizens who have enlisted community media for their own purposes are empowered in terms of their capacity to participate more fully in democratic processes. Here, we are talking about 'communicative democracy' through media. Empowerment at this level refers to the impact of community radio and television in enhancing broader societal concepts, especially ideas related to citizenship, democracy and the public sphere. These are familiar terms in literature on community media and the media generally. They are terms which, at first glance, seem somewhat removed from the day-to-day efforts of media workers – for example, an Indigenous broadcaster working in isolation in a regional town or a producer for a sub-Saharan African community fashioning a weekly half-hour programme with limited or no resources – and the listening habits of their audiences. However, it is precisely individuals' engagement with these micro-instances of participation that make these terms relevant to the processes of community media production (Bickford 1996). The very nature of community media and the multiplicity of ways in which they function complicate attempts to frame these processes. Rodriguez (2001: 160–161) expands on this:

> Too many analyses of the democratization of communication lack acceptance and understanding of the diffuse nature of power struggles and negotiations. Only when we learn to design theories and methods able to accompany the fluidity of citizens negotiating power will we do justice to people and their actions of shaping everyday lives. What we commonly do – formulating a theory of how social change should happen and dissecting specific cases in relation to such criteria – will continue our myopic understanding of citizens' media…[It is] this explosion of communication at the local level that makes citizens' media into empowering tools for democracy. The disruption of established relations of power is a 'messy' enterprise, and our attempts to impose order and organization will only cause our alienation from these processes.

In the spirit of this challenge, we need to consider the links between community media and civil society. In this configuration, community radio and television are situated between the domain of private economic organizations (for profit) and private personal and family relations – and public state-owned economic organizations and state and quasi-state organizations. As intermediate organizations (like charities, political parties, pressure groups, etc.), community media thus function as a part of civil society that is crucial to democracy by fostering citizen participation in public life (Carpentier et al. 2003: 58–59). As we suggested earlier, the instances of 'micro-participation', enabled by Indigenous and ethnic community broadcasting, contribute to broader 'macro-participation' as audiences actively adopt civic attitudes and actions thus performing a pivotal role in a healthy democracy. This is particularly important when participants are able to offer alternatives to the ideas and assumptions purveyed by dominant media. Carpentier et al. conclude (2003: 60): 'Community media can overcome the absolutist interpretation of media neutrality and impartiality, and offer different societal groups and communities the opportunity for extensive participation in public debate and for self representation in the (or a) public sphere.'

The distinction between community media, the state and the market fosters social antagonisms which do not necessarily capture community media's role, or potential role, in broader society. The antagonistic relations characteristic of community media which, on numerous fronts, philosophically oppose the state, the market and mainstream media, places community radio and television in a position of 'discursive isolation', unable to engage with some of the most powerful and critical discourses and their attendant institutions (such as the state, the market and the media) in any meaningful sense. We suggested earlier that the intersection of community public spheres with the broader public sphere creates the opportunity for such dialogue.

Carpentier et al. (2003) offer a solution which they suggest as a defining element of community media per se. It is based on a more fluid conception of state and civil society relations, applying Deleuze and Guattari's (1987) theory of the rhizome. Rhizomatic thinking is characterized as non-linear, anarchic and nomadic, connecting any point to any other point (Deleuze and Guattari 1987, cited in Carpentier et al. 2003: 61). The relevance of the rhizome to community media is to 'highlight the role of community media as the crossroads of organizations and movements linked with civil society [and to]…incorporate the high level of contingency that characterizes community media'. They conclude (Carpentier et al. 2003: 61):

> Both their embeddedness in a fluid civil society (as a part of a larger network) and their antagonistic relationship towards the state and the market (as alternative to mainstream public and commercial media) make the identity of community media highly elusive. In this approach it is argued that this elusiveness and contingency, as is the case for a rhizome, forms its main defining elements.

This theoretical approach concurs with recent applications of radical democratic theory to community media (Rodriguez 2001) where power is enacted and citizenship expressed in a multiplicity of forums including political action in the quotidian. Rodriguez (2001: 158) describes it in similar terms:

> citizens' media are similar to living organisms that evolve and develop uniquely in permanent interaction with their complex environments/contexts: at some point they strengthen their struggle against one target, but later they can abandon a target and take on a new one, which, in turn, can be abandoned to focus on a third one. It is in the play of articulated historical conflicts and struggles where the richness of citizens' media resides, in terms of their potential as forces of resistance. But this same richness will be overlooked if we attempt to see citizens' media as one-dimensional static platforms aimed at unified goals.

In part, the rhizomatic approach questions some of the radical foundations of community media, arguing that their antagonistic relationship with the state and the market neglects their bridging position between the state and civil society. Our experience is that community radio stations, in particular, often find themselves in an uneasy situation of compromising their principled stance towards the state and the market while consistently seeking either funding (from the state) and sponsorship (from the market). Their supposed distance from the state and the market is further complicated by the range of community groups – state, quasi-state and private organizations – which produce programming through the stations for broadcast to local communities. Community broadcasting enables these organizations to access and participate in dialogue with their audiences at the local level.

Conclusion

In this chapter, we have traced some trends in media theory and suggested some applications and adjustments to accommodate community media. While community media shares much with other media, their distinguishing characteristic is the nature of the audience-producer boundary. This revised relationship between producers and consumers is at the core of community media's empowering potential. Empowerment is enabled by the dissolution of the traditional power relations between media producers and their audiences and in the dismantling of the hierarchy of production and reception. This is the basis of all empowerment processes inherent in the community media sector. It is the fundamental characteristic which distinguishes community media from mainstream media processes.

Community broadcasting in Australia and elsewhere is challenging some of the negative manifestations of globalization – homogenization of content, for example – and instead seeks to promote citizenship by empowering diverse cultures to access the public sphere. Indigenous and ethnic community cultures that are either neglected or marginalized – almost by definition – are thus given a voice at the community level. Community radio and television contribute actively to the creation of what we have termed 'community public spheres', which overlap and interact with the broader public sphere to build and maintain meaningful local and national cultural agendas. Media are powerful elements in the representation of culture and as such, participation in the processes of media production and reception by diverse communities is an empowering experience. At the level of 'community', media create and then empower social groups to represent their own cultures or ways of life. In terms of empowerment and the media, community broadcasters serving Indigenous and ethnic communities 'disturb' the established power base of the mainstream media. Community radio and television are central elements in the representation of cultures which are routinely either misrepresented or ignored by mainstream media. The efforts of community media producers and their audiences are able to interrupt 'common sense' mainstream media representations by offering alternatives which showcase the diversity of Australian culture at the local level. The dissemination of different ideas and assumptions about the world and our place in it validates a 'whole way of life' for millions of Australians who engage in the processes of community broadcasting. This happens by empowering not only diverse communities of interest in terms of their ability to assert their own cultural identity and ideologies within community public spheres, but also by articulating these ideas to broader public sphere activity through both community and mainstream media networks. Participation in the processes of community broadcasting by Indigenous and ethnic community producers and audiences facilitates the enactment of citizenship and participation in democracy. The very nature of the sector enables this kind of engagement by citizens – more often accustomed to being marginalized – in the public life of their communities.

Conclusion

Indigenous and ethnic community broadcasting in Australia emerged in the early 1970s as a direct response to continuing mainstream media misrepresentation of the complexity and multiplicity of cultures encompassed by these broad 'minority' categories. They grew out of the fledgling 'public' radio movement which began precisely to democratize the air waves by creating spaces for disenfranchised and disadvantaged communities of interest. More than 35 years later, the sector has become arguably the most popular in the world with almost 30 percent of all listeners in Australia aged above fifteen tuning in weekly (McNair Ingenuity 2008).

Although comparable quantitative survey research has not been carried out specifically for either Indigenous or ethnic radio and television audiences, the evidence from both the McNair Ingenuity studies and our own research suggests that audiences for these specialist sub-sectors are significantly higher per capita. Based on many years' engagement with Indigenous communities and the more recent specific exploration of audiences for Indigenous-produced radio and television across Australia, it is clear that few – if any – do not engage regularly with their local broadcasting services. We make a similar assertion for ethnic community radio and its reach into the particular communities of interest it serves. In addition, these media perform an important agenda-setting role because of the primary importance of oral communication in these communities, placing them in an ideal position to facilitate the complex 'local talk' narratives that operate at community level – someone hears something on a community radio station and then is able to spread the message through their own social networks. As we suggested earlier, this plays a significant role in creating public consciousness by offering alternatives to ideas and assumptions propagated in the mainstream media that tend to be constructed within 'narrow frames of mediated discourse' (McCallum 2007: 27). As such, Indigenous and ethnic broadcasting represents a key cultural resource, deeply implicated in the process of 'imagining' Australia through various processes.

Much of the data presented in this book comes from an analysis of Indigenous and ethnic community broadcasting audiences canvassed during the first qualitative study of the two sectors. Our decision to adopt qualitative methods such as interviews and focus group during our long research engagement with the community broadcasting sector has enabled a deeper exploration of the relationships between audiences, producers and the communities in which they are active. Drawing from Native Canadian experiences in the communication policymaking process, Ramirez (2007: 92) reminds us of an important, often absent, element:

People's perceptions about a project or technology can integrate a number of dimensions that are otherwise difficult to discover. How have people witnessed change? The significance of this is that policy decision-making rarely waits for evaluation of project impacts.

He argues that the challenge for policymakers in responding to this could be to 'create spaces for experimentation' where 'people's participation' is embedded in – and at the heart of – such processes (Pimbert 2004; Ramirez 2007: 92). Our approach set out to create such spaces where all stakeholders – Indigenous, ethnic, generalist and government community broadcasting industry representatives – were able to participate in the research and by association, the subsequent policymaking process. This activity took place through a project advisory committee – a pivotal element of our overall approach which not only produced a rewarding and cooperative working environment, but also enabled specialized knowledges to inform ways of dealing with the formidable challenges inherent in cross-cultural research. This idea initially was based on the very nature of the community broadcasting sector itself with its philosophy of inclusiveness and flexibility. Our aim has been to engage all stakeholders, along with ourselves, in a research and learning process that set out to 'appreciate' rather than to merely 'evaluate' (Ramirez 2007: 92).

Audiences for Indigenous radio and television identify 'their' media as essential services which play a central role in the organization and facilitation of community life on multiple levels. They maintain social networks and play a strong role in educating young and old alike. They provide alternative sources of news and information for their audiences, countering ignorance and stereotypes of Indigenous people and issues that remain commonplace practice in mainstream media. These media play an important role in promoting cross-cultural dialogue and in boosting Indigenous self-esteem with support for the strong Indigenous music and arts industry a primary function. Specialist ethnic programming on generalist community radio stations or full-time ethnic community radio stations attract audiences who perceive that programming plays a central role in maintaining their cultures and languages. It maintains community connections and networks, enabling listeners to hear music, news and other information unavailable through other media. Audiences for ethnic community radio are particularly interested in hearing news and information relevant to their lives in Australia, along with that from their home countries and from neighbouring countries and regions.

Empowerment

The various ways in which Indigenous and ethnic audiences engage with community radio and television programmes represents empowerment at the levels of community, media and society. This is the overwhelming conclusion we have reached following many years' engagement with the Australian community broadcasting sector. In our earlier studies involving station managers, news and general volunteers – and now audiences – it is clear that this encapsulates the sector's operations, functions and services. The complex processes that define community broadcasting enable audiences, community organizations, volunteers and managers alike to 'live their lives in different ways' through the support networks inexorably bound up in the processes of community media (Grossberg 1987: 95). This happens through the creation and maintenance of ideas and assumptions more in tune with those of audiences seeking affirmation of their cultural identities in the face of global cultural hegemony. This 'inherently interpersonal process' creates new spaces or community public spheres which, in turn, facilitate greater engagement with the broader public sphere (Summerson Carr 2003: 18).

It may be, too, that Indigenous and ethnic community broadcasting offers the only effective way of engaging with many of the people at risk in terms of mental health. The evidence suggests that these media are helping their audiences to counter feelings like shame, depression, sadness and anger that stem directly from stereotyped and ill-informed representations of communities, particularly those on the margins of society. Although the evidence for this is strongest in ethnic and Indigenous communities, generalist community radio audiences also acknowledging the 'healing' which flows from their participation. Indigenous and ethnic community radio and television play a significant role in promoting feelings of pride, self-esteem and happiness amongst their audiences. This is especially empowering because of a weakening of the traditional barrier between audiences and producers of community radio and television in Australia (Meadows et al. 2008). Again, although this is more apparent with Indigenous and ethnic communities, it suggests that it is the very nature of this *process* that places community broadcasting in a privileged relationship with its audiences. There is clearly a high level of trust that enables a more open acceptance of alternative ideas and assumptions than those that tend to prevail in the mainstream. This is especially the case when community perceptions of what is happening in the 'real world' do not accord with those being promoted primarily by media with largely commercial imperatives.

The ability of the processes of community radio and television production to foster social inclusion is clear across all levels of the sector (Meadows et al. 2007). The essential service nature of Indigenous and ethnic radio and television has enabled a dialogue between audiences and producers that is the foundation of a 'more engaged and participatory culture' (Langton 1993; Deuze 2006: 271). The Australian community broadcasting sector as a whole is making a significant contribution to countering mental illness. This is more apparent in marginalized Indigenous and ethnic communities and demands further investigation within the community media sector globally. It seems apparent that the existing role being played by community broadcasting in Australia could be further enhanced if health care providers adopted a more participatory approach in working with individual stations and communities to achieve common goals.

The audience-producer relationship

One of the dominant elements that emerged from this research is evidence to support an assertion of either a weakening or absence of a barrier between audiences and producers of Indigenous and ethnic community radio and television. The evidence of a collapse of this barrier is strongest in Indigenous communities, exemplified in expressions that consistently described local radio and television as 'ours'. Others talked about feeling 'absolutely more comfortable' listening to Indigenous radio because of its ability to provide the cultural context and understanding that is missing from mainstream media. Communication between producers and audiences happens in many ways: primarily through music, but perhaps more importantly, 'talking about place' (Interview, Yuendumu 2006). As one listener to CAAMA Radio concluded (Focus Group, CAAMA, Alice Springs, 2006): 'It's Aboriginal radio for Aboriginal people; people who take greater pride in being Aboriginal people especially grassroots people.' Another important element which emerged, too, in commentary on the nature of news and information, is the absence of simplistic media representations. Many participants and interviewees told us that this was because Indigenous people were in control. It was also attributed to the nature of Indigenous radio and television enterprises on the mainland, or as in this case, throughout the islands of the Torres Strait (Interview, TSI, 2005): 'They're very open in their [approach]. If you've got something you want to put on the radio, they call in, you know, talk about your idea. If it's community news or, you know, you go into the studio and do all of that.' Many of the participants in our audience focus groups and interviews identified the importance of stations communicating with their audiences at their level – 'a lingo that you can get your head around' as one CAAMA listener put it (2006). The ways in which Indigenous broadcasting outlets have facilitated links between Indigenous prisoners and their families is widespread and another important example of inclusion for this particularly marginalized section of the Australian community. With Indigenous imprisonment rates running at around fourteen times those of non-Indigenous Australians, this service by the community broadcasting sector – and stations with Indigenous-produced programmes in particular – becomes crucial to the rehabilitation process so elusive in the Australian and Canadian prison environments (Anderson 2008). As one participant concluded (Focus Group, CAAMA, Alice Springs, 2006): 'It keeps the dialogue going between people.'

For the majority of audiences for Indigenous radio and television, it is simply about having confidence and feeling comfortable listening to and/or watching programmes with which they can identify and trust. Others talk about the connection between themselves and producers as a 'talking relationship' or simply 'Black voices; Black issues' (Interview, Torres Strait, 2005; Palm Island, 2006). Audiences around Australia identify the presentation of a wide variety of programming types and styles – within an Indigenous framework. People commonly described 'their' radio as 'truthful' and straightforward. As one Melbourne listener observed (Focus Group, 3KND Melbourne, 2005): 'There's something for everybody. I really like that and no-one feels excluded. Well, no-one basically is excluded, you know.' A young Indigenous woman in another focus group acknowledged that 'pretty much all the elders in Inala listen to 98.9', confirming its 'authorization', like other Indigenous stations, by key community figures (Focus Group, 98.9FM, 2006). This was a common theme around the country: the importance of seeking confirmation from those in the community who have the greatest respect.

Perhaps the strongest support for a collapse of the barrier between audiences and producers in Indigenous broadcasting, in particular, comes from the very nature of Aboriginal and Torres Strait cultures themselves. The extended kinship structures that define them, along with the relatively small and highly networked social relationships that bind communities together mean that familiarity is an important element of Indigenous identity. Positioning somebody in existing social networks is a crucial process that determines how one person relates to another. Although generally this has greater impact in remote communities which have had minimal contact with the non-Indigenous world, it is a feature of Indigenousness that remains strong. But even apart from these crucial familial links, Indigenous people are inevitably drawn together as part of a broader political struggle against racism, discrimination and dispossession. All of these factors would suggest the existence of an intimate dialogue between Indigenous people – some of whom happen to be producers while others participate in the communication process as listeners and/or viewers. The intimate nature of the networks that bind individuals, families, clans, communities and nation mitigate against the formation of imposed barriers in the first place. The various ways in which Indigenous people globally have appropriated information and communication technologies to suit their own purposes reminds us that the technologies themselves do not necessarily come with instructions on how they should be used (Michaels 1986; Kulchyski 1989; Ginsburg 1991; Meadows 1993; Molnar and Meadows 2001; Deger 2007; Wilson and Stewart 2008). This is nowhere more apparent than in the ways in which Indigenous media producers engage with their audiences in multifarious cultural settings across the Australian continent.

Ethnic community radio audiences used similar examples to highlight the intimate associations they have built with their own programme producers and presenters – often the same person. It was clear from our research that these people were held in high esteem within particular cultural communities and were invested with a high level of trust and authority to speak on behalf of communities on various issues. Of course, they were all well-known personally by most listeners or if they weren't, there was a perception that they helped to bring listeners together. The idea that presenters were 'one of us' was very strongly expressed, with no suggestion of a barrier between them and their audiences. In every focus group discussion we conducted, the joy of hearing a familiar voice or music on radio was a commonly cited example that made audiences 'feel better' and part of their own cultural community. One Macedonian listener described the transition from feeling depressed on arrival here to one of joy: 'I was happiest when I heard the Macedonian radio and [then] Australia was very nice.' Others talked about the camaraderie that stems from being aware of a supportive cohort and having easy access to it, as this comment from the Macedonian focus group (2006) suggests: 'We can call in and you know, and share our feelings with others and we can recognize their voice but…we can call in and talk and share our feelings and it makes us feel good about that.'

The isolation that often stems from immigration was expressed widely by the ethnic community radio audiences we canvassed. It was strongest, as expected, amongst refugee communities who viewed the producer-presenter of their weekly radio programme in Melbourne with extraordinary respect – and yet felt this was perhaps the only place they could go to say what they wanted, when they wanted. The description of feeling as if you are 'deaf and dumb' when you first arrive in another country which uses a foreign language was an analogy used by many. Programmes started by 'ordinary people' in specific communities to counter social isolation meant that although they are considered to be in a privileged position in terms of their production-presenting roles, they are still considered to be very much part of their own communities by their audiences. One Chinese listener expressed it like this (Focus Group, 2006): 'You feel comfortable to talk to people you actually know.' This feeling of wellbeing flowing from familiarity is a common theme emerging from ethnic language focus groups and interviews.

In several ways, the discovery of local language programmes by ethnic community audiences has helped to build social cohesion where this was notably absent in their homeland. One stark example comes from Sudan where refugees from different warring regions acknowledged that they are able to come together on community radio in their newly adopted country where the concepts of 'North' and 'South' do not exist. In this way, such programmes engender processes that extend far beyond the mere production and presentation of programmes. As suggested by the overwhelming commentary we have gathered, both production *and* reception are empowering processes at many different levels.

It is clear that ethnic community radio programmes and stations play an important role in 'creating' or 'maintaining' community spirit, social life and connections between members of the same community. Some listeners feel the provision of a music request and talkback show is an important contributor to the maintenance of such community networks, while others identify the establishment of a programme 'fan club', or regular organization of community gatherings as evidence that a particular radio programme is assisting in the maintenance of community connections. The Sudanese focus group discussed the importance of its weekly radio programme in creating such links and this outcome is perhaps more important to emerging communities. Established communities seem to have multiple avenues through which to be in touch with community members – regular church gatherings, cultural events, community clubs and so on in which radio is not necessarily directly involved. For emerging communities, however, these organized social groups are often non-existent or newly established and so radio provides a more important source of 'community glue'. It is perhaps here that their similarities to the processes that define Indigenous radio and television are most apparent. For many, this is the only medium they have to enable dialogue beyond word of mouth.

This primary connection role was evident in all of the focus group discussions and as such, was considered by audiences to be the only place where this type of activity could happen in a way that extended its reach beyond local community networks such as social clubs and churches. People in the Sudanese focus group spoke about hearing on radio the names of others they had no idea were in Australia and of using the programme presenters to track them down. The ethnic community radio network enables the small Tongan community in Adelaide to link up with other Tongan enclaves on Australia's eastern seaboard.

In these ways, ethnic community radio can be seen as much more than a programme production process. Like community broadcasting in general, it is far more concerned with the processes that lead to production and the activities of their audiences. Essentially, community radio is one of a range of cultural activities that enable communities to create, re-create and maintain their own cultures. Although it should be seen alongside other important cultural institutions such as schools, clubs, societies, libraries, etc., the symbolic power inherent in media processes engenders it with particular significance. As countless stories of arrogance and overindulgence stemming from mainstream media 'success' by celebrities testify, corruption tends to flourish in such environments. And while we are not suggesting that the Indigenous and ethnic community broadcasting is free from such influences, the close-knit nature of the communities involved – and the intimate relationship that exists between audiences and producers – means that such instances are quickly dealt with in the rare cases they arise. It is precisely because of the absence or near-absence of a barrier between these cohorts that enables an open dialogue unlike the closed worlds of commercial and publicly funded or 'big' media where audiences' voices are largely inconsequential.

Developing dialogues

The overwhelming view across Australia is that Indigenous and ethnic community broadcasting is grossly underfunded, given the important cultural work that it undertakes. As we suggested earlier in this book, the policy process remains largely tied to 'hard' economic measures such as audience numbers and hours of programmes produced per dollar rather than taking into account the significant cultural activity that most effectively promotes social cohesion. It is clear that Indigenous and ethnic community radio and television are the most effective ways of reaching audiences who have either rejected the frameworks of mainstream media or who speak English as a second, third or fourth language – or not at all. In both Indigenous and ethnic communities, much of the emphasis is on young people who are growing up in 'two cultures' – their own and either an adopted or imposed one – and who need encouragement to see the value of both. And while criticism of the mainstream – the media, in particular – is strongest amongst Indigenous people, both Indigenous and ethnic community radio audiences have clearly established an intimate relationship with their 'media'.

Audiences suggest that existing evidence of the successes in remote Indigenous communities where young people have been diverted away from substance abuse into media-related work demonstrate that the industry has an enormous potential to offer alternative pathways – if it is funded appropriately. Audiences want better training opportunities for emerging broadcasters with a career path for those who want to continue to work with their own communities. There is a strong feeling that despite an increase in the number of young people training within the sector to undertake skilled jobs, there are few paid media options for them to pursue without moving into the mainstream. This comment from a young media worker from the Torres Strait perhaps underlines what it means to be working in the industry for the many hundreds of other broadcasters, young and old, whose commitment to their communities was acknowledged and praised by audiences around Australia (Interview, Batchelor, 2004):

> And I can honestly say that in 2005, it is going to be my 30th birthday, and I'm actually living my dream. To think that when I first came back here, I said, 'Gee, I really like that' [Torres Strait Radio]. Ten years later I said, 'Gee, I wouldn't mind doing that'...Now it makes me think I'm living my dream and I'm going to be there celebrating their 20th birthday. And it'll go down in history, as me and a couple of other colleagues of mine, being a part of that radio in Torres Strait.

From our most recent engagement with Indigenous media audiences, producers, sector organizations and representatives, it is clear that there is widespread concern about whether the industry does have a future. The launch of NITV on a shoestring budget in 2007 has offered some options but at what expense? The demise of ICTV to make way for this sorely needed enterprise seems a grim irony in an industry that needs a variety of approaches to meet the needs of its diverse audiences. Several callers to the radio programme, *Talk Black*, along with a significant number of listeners and viewers around Australia, voiced their suspicions that it was deliberate government policy to keep the sector underfunded. This response sums up the thoughts of many (*Talk Black* 2005):

> I think that the Federal government should take a lot of blame for not creating positions within the Indigenous radio stations and that's because of the lack of funding. I found that there is a lot of emphasis on studying radio, getting into colleges but where do they go when they finish?

A more cynical observer was not alone in drawing this conclusion (*Talk Black* 2005): 'Doesn't matter what they are going to do, at the end of this enquiry [this study] they are going to hammer youse, because they have hammered everything else.' These were not isolated observations. The audiences taking part in our study were generally very well-informed about issues within the sector, again confirming the close relationship they have with their local media organizations. This is further support for the idea of an absence of a real audience-producer barrier across the Indigenous media sector. The critical role being played by talkback radio in its various programme formats has clearly captured audiences around the country – and they want more time allocated to this to enable more dialogue. There was a call by several focus groups for greater support for local musicians, especially emerging artists, and this comment is typical of many on this topic:

> They're doing a pretty good job as it is but it could always be better...There's heaps of Indigenous artists out there who are really talented people and they should be played more. That's what it's all about as far as I'm concerned – giving the little bloke a go (Focus Group, 98.9FM, 2006).

Other issues raised included suggestions that stations could become more involved in organizing local community activities like dances, music events and needed to promote themselves more actively in their local communities – and to both Indigenous and non-Indigenous audiences. Another suggestion was for stations to introduce more traditional, local languages into their programming where possible. These comments relate particularly to urban-based stations canvassed in Cairns, Townsville, Brisbane and Melbourne. Audiences want the extension of local news and information sources to include those often ignored, as this exchange suggests:

> Participant 1: Reach out to the parkies [itinerant park dwellers] and get their views too – they're very knowledgeable. They got a lot of brains – it's just because of the alcohol.
> Participant 2: A lot of parkies, they come down here and people say they're bludging, but a lot of them can't go back to their communities because of family feuds, things like that.
> Participant 1: Got to reach out.
> Participant 2: A lot of them keep in contact with family through the station (Interview, Townsville, 2005).

A greater level of government recognition and support along with better levels of funding were suggestions emerging from audiences for ethnic community radio. But perhaps the most strident claims were for more access to the airwaves. It is difficult to see how this might be easily resolved with around 100 different community language groups vying for attention on just 123 ethnic radio stations. And although an additional 30 hours of programming time is available through generalist community radio stations, this comes nowhere near meeting the needs, particularly of emerging and refugee communities, some of which have just 30 minutes each week to address the pressing concerns that confront their audiences. One of the problems is that established communities like the Greeks, Italians and Chinese are generally well catered for with good access to radio along with the largest circulation ethnic newspapers in Australia. There is a general feeling against 'taking back' air time from other communities who have fought for access for decades, in some cases. Expanding the already cluttered FM spectrum is also unviable with some – mainly policymnakers – suggesting digital radio as a possible solution. However, with a realistic switchover a decade away, it offers little hope for the current needy organizations. It seems more likely that web-streaming will offer a low-cost option although this assumes audience access to broadband, something which is far from a reality in most disadvantaged communities. Nevertheless, more creative solutions, such as the mixed media use by Indigenous broadcasters in the APY Lands may offer a solution.

Radio broadcasts in community language rate as the second-most preferred way for ethnic communities to receive government information. This indicates calls for more airtime have a significant basis beyond the cultural work we have identified these programmes are already performing. Ethnic communities themselves identify radio broadcasts in community languages as the fourth most *common* way to access government information, reflecting the growing influence of well-educated second, third and fourth generation children of migrant parents who have increasingly adopted mainstream media as their primary source of information. Nevertheless, as one Greek Seniors' focus group participant reminded us, the 'common language' that is used in radio broadcasts makes it accessible to all listeners. Brochures and newspapers produced in language might only be accessible to well-educated or younger members of the community as many older migrants still have poor literacy skills. This shift in emphasis is a particular characteristic of more established ethnic communities and perhaps an argument to 'pass on' airtime to those more in need when the opportunity arises.

Indigenous imaginings

Australia's First Nations people claim the longest continuous surviving culture on the planet with the country as a whole arguably amongst the most multicultural nations on earth. The European invasion more than two centuries ago wreaked havoc on the estimated 250 different Aboriginal nations that had eked out an existence for possibly 100,000 years. The racist treatment of Indigenous peoples that is a hallmark of Australia's 'settlement' process set up a framework for thinking about Aboriginal people that has proven difficult to shift, despite the many examples of cooperation between Indigenous and non-Indigenous people (Meadows 2001). Continuing mainstream media misrepresentation of Indigenous people and issues reflects this seeming inability for the 'parallel voices' of Indigenous and non-Indigenous Australia to establish an effective and productive dialogue (Langton 1993). While there have been notable acts of reconciliation and sharing along the way, the majority of Australia's Indigenous people remain disadvantaged in terms of almost every social indicator. It perhaps helps to explain the task that continues to confront Indigenous people seeking to gain control of the means of production of their own images and voices. The emergence of Indigenous radio and television has been a major element in giving diverse cultures the opportunity to imagine their own albeit limited futures. Access to the airwaves has been a long struggle and as the controversial emergence of NITV confirms, the resources made available for such important ventures are miniscule when compared with similar First Nations' television enterprises in New Zealand and Canada (APTN 2007; Maori Television 2008). And distinct from both of these countries, Australia has yet to include a clause in its *Broadcasting Services Act* that recognizes the special place of Indigenous languages and cultures in the Australian broadcasting environment.

Audiences for Indigenous media across Australia have revealed themselves to be as diverse as the media over which they believe they have ownership. Indigenous radio and television are integral parts of Indigenous culture and as such, central organizing elements of communities where they are active. These audiences see their media as essential services, offering them far more than news and information about their communities and the outside world. There are no other media in Australia that fulfil or that could fulfil the role currently being played by the existing Indigenous media industry – and an industry it has clearly become. Audiences confirm that it is an enduring symbol of community empowerment: 'Our voices', 'our images', 'the *Anangu* way', 'Black voices, Black issues'. Indigenous media play a critical role in maintaining cultures and languages through the intimate relationships they have with their diverse communities. Based on the evidence adduced here, the absence of the audience-producer barrier is a defining characteristic of Indigenous media in Australia. This has led to innovative uses of a range of technologies: radio (particularly talkback, language and music), video through the former ICTV and UHF radio and a fledgling National Indigenous Television service. It is also clear that these developments have come about because communities have identified a functional need for these technologies to maintain and expand existing traditional communication systems.

Audiences have made it very clear that they regard Indigenous radio and television as powerful media for education, particularly for children and thus, their future. This emphasis on education emerged across all of the themes we have identified here and in many ways, offers a holistic concept of the ultimate goals of Indigenous media in whatever form. Clearly, educating the next generation is the focus but the media's educative role extends across cultures, with non-Indigenous audiences seen as playing a vital role in learning more about Indigenous cultures, thus contributing to the process of reconciliation. At all of our visits to regions around Australia over the course of this research, audiences consistently and spontaneously raised the notion that Indigenous media provide a cultural bridge between Indigenous and non-Indigenous Australia. Audiences told us that this element has great potential for future development, particularly through access to remote Indigenous video productions for the broader Australian population. Although this had begun to be addressed by NITV at the time of writing, the potential offered by the former ICTV is a cultural resource that has been unfortunately overlooked in the name of political expediency. Regardless, it is important to note that participants stressed that Indigenous media's primary role was to provide an essential service to Indigenous people – additional outcomes must follow from this.

Audiences in all regions involved in this study expressed their dissatisfaction with mainstream media representation – and equally, lack of representation – of Indigenous issues in ways that might engage them. Apart from some passing references to acceptable and occasional coverage of relevant issues by the ABC and SBS, audiences we canvassed are unanimous in their conclusions that mainstream media in Australia have failed Indigenous people. This is an alarming finding – that in 2008, the major sources of information for most Australians remain unable or unwilling to address this void in their programming policies. Support for Indigenous media in Australia is, according to our audience research, still largely driven by perceptions of negative coverage of Indigenous affairs in the mainstream media. Research over the past two decades suggests that this has not changed and it should be of concern (Michaels 1986; Mishra 1988; Langton 1993; Meadows 1994; West 1994; Hippocrates et al. 1996; Molnar and Meadows 2001; Meadows 2005). As a result, Indigenous media remain the primary sources of information for communities about issues of relevance to them, apart from word of mouth. Indigenous media are identified by audiences as 'theirs' and the only places where they are able to speak out without fear of censorship. The several hugely popular talkback programmes on Indigenous radio clearly perform this role. As audiences participating in this study concluded, for this reason alone, the role of the Indigenous media sector should be recognized and adequately resourced.

Audience feedback underlined the crucial role being undertaken by the Indigenous media sector in supporting, virtually single-handed, the burgeoning Indigenous music industry. Without Indigenous radio, local bands would never get out of the garage. Music and dance, both traditional and contemporary, are featured at every major Indigenous cultural festival in the country. And there is a myriad of young people who have immersed themselves in the industry either as listeners or as producers. Music production, like media, is one of the few available career options for young people in Indigenous communities wherever they might be. And like broadcasting, it presents alternatives to young people easily lured into substance-abuse and self-harm. The outcomes that flow from the maintenance and expansion of the Indigenous music industry are clear but it is Indigenous media that are leading the way.

Concerns by audiences over inadequate sector funding were widespread and across all regions. There is strong evidence that the sector is offering real alternatives for young people wanting to become involved in media production and steady enrolments at tertiary training institutions such as Batchelor College in the Northern Territory attest to this. However, the relatively few full-time paid positions available across the industry have limited opportunities for young broadcasters seeking a career path. In short, audiences reported that there are few career paths, essentially because of a lack of funding. Historically, volunteerism at the levels of those in the generalist community radio sector, has not been part of contemporary Indigenous culture, although there *are* many regular volunteers in Indigenous media. Nevertheless, there is an almost total reliance on alternative funding sources such as 'work for the dole' (CDEP) to support or 'top-up' wages for local RIBS broadcasters. Suggestions in 2007 that this system might be removed sent shockwaves through the sector; but for now, at, least, it remains an option.

Conclusion

At the time of our audience research, the extension of the now defunct ICTV signal into remote Indigenous communities was being enthusiastically received, but even then, there were significant concerns about 'outside interference' with 'our TV'. Audiences, particularly those who have become used to their own local television service – in the APY lands, central Australia and the Pilbara–Kimberley regions – were worried that deliberations over the introduction of a National Indigenous Television Service would marginalize them. They saw this as particularly ironic given that communities centred around Ernabella and Yuendumu 'invented' Indigenous television more than 25 years ago (Michaels 1986). Clumsy management of this has led to an almost inevitable 'bush–city' divide. ICTV was clearly offering remote communities and those able to receive it via satellite (the signal was unscrambled in 2006 for general viewing) an innovative alternative to mainstream television programming. Audiences in urban and regional centres (including Darwin, Alice Springs and Broome) wanted access to the ICTV signal. Many in this audience cohort who had seen ICTV, believed it could have played a major role in challenging stereotypes about Indigenous Australia which, they reminded us constantly, remain prevalent in mainstream media portrayals. ICTV represented the most significant advance for remote Indigenous communities in the past twenty years in terms of its potential to contribute to the maintenance of languages and cultures, boosting self-esteem and making a significant contribution to reinforcing a sense of identity amongst its diverse audiences. It had already begun to achieve this when it was unceremoniously switched off in July 2007 to make way for NITV. And while there is no doubt that Australia needs such a national Indigenous television service, it cannot fill the void left by the demise of ICTV. The two entities are targeting very different audiences although there could have been some productive overlap. But it may yet become a reality: moves to re-create ICTV as an Internet-streamed service which could then be re-broadcast locally by RIBS communities was under development at the time of writing. Watch this space!

The evidence offered by the audiences for Indigenous media we have canvassed both complements previous research into the sector and advances our knowledge significantly. We can confidently say that the Australian Indigenous media industry is providing an essential service for a diverse range of communities across the country. It is much more than simply a purveyor of news, information and music, although it is the *only* source of relevant information for these. Indigenous media enterprises are part of Indigenous cultures. By their very nature, they fulfil multiple roles within their communities – unique, complex roles that are simply beyond the capacity or will of existing mainstream organizations.

Cultural crossroads

Audiences for ethnic community radio programmes produced by a range of communities around Australia are overwhelmingly supportive of the information and entertainment services provided by these media. They are grateful to both the stations and individual presenters and producers for the contributions they make to the community, and to issues they consider are essential to community life – maintenance of culture and language, enjoyment of traditional music, creation and maintenance of community networks, provision of local community news and essential 'settlement' information and provision of news from home to help with feelings of anxiety and homesickness.

Community radio news for ethnic communities serves the multiple purposes of informing people about local community events and gossip, as well as providing important information about legal issues, visas and Australian culture for new migrants and older people with poor English skills. The role of music in the lives of all the community radio listeners we have spoken to is strong, with many ethnic focus group participants speaking passionately about the impact that traditional music programming has on their general feelings of wellbeing and happiness. Music programming is essential to their enjoyment of ethnic radio and is inexorably connected to maintenance of culture and language. Indeed, 'hearing your own language' is the most commonly expressed reason for listening to ethnic community radio and the further experience of 'hearing music in your own language' only serves to increase the importance of such programmes. Music is used for entertainment, to improve and maintain language skills, to communicate with other community members through request programmes and to reignite memories of home.

These results suggest that ethnic audiences are as passionate about spoken-word language programming – particularly news and information – as music. This conclusion, drawn from our audience study, led to a policy change which saw music programmes also attracting funding support from the Community Broadcasting Foundation (CBF) alongside spoken-word programming. Our research revealed that music is not used merely as a form of entertainment in ethnic community radio programming – it performs an important role in cultural and language maintenance. While some balance between spoken-word language programming and music programming is certainly needed, focus group participants place equal 'cultural' value on spoken-word language and language through music.

Almost four decades ago, the idea of Australian multiculturalism was first 'imagined' and adopted as government policy. The coincidental emergence of the community radio sector had the support of all major political parties, acknowledging the shift of Australian identity from one dominated by traditional ties to England and Europe to a more realistic cultural melange. Indigenous people have long argued that their First Nation status places them apart from settler cultures and as such, have generally been opposed to being included under the banner of 'multiculturalism'. And thus the search continues for consensus on an approach for an 'inclusive multiculturalism' – a democratic pluralism – that encompasses citizen empowerment, respect for cultural difference, social integration, recognition of cultural identity and a need for community belonging and membership that extends to Indigenous and ethnic communities alike (Jayasuriya 2008). The history of Australian race relations will loom large in any such venture. For example, the gradual expansion of the embryonic community radio sector did not automatically extend access to the groups in the Australian community most in need. And while specialist ethnic radio stations were set up in Sydney and Melbourne in the mid-1970s, Indigenous communities had to struggle for access, gaining their first specialist community station in 1980, the same year that the Special Broadcasting Service (SBS) was set up to service ethnic media audiences. SBS television was launched in 1984, gradually rolling out as a national service over the next decade or so. Significantly, the first attempt to launch a national Indigenous television service in Australia was in 2007!

Stepping stones

The Australian community broadcasting sector is on the move by any measure. Its steadily increasing audience numbers have been confirmed in quantitative surveys over the past six years (McNair Ingenuity 2004; 2006; 2008); the important cultural role it plays from the perspectives of station managers, news and general volunteers is evident from both quantitative and qualitative research (Forde et al. 2002); and now its diverse audiences emphasize the multiple social, cultural and political roles played by its various elements (Meadows et al. 2007). So what does all this mean?

It is clear that the Australian community broadcasting sector as a whole is a key cultural resource that is making a significant contribution to fostering dialogue between the complex cultural elements that 'imagine' Australia as a nation (Anderson 1984). The Indigenous and ethnic community radio and television 'sub-sectors' we have considered in this book are arguably the most dynamic elements of this diverse network. In many ways, they epitomize the very reason that community broadcasting was set up in Australia – to afford access to the air waves by marginalized communities. But they are also places where the processes of community media are perhaps most visible. As such, they represent a way of thinking about the broader sector by using these as 'lenses', allowing all of us to 'see' more clearly. A primary reason for focusing on these particular media is because of the belief we have formed that they are part of a unique process. We have been invited to explore some of the elements that create, drive and sustain it. It is the first time that a book on community media has been able to draw from such extensive, primary data from the entire community broadcasting production and reception process of a single national entity. We hope that the empowering narratives that have emerged from our analysis will strengthen the resolve of community media workers elsewhere, perhaps drawing from the experiences to continue with their own important work.

In the light of the evidence we have gathered, we suggest the need to consider the nature of audience-producer relationships as a principle defining characteristic of community broadcasting – and community media more broadly. Despite the empowering nature of these media on many levels, we have been able to identify the 'transparency' of the audience-producer boundary along a continuum – from the most intimate relationships in Indigenous community radio and television to some that are perhaps less so in the ethnic community radio sector. And while this does not diminish in any way the work that all are doing, it suggests a way of contextualizing the processes involved, offering an insight into why particular 'repertoires of conduct' prevail and how dialogue between disparate communities of interest might be enhanced (Mercer 1989; Langton 1993). Almost without exception, theorizing of community media thus far has been based on almost every element of the media production process – except detailed, qualitative audience analysis. We hope that the start we have made in this book goes some way towards encouraging others to not only question our conclusions, but also to advance thinking on this important social phenomenon. Community broadcasting in Australia represents the full range of experiences emerging from countless sites around the world. We have been in a privileged position to be able to explore some of the questions raised by previous scholars and hopefully, this will inspire many more to extend this work, particularly with a strong audience research dimension. We can only hope that recognition of the cultural role being played by these two active and inspirational arms of the Australian community broadcasting sector receive the recognition they deserve from policymakers. It seems that audiences have already cast their votes: it is now up to our political representatives to follow their lead.

References

ABC News Online, 'Palm Island riot accused found not guilty', 22 March 2007, available at http://www.abc.net.au/news/newsitems/200703/s1879134.htm <viewed 20 February 2009>.

Aboriginal and Torres Strait Islander Commission, *Digital Dreaming: A National Review of Indigenous Media and Communications – Executive Summary*, Canberra, ATSIC, 1999, available at http://pandora.nla.gov.au/pan/41033/20060106-0000/ATSIC/programs/Broadcasting/Digital_Dreaming/default.html <viewed 20 February 2009>.

Aboriginal People's Television Network, home page, available at http://www.aptn.ca/images/stories/corporatepdfs/Financial/AnnualReport2007FINAL.pdf <viewed 16 March 2009>.

Agence France Presse, 'Aborigines wild over Guinness Book listing', 14 November 1998, available at http://www.indianexpress.com/res/web/pIe/ie/daily/19981114/31850314.html <viewed 20 February 2009>.

AIATSIS and FATSIL, *National Indigenous Languages Survey Report 2005*, Canberra, Australian Institute of Aboriginal and Torres Strait Islander Studies in association with the Federation of Aboriginal and Torres Strait Islander Languages, 2005.

AICA, Australian Indigenous Communications Association background information, available at http://www.aicainc.org.au/Html/index.html <viewed 20 February 2009>.

Alacorn, C., 'RTV is old news while CTS get the boot', *B & T Magazine*, 13 September 2004, available at http://bandt.com.au/news/68/Pc026968.asp <viewed 20 February 2009>.

Alvarez, C., 'Australian and Pacific Islands miles apart on radio legislation', *Interadio*, 8:1 (1997), pp. 24–25.

AMARC, World Association of Community Radio Broadcasters, available at http://www.amarc.org/ <viewed 3 March 2009>.

Anderson, B., *Imagined Communities: Reflections on the Origin and Spread of Nationalism*, London, Verso, 1984.

Anderson, H., 'Raising the Civil Dead: Prisoners' Radio in Australia and Canada', unpublished PhD dissertation, Brisbane, Faculty of Arts, Griffith University, 2008.

Ang, I., 'In conversation with Mary Zounazi', *Foreign Dialogues*, Part 3, 'Out of Bounds', ABC Radio National, 21 February 1999, available at http://www.abc.net.au/rn/arts/radioeye/transcripts/stories/s53213.htm <viewed 10 March 2009>.

Ang, I., *Desperately Seeking the Audience*, Routledge, London, 1991.

Ang, Ien, Brand, J. E., Noble, G. and Wilding, D., *Living Diversity: Australia's Multicultural Future*, Humanities and Social Sciences Papers, Gold Coast, Bond University, 2000.

Atton, C., *Alternative Media*, London, Sage, 2002.

Atton, C., and Couldry, N., 'Introduction', in *Media Culture and Society*, 25 (2003), pp. 579–586.

Australian Bureau of Statistics, *Adult Literacy and Life Skills Survey, Summary Results, Australia, 2006*, availableathttp://www.abs.gov.au/ausstats/abs@.nsf/Latestproducts/4228.0Main%20Features22006%20(Reissue)?opendocument&tabname=Summary&prodno=4228.0&issue=2006%20(Reissue)&num=&view= <viewed 3 March 2009>.

Australian Communications and Media Authority, *Price Based Allocation of Low Power Open Narrowcasting (LPON) Transmitter Licences: Applicant Information Package*, Belconnen, Australian Government, 2008, available at http://www.acma.gov.au/webwr/_assets/main/lib310196/lpon_info_pack_chapters1-4.pdf <viewed 20 February 2009>.

Australian Communications and Media Authority, *Communications Report 2005-2006*, Melbourne, ACMA, 2006, available at www.acma.gov.au/CommsReport <viewed 20 February 2009>.

Australian Communications and Media Authority, *Digital Media in Australian Homes*, Canberra, ACMA, 2005, available at http://www.acma.gov.au/acmainterwr/_assets/main/lib100068/digitalmedia.pdf <viewed 20 February 2009>.

Australian Communications and Media Authority, *Survey of the Community Broadcasting Sector 2002-2003*, Canberra, ACMA, Sydney, 2003.

Australian Press Council, *State of the news media report*, Australian Press Council, 2006, available at http://www.presscouncil.org.au/snpma/ch07.html <viewed 2.4.08>.

Avison, S. and Meadows, M., 'Speaking and hearing: Aboriginal newspapers and the public sphere in Canada and Australia', *Canadian Journal of Communication*, 25 (2000), pp. 347-366.

Bailey, O. G., Cammaerts, B. and Carpentier, N., *Understanding Alternative Media*, Maidenhead, Open University Press, 2008.

Baker, R. and Hinton, R., 'Do focus groups facilitate meaningful participation in social research?', in R. S. Barbour and J. Kitzinger (eds), *Developing Focus Group Research: Politics, Theory and Practice*, London, Sage Publications, 1999, pp. 79-98.

Barclay, B., *Our Own Image*, Auckland, Longman Paul, 1990.

Barlow, D. M., 'Understanding access and participation in the context of Australian community broadcasting', *Communications*, 24:1 (1999), pp. 85-104.

Barlow, D. M., 'Whither non-profit community media?', *Culture and Policy*, 8:3 (1997), pp. 119-137.

BBS, Media Survey, Brisbane, BBS Public Relations, 2008.

Bear, A., 'The emergence of public broadcasting in Australia', *Australian Journal of Communication*, 4 (1983), pp. 21-28.

Bear, A., 'Public broadcasting in Australia', *Studies in Continuing Education*, 2 (1979), pp. 1-20.

Beecher, E., 'Look to the future', *The Walkley Magazine*, 50 (2008), pp. 14-15.

Benhabib, S., 'The democratic movement and the problem of difference', in S. Benhabib (ed.), *Democracy and Difference: Contesting the Boundaries of the Political* (Princeton, Princeton University Press, 1996), pp. 3-18.

Bickford, S., *The Dissonance of Democracy: Listening, Conflict and Citizenship*, New York, Cornell University Press, 1996.

Biliki, R., Leeming, D. and Agassi, A., *People First Network: Solomon Islands' Rural Community Email Network for Peace and Development, Final Report, March 2005*, Honiara, Rural Development Volunteers Association (RDVA), available at http://www.peoplefirst.net.sb/Downloads/Japanese_grassroot_FinalReport.pdf <viewed 3 March 2009>.

Bosch, T., 'Community radio in post-apartheid South Africa: The case of Bush Radio in Cape Town', *Transformations*, Issue no. 10 , February, 2005, available at http://transformations.cqu.edu.au/journal/issue_10/article_05.shtml <viewed 20 February 2009>.

Bowd, K., 'Interviewing the interviewers: Methodological considerations in gathering data from journalists', *Australian Journalism Review*, 26:2 (2004), pp. 115-123.

Brady, M., 'Some problems of method and theory in Aboriginal research', in Peter Cashman (ed.), *Research and the Delivery of Legal Services* (Sydney, Law Foundation of New South Wales, 1981), pp. 281-285.

References

Broadcasting Services Act (1992) available at http://www.austlii.edu.au/au/legis/cth/consol_actbsa 1992214/ <viewed 20 February 2009>.

Brough, M., Gorman, D., Ramirez, E. and Westoby, P., 'Young refugees talk about wellbeing: A qualitative analysis of refugee youth mental health from three states', *Australian Journal of Social Issues*, 38:2 (2003), pp. 193–208.

Browne, D. R., *Ethnic Minorities, Electronic Media and the Public Sphere: A Comparative Study*, Cresskill, NJ, Hampton Press, 2005.

Browne, D. R., *Electronic Media and Indigenous Peoples: A Voice of Our Own?* Ames, Iowa State University Press, 1996.

Camara, M., 'Giant too big for its britches', *Interadio*, 8:1 (1996), pp. 20–21.

Carpentier, N. and de Cleen, B., *Participation and Media Production: Critical Reflections on Content Creation*, London, Cambridge Scholars Publishing, 2007.

Carpentier, N., Lie, R. and Servaes, J., 'Community media: Muting the democratic Media discourse?' *Continuum*, 77:1 (2003), pp. 52–68.

Castillo, A., 'They shall not pass: Cultural diversity in Australian newsrooms', *Australian Mosaic,* 5:1 (2004), pp. 16–17.

Catterall, M. and Maclaran, P., 'Focus group data and qualitative analysis programs: Coding the moving picture as well as the snapshots', *Sociological Research Online*, 2:1 (1997), available at http://www.socresonline.org.uk/2/1/6.html <visited 20 February 2009>.

CB Online, *Community Broadcasting Database: Public Release Report 2006*, available at http://www.cbonline.org.au/index.cfm?pageId=37,0,1,0 <viewed 23 November 2006>.

CB Online, *Community Broadcast Database: Survey of the Radio Sector 2003–2004 Financial Year*, Full Report, Sydney, Community Broadcasting Association of Australia, 2006.

CB Online, *Value our Voices: Strengthen Community Broadcasting,* 2009/10 federal budget submission by the Community Broadcasting Association of Australia, National Ethnic & Multicultural Broadcasters Council, Australian Indigenous Communications Association, RPH Australia, Christian Media Australia, Community Broadcasting Foundation, October 2008, available at http://www.cbonline.org.au/%5Cmedia%5CValueVoicesOct08amended.pdf <viewed 20 February 09>.

Centrelink, *DBM Consultants: Communications Effectiveness Module - Abstract*, provided to the authors in confidence, Sydney and Melbourne, DBM Consultants, 2003.

Chand, A., 'Ethnic media and Fijian Indians in Sydney', *Australian Journalism Review*, 26:1 (2004), pp. 145–154.

Chitty, N. and Rattichalkalakorn, S., *Alternative Media: Idealism and Pragmatism*, Penang, Southbound, 2007.

Chitty, N., Personal communication, Macquarie University, 2006.

Chomsky, N., 'What makes mainstream media mainstream?' *Z Magazine*, from a paper delivered to the Z Institute, June 1997, available at http://www.zmag.org/zmag/articles/chomoct97.htm <viewed 3 March 2009>.

Coben, D., 'Common sense or good sense? Ethnomathematics and the prospects for a Gramscian politics of adults' mathematics education', 2005, available at http://www.nottingham.ac.uk/csme/meas/papers/coben.html <viewed 20 February 2009>.

Cohen, E., 'Voices of our land: Ethnic radio and the complexity of diasporic practices in multicultural Australia', *Humanities Research*, 10:3 (2003), pp. 125–148.

Commonwealth of Australia, *Ready, Get Set, Go Digital: A Digital Action Plan for Australia*, Canberra, Commonwealth of Australia, 2006.

Community Media Association, 'About Community Media', 2009, available at http://www.commedia.org.uk/about-community-media/community-radio/ <viewed 20 February 2009>.

Coonan, H., 'Media laws proclaimed', news release from the Department of Communication, Information Technology and the Arts, 29 March 2007, available at http://www.minister.dcita.gov.au/coonan/media/media_releases/media_laws_proclaimed?SQ_DESIGN_NAME=printer_friendly <viewed 3 March 2009>.

Corker, J., 'BRACS: Destined to Fail?', *Media Information Australia*, 51 (1989), pp. 43–44.

Couldry, N., 'Mediation and alternative media, or relocating the center of media and communication studies', *Media International Australia*, 103 (2002), pp. 24–31.

Coupe, B. and Jakubowicz, A., *Nextdoor Neighbours: A Report for the Office of Multicultural Affairs on Ethnic Group Discussions of the Australian Media*, Sydney, University of Technology Sydney, 1992.

Coyer, K., Dowmunt, T. and Fountain, A., *Alternative Media Handbook*, London, Taylor and Francis, 2007.

Criterion Research, *Community Consultation: Focus Group Results*, Report to Strathcona County and KPMG Consulting, August, 2002.

Cunningham-Burley, S., Kerr, A. and Pavis, S., 'Theorizing subjects and subject matter in focus group research', in R. S. Barbour and J. Kitzinger (eds), *Developing Focus Group Research: Politics, Theory and Practice* (London, Sage, 1999), pp. 186–199.

Curran, J. and Gurevitch, M. (eds), *Mass Media and Society 4th Edition*, London, Hodder Education, 2005.

Daniels, G. L., 'The role of Native American print and online media in the "era of big stories": A comparative case study of Native American outlets' coverage of the Red Lake shootings', *Journalism*, 7:3 (2006), pp. 321–342.

Davies, N., *Flat Earth News*, London, Chatto and Windus, 2008.

Davis, M., *Gangland: Cultural Elites and the New Generationalism*, Sydney, Allen & Unwin, 1997.

Day, G., *Community and Everyday Life*, New York, Routledge, 2006.

De Wit, P., Personal communication from the director of OLON, May 2007.

Deger, J., Shimmering Screens: Making Media in an Aboriginal Community, Minneapolis, University of Minnesota Press, 2007.

Department of Immigration and Citizenship, *Australian Multiculturalism for a New Century: Towards Inclusiveness*, Canberra, available at http://www.immi.gov.au/media/publications/multicultural/nmac/ <viewed 10 March 2009>.

Department of Immigration and Citizenship, *Population Flows: Immigration Aspects 2007–2008 Edition*, Canberra, available at http://www.immi.gov.au/media/publications/statistics/popflows 2007-08/ <viewed 10 March 2009>.

Deuze, M., 'Ethnic media, community media and participatory culture', *Journalism*, 7:3 (2006), pp. 262–280.

Dowmunt, T., *Channels of Resistance: Global Television and Local Empowerment*, London, BFI Publishing and Channel Four Television, 1993.

Downing, J., 'Audiences and readers of alternative media: The absent lure of the virtually unknown', *Media, Culture & Society*, 25 (2003), pp. 625–645.

Downing, J., *Radical Media: Rebellious Communication and Social Movements*, Thousand Oaks, Sage, 2001.

Downing, J., *Radical Media: The Political Experience of Alternative Communication*, Boston, South End Press, 1984.

Downing, J. and Fenton, N., 'New media, counter publicity and the public sphere', *New Media and Society*, 5:2 (2003), pp. 185–202.

Downing, J. and Husband, C., *Representing Race: Racisms, Ethnicity and the Media*, London, Sage, 2005.

Dreher, T., 'Speaking up and talking back: News media interventions in Sydney's "othered" communities', *Media International Australia*, 109 (2003), pp. 121–137.

Eades, D., 'You gotta know how to talk…Information seeking in South East Queensland Aboriginal society', in J. B. Pride (ed.), *Cross-cultural Encounters: Communication and Mis-communication* (Melbourne, River Seine Publications, 1985), pp. 91–109.

Elghul-Bebawi, S., 'The relationship between mainstream and alternative media: A blurring of the edges?', in J. Gordon (ed.), *Notions of Community: A Collection of Community Media Debates and Dilemmas* (Bern, Peter Lang, 2009), pp. 17–32.

Ethnic Broadcasting Association of Queensland (EBAQ), *Messages from the Past: Voices to the Future – Communications Linking and Sustaining Multicultural Queensland*, Brisbane, Radio 4EB, EBAQ, 2002.

European Broadcasting Union, 'EBU president sees public broadcasters "at the heart of e-Europe"', EBU News Release, Brussels, 27 March 2001.

European Parliament, Texts adopted by Parliament Thursday, 25 September 2008, Brussels (Provisional edition), Community Media in Europe, available at http://www.europarl.europa.eu/sides/getDoc.do?type=TA&reference=P6-TA-2008-0456&language=EN <visited 3 March 2009>.

Everitt, A., *An Interim Evaluation of 15 Access Radio Projects*, The Radio Authority Online, September 2002, available at www.ofcom.org.uk/static/archive/rau/publications–archive/word–doc/communications–bill/Interim%20Report%20–%20%20exec%20summary.doc <viewed 3 March 2009>.

Ewart, J., 'Capturing the heart of the region – how regional media define a community', *Transformations*, 1 (2000), pp. 1–13.

FAIRA, 'Shameful white history of Palm Island', Foundation for Aboriginal and Islander Research Action archives, 1999, available at http://www.faira.org.au/lrq/archives/199901/stories/shameful-white-history.html <viewed 20 February 09>.

Fairbairn, J., *Community Media Sustainability Guide: The Business of Changing Lives*, Arcata, Internews Network, 2009.

Forde, S., 'The changing face of the Australian newsroom: Cultural and ethnic diversity among Sydney journalists', *Australian Journalism Review*, 27:2 (2005), pp. 119–134.

Forde, S., 'Community radio and "progressive" politics: Australian community radio and its shift to the right', paper presented at *Predicting Pathways and Pulling Together*, Radiocracy Conference, Durban, South Africa, 20–24 September 2001.

Forde, S., '"Journalistic practices and newsroom organisation in the independent and alternative press", *Australian Journalism Review*, 21:3 (1999), pp. 60–79.

Forde, S., 'The development of the alternative press in Australia', *Media International Australia*, 87 (1998), pp. 114–133.

Forde, S., 'Reviving the Public Sphere: The Australian Independent and Alternative Press Industry', unpublished PhD thesis, Brisbane, University of Queensland, 1998.

Forde, S., 'A descriptive look at the public role of Australian independent alternative press', *AsiaPacific MediaEducator*, 3 (1997), pp. 118–130.

Forde, S., Meadows, M., and Foxwell, K., 'The Australian community radio sector', European Journal of Communication Research, 28:3 (2003), pp. 231–252.

Forde, S., Meadows, M., and Foxwell, K., 'Through the lens of the local: Public arena journalism in the Australian community broadcasting sector', *Journalism*, 4:3 (2003), pp. 317–342.

Forde, S., Foxwell, K. and Meadows, M., 'Creating a community public sphere: Community radio as a cultural resource'. *Media International Australia*, 103 (2002), pp. 56–67.

Forde, S., Meadows, M., and Foxwell, K., *Culture, Commitment, Community: The Australian Community Radio Sector*, Brisbane, Griffith University, 2002.

Forde, S., Foxwell, K. and Meadows, M., 'Commitment to community: Results from a national survey of the community radio sector', *ABA Update*, 100 (2001), pp. 16–22.

Foster, L. and Stockley, D., *Australian Multiculturalism: A Documentary History and Critique*, Clevedon, Multilingual Matters, 1988.

Foucault, M., *Discipline and Punish: The Birth of the Prison*, London, Allan Lane, 1977.

Foundation for Development Corporation, 'The promotion of culture in the ACP region: Together, shaping our future', background paper, Brisbane, 31 May 2004.

Foxwell, K., Ewart, J., Forde, S. and Meadows, M., 'Sounds like a whisper: Australian community broadcasting hosts a quiet revolution', *Westminster Papers in Communication and Culture*, 5:1 (2008), pp. 5–24.

Fraser, N., 'Rethinking the public sphere: A contribution to the critique of actually existing democracy', in C. Calhoun (ed.), *Habermas and the Public Sphere* (Cambridge, MIT Press, 1999), pp. 109–142.

Fraser, N., 'Rethinking the public sphere: A contribution to the critique of actually existing democracy', in B. Robbins (ed.), *The Phantom Public Sphere* (Minneapolis, University of Minnesota Press, 1993), pp. 1–32.

Friere, P., *Pedagogy of the Oppressed*, New York, Continuum, 1983.

Fuller, L., (ed.) *Community Media: International Perspectives*, London, Palgrave Macmillan, 2007.

Gardiner-Garden, J. and Chowns, J., *Media Ownership Regulation in Australia*, Parliament of Australia – Parliamentary Library, 2006, available at http://www.aph.gov.au/library/intguide/SP/Media_Regulation.htm <viewed 20 February 2009>.

Garrett, P., Interview at Garma Festival, Northern Territory, 7 August 2005.

Geertz, C., *The Interpretation of Cultures: Selected Essays*, New York, Basic Books, 1973.

Geurts, J. and Joldersma, C., 'Methodology for participatory policy analysis', *European Journal of Operational Research*, 128 (2001), pp. 300–310.

Gibbs, A., 'Focus groups', *Social research Update*, 19 (1997), available at http://sru.soc.surrey.ac.uk/SRU19.html <viewed 20 February 2009>.

Gibson, K. and Cameron, J., 'Transforming communities: Towards a research agenda', *Urban Policy and Research*, 19:1 (2001), pp. 7–24.

Gillard, P., 'Shaping audiences online: Principles of audience development for cultural institutions', *Media International Australia*, 94 (2000), pp. 117–130

Ginsburg, F., 'Resources of hope: Learning from the local in a transnational era', in C. Smith and G. K. Ward (eds), *Indigenous Cultures in an Interconnected World* (St Leonards, Allen and Unwin, 2000), pp. 27–47.

Ginsburg, F., 'Indigenous media: Faustian contract or global village?' *Cultural Anthropology*, 6:1 (1991), pp. 92–112.

Girard, B., *A Passion for Radio: Radio Waves and Community*, Montreal, Black Rose Books, 1992.

Girard, B. and van der Spek, J., *The Potential for Community Radio in Afghanistan: Report of a Fact-finding Mission: October 5 to 22, 2002*, available at www.comunica.org/afghanistan/cr_afghan.pdf <viewed 3 March 2009>.

References

Glaser, B. G. and Strauss, A. L., *The Discovery of Grounded Theory: Strategies for Qualitative Research*, Chicago, Aldine Publishing, 1967.

Gordon, J., (ed.) *Notions of Community: A Collection of Community Media Debates and Dilemmas*, Bern, Peter Lang, 2009.

Gordon, J., 'Community radio, funding and ethics: the UK and Australian models', in J. Gordon (ed.), *Notions of Community: A Collection of Community Media Debates and Dilemmas* (Bern, Peter Lang, 2009), pp. 59–79.

Gordon, J., Panel discussion at the Radio Conference, Lincoln, UK, 16–19 July 2007.

Goudie, D., Interview, Townsville Cultural Festival, 2005.

Gramsci, A., *The Antonio Gramsci Reader: Selected Writings 1916–1935*, D. Forgacs (trans. and ed.), New York, Shocken Books, 1988.

Gramsci, A., *Selections from the Prison Notebooks*, edited and translated by Q. Hoare and G. Nowell Smith (trans. and ed.), London, Lawrence and Wishart, 1971.

Green, L., 'Focusing upon interview methodologies', *Australian Journal of Communication*, 26:1 (1999), pp. 35–46.

Grossberg, L., 'The context of audiences and the politics of difference', *Australian Journal of Communication*, 16 (1989), pp. 13–36.

Grossberg, L., 'Putting the pop back into postmodernism', in A. Ross (ed.), *Universal Abandon? The Politics of Post-Modernism* (Minneapolis, University of Minnesota Press, 1988), pp. 167–190.

Grossberg, L., 'Critical theory and the politics of empirical research', in M. Gurevitch and M. Levy (eds), *Mass Communication Review Yearbook* Volume 6 (London, Sage, 1987), pp. 86–106.

Gutierriez, F., 'Introduction', *Journalism*, 7:3 (2006), pp. 259–261.

Guzman, I. M., 'Competing discourses of community: Ideological tensions between local general market and Latino news media', *Journalism*, 7:3 (2006), pp. 281–298.

Hall, S., 'The rediscovery of "ideology": Return of the repressed in media studies', in M. Gurevitch, T. Bennett, J. Curran and J. Woollacott (eds), *Culture, Society and the Media* (London, Methuen, 1982), pp. 56–90.

Hall, S., 'Cultural studies: two paradigms', *Media, Culture and Society*, 2 (1980), pp. 57–72.

Hamilton, J., *All the News That's Fit to Sell: How the Market Transforms Information into News*, Princeton, Princeton University Press, 2004.

Hartley, J. and McKee, A., *Telling Both Stories: Indigenous Australia and the Media. Proceedings of the National Media Forum*, Perth, Arts Enterprise: Edith Cowan University, 1996.

Hemple, J., 'Packaging Indigenous media: An interview with Ivan Sanjines and Jesus Tapia', *American Anthropologist*, 106:2 (2004), pp. 354–363.

Hepi, A., Sports Producer, Interview at 4K1G, Townsville, 28 November 2005.

Herman, E. S. and McChesney, R. W., *The Global Media: The New Missionaries of Corporate Capitalism*, Cassell, London, 1997.

Hippocrates, C., Meadows, M. and van Vuuren, K., *Race Reporter*, a study funded by the Queensland Anti-Discrimination Commission, Brisbane, November, 1996.

Hirner, W., *Independent Radio in Central and Eastern Europe: Country by Country Reports*, AMARC Europe, March 1996.

Hochheimer, J. L., 'Organising community radio: Issues in planning', *Communications*, 24:4 (1999), pp. 443–455.

Hollander, E., Personal communication, Nijmegen, The Netherlands, 19 June 2007.

Horsfall, D., Byrne-Armstrong, H. and Higgs, J., 'Researching critical moments', in H. Byrne-Armstrong, J. Higgs and D. Horsfall (eds), *Critical Moments in Qualitative Research* (Oxford, Butterworth Heinemannn, 2001), pp. 3–13.

House of Representatives Standing Committee on Communication, Transport and the Arts, *Local Voices: An Inquiry into Local Radio*, Canberra, Parliament of the Commonwealth of Australia, 2001.

Howley, K., *Community Media: People, Places and Communication Technologies*, Cambridge, Cambridge University Press, 2005.

Ishikawa, S., 'Promoting community culture: Growth of community FM radio in Japan', paper presented to the MacBride Round Table, Seoul, 1996.

Jakubowicz, A. and Seneviratne, K., *Ethnic Conflict and the Australian Media*, University of Technology Sydney, Australian Centre for Independent Journalism, 1996.

Jayasuriya, L., 'Australian multiculturalism reframed', *The New Critic*, 8 (2008), available at http://www.ias.uwa.edu.au/new-critic/eight/jayasuriya <viewed 31 March 2009>.

Johnson, F., *What's Going on in Community Media*, Washington, Benton Foundation, 2007.

Josiah, J., 'Community broadcasting in the Caribbean: Collaboration and exchange via the internet', unpublished paper presented at the Pre-Conference Seminar on Mixed Media in Latin America and the Caribbean, Tampa, Florida 23–24 September 2000.

Kauranen, R. and Tuori, S., *Mapping Minorities and their Media: The National Context – Finland*, 2001, available at http://www.lse.ac.uk/collections/EMTEL/Minorities/papers/finlandreport.doc <viewed 20 February 2009>.

Kawakami, T., 'Community FM radio in Japan', paper presented at the OurMedia conference, Sydney, Australia, 10 April 2007.

Kawakami, T., Personal communication, Brisbane, 2006.

Kellner, D.M. and Durham, M.G., 'Adventures in Media and Cultural Studies: Introducing the KeyWorks', in M. G. Durham and D.M. Kellner (eds), *Media and Cultural Studies: KeyWorks* (Oxford, Blackwell Publishing, 2006), pp. ix–xxxviii.

Kelly, L., 'Channelling success: Why more people are switching on to Community TV', Arts Hub Australia, 10 May 2006, available at http://www.artshub.com.au/au/news.asp?sId=94374 <viewed 20 February 2009>.

Kern European Affairs, 'The state of community media in the European Union', a study requested by the European Parliament's Committee on Culture and Education, September 2007, available at http://www.europarl.europa.eu/meetdocs/2004_2009/documents/dv/691/691771/691771en.pdf <viewed 23 March 2009>.

Kitzinger, J. and Barbour, R. S., 'Introduction: The challenge and promise of focus groups', in R.S. Barbour and J. Kitzinger (eds). *Developing Focus Group Research: Politics, Theory and Practice* (London, Sage Publications, 1999), pp. 1–20.

Kivikuru, U., 'Top-down or bottom-up?' *International Communication Gazette*, 68:1 (2006), pp. 5–31.

Kleinwächter, W., 'From the mountains of visions to the valleys of reality: New legal frameworks for broadcasting in Eastern and Central Europe', *Canadian Journal of Communication Online*, 20:1 (1995).

Klocker, N. and Dunn, K., 'Who's driving the asylum debate?' *Media International Australia*, 109 (2003), pp. 71–92.

Knight, V., 'An investigation into the mass communication consumption in a closed male young offenders institution', *Particip@tions*, 2:1 (2005), available at http://www.participations.org/volume%202/issue%201/2_01_knight.htm#_edn7 <viewed 20 February 2009>.

Kulchyski, P., 'The postmodern and the paleolithic: Notes on technology and Native community in the far North', *Canadian Journal of Political and Social Theory*, 13:3 (1989), pp. 49–62.

Langton, M., *"'Well, I heard it on the radio and I saw it on the television": An Essay for the Australian Film Commission on the Politics and Aesthetics of Filmmaking by and about Aboriginal People and Things*, Sydney, Australian Film Commission, 1993.

Lewis, J., *Constructing Public Opinion – How Political Elites Do What they Like and Why we Seem to Go Along with It*, New York, Columbia University Press, 2001.

Lewis, P., *Promoting Social Cohesion: The Role of Community Radio*, report prepared for the Council of Europe's Group of Specialists on Media Diversity, Strasbourg, Council of Europe, 2008.

Lewis, P., Personal communication, The Radio Conference, Lincoln, UK, 16–19 July 2007.

Lewis, P. and Scifo, S., (eds) *Finding and Funding Voices: The Inner City Experience. An International Colloquium*, London, London Metropolitan University, 2007, available at http://www.communitymedia.eu/events/finding-and-funding-voices/Finding_and_Funding_Voices-Report.pdf <viewed 26 March 2009>.

Lin, W. and Song, H., 'Geo-ethnic storytelling: An examination of ethnic media content in contemporary immigrant communities', *Journalism*, 7:3 (2006), pp. 362–388.

Little, A., *The Politics of Community – Theory and Practice*, Edinburgh, Edinburgh University Press, 2002.

Lopez-Vigil, J., 'Giddy-up democracy!' *Interadio*, 8:1 (1996), pp. 8–9.

Luckman, S., 'People like that: Images of multiculturalism in the media', *Australian Mosaic*, 5:1 (2004), pp. 24–26.

Lui, G., 'Torres Strait: Towards 2001', *Race and Class*, 35:4 (1994), pp. 11–20.

Lyons, G., 'Aboriginal perceptions of courts and the police: A Victorian study', *Australian Aboriginal Studies*, 2 (1983), pp. 45–59.

Lyons, G., 'Surveying Aboriginal opinion concerning the law: Some methodological considerations', in P. Cashman (ed.), *Research and the Delivery of Legal Services* (Sydney, Law Foundation of New South Wales, 1981), pp. 253–279.

McNaughten, P. and Myers, G., 'Focus groups', in C. Seale, G. Gobo, J. F. Gubrium and D. Silverman (eds), *Qualitative Research Practice* (London, Sage, 2004), pp. 65–79.

Magno, A., 'Seeing is believing: Using new technologies to change the world', videotape/website produced by Necessary Illusions, CBS Newsworld and SRC/RDI, 2002, available at http://www.seeingisbelieving.ca/ <viewed 22 February 2009>.

Manne, R., 'Comment', *The Monthly*, November (2006), pp. 10–13.

Manning, P., *Us and Them: A Journalist's Investigation of Media, Muslims and the Middle East*, Sydney, Random House, 2006.

Maori Television, *Annual Report 2008*, available at http://corporate.maoritelevision.com/publications/MT_AR_2008.pdf <viewed 20 February 2009>.

Marmot, M., *The Status Syndrome: How Social Standing Affects our Health and Longevity*, New York, Times Books/Henry Holt, 2004.

Marr, D. and Wilkinson, M., *Dark Victory, 2nd edition*, Sydney, Allen and Unwin, 2004.

Martin-Barbero, J., 'Communication from culture: The crisis of the national and the emergence of the popular', *Media, Culture and Society*, 10 (1988), pp. 447–465.

Mattelart, A., *Mapping World Communication: War, Progress, Culture*, Minneapolis, University of Minnesota Press, 1994.

McCallum, K., 'Public opinion about Indigenous issues in Australia: Local talk and journalistic practice', *Australian Journalism Monographs*, 8, Brisbane, Griffith University, 2007.

McCauley, M., *NPR: The Trials and Triumphs of National Public Radio*, New York, Columbia University Press, 2005.
McChesney, R., *The Problem of the Media: US Communication Politics in the 21st Century*, New York, Monthly Review Press, 2004.
McChesney, R., 'The problem of journalism: A political economic contribution to an explanation of the crisis in contemporary US journalism', *Journalism Studies*, 4:3 (2003), pp. 299–329.
McChesney, R., *Corporate Media and the Threat to Democracy*, Open Pamphlet Series, Seven Stories Press and Open Media, 1997, available at http://www.thirdworldtraveler.com/Media/CorpMedia_McChesney.html <viewed 26 February 2007>.
McChesney, R., *Rich Media, Poor Democracy*, The New Press, 1999, available at http://www.thirdworldtraveler.com/McChesney/RichMedia_PoorDemocracy.html <viewed 22 February 2009>.
McChesney, R. and Nichols, J., 'Who'll unplug big media? Stay tuned', *The Nation*, 29 May 2008, available at http://www.thenation.com/doc/20080616/mcchesney <viewed 3 March 2009>.
McKinnon, K., 'Chairman's foreword', in *Annual Report No. 28* (Sydney, Australian Press Council, 2004), pp. 3–6.
McNair Ingenuity, Community Broadcasting Audience Survey 2008, available at http://www.cbonline.org.au/media/McNairListners2008/FullNationalListenerSurvey2008.pdf <viewed 22 February 2009>.
McNair Ingenuity Research, *Community Radio Listener Survey – Summary Report of Findings*, available at www.cbonline.org.au, 2004, 2006, 2008.
McQuail, D., *McQuail's Mass Communication Theory*, London, Sage Publications, 2005.
Mdlalose, S., 'Starting an evolution: The NCRF trains for the future', *Interadio*, 9:1 (1997), p. 14.
Meadows, M., 'Electronic dreaming tracks: Indigenous community broadcasting in Australia', *Development in Practice* (forthcoming), 2009.
Meadows, M., 'Journalism and Indigenous public spheres', *Pacific Journalism Review*, 11:1 (2005), pp. 36–41.
Meadows, M., *Voices in the Wilderness: Images of Aboriginal people in the Australian media*, Westport, Greenwood Press, 2001.
Meadows, M., 'Deals and victories: Newspaper coverage of Native title in Australia and Canada', *Australian Journalism Review*, 22:1 (2000), pp. 81–105.
Meadows, M., 'A 10-point plan and a treaty', *Queensland Review*, 6:1 (1999), pp. 50–76.
Meadows, M., 'The way people want to talk: Indigenous media production in Australia and Canada', *Media Information Australia*, 73 (1994), pp. 64–73.
Meadows, M., 'Getting the right message across: Inadequacies in existing codes make imperative the development of a code of conduct for Australian journalists reporting on race', *Australian Journalism Review*, 10:1&2 (1988), pp. 140–153.
Meadows, M., 'The jewel in the crown: The coming of television to the Torres Strait could be as significant as the impact of religion there, 117 years ago', *Australian Journalism Review*, 10:1&2 (1988), pp. 162–169.
Meadows, M. and Foxwell, K., 'Community broadcasting and mental illness: An audience study', *Australian Journalism Review* (forthcoming), 2009.
Meadows, M. and Molnar, H., 'Bridging the gaps: Towards a history of Indigenous media in Australia', *Media History*, 8:1 (2002), pp. 9–20.
Meadows, M. and van Vuuren, K., 'Seeking an audience: Indigenous people, the media and cultural resource management', *Southern Review*, 31:1 (1998), pp. 96–107.

References

Meadows, M., Forde, S., Ewart, J. and Foxwell, K., 'A catalyst for change: Australian community broadcasting audiences fight back', in J. Gordon (ed.), *Notions of Community: A Collection of Community Media Debates and Dilemmas* (Bern, Peter Lang, 2009), pp. 149–172.

Meadows, M., Forde, S., Ewart, J. and Foxwell, K., 'A quiet revolution: Australian community broadcasting audiences speak out', *Media International Australia*, 129 (2008), pp. 20–32.

Meadows, M., Forde, S., Ewart, J. and Foxwell, K., *Community Media Matters: An Audience Study of the Australian Community Broadcasting Sector*, Brisbane, Griffith University, 2007, available at http://www.cbonline.org.au/index.cfm?pageId=51,0,1,0 <viewed 22 February 2009>.

Meadows, M., Forde, S., Ewart, J. and Foxwell, K., 'The untapped potential of participation: New methods for evaluating audiences in the community media sector', *Australian Studies in Journalism*, 16 (2006), pp. 74–100.

Media, Entertainment and Arts Alliance, *Annual Report 2006–2007*, Redfern, MEAA, 2007.

Media Watch, *Community or Commercial TV?* Australian Broadcasting Corporation, 11 November 2002, available at http://www.abc.net.au/mediawatch/transcripts/041102_s4.htm <viewed 22 February 2009>.

Medrado, A., 'Sounds of the Favela: Community radio in public spaces', paper presented at the International Association for Mass Communication Research, Stockholm, Sweden, July 2008.

Mercer, C., 'Antonio Gramsci: E-Laborare, or the Work and Government of Culture', paper delivered at TASA conference, La Trobe University, Melbourne, December, 1989.

Michaels, E., 'A model of teleported texts (with reference to Aboriginal television)', *Continuum*, 3:2 (1990), pp. 8–31.

Michaels, E., *Aboriginal Invention of Television Central Australia 1982–1985*, Canberra, Australian Institute of Aboriginal Studies, 1986.

Michaels, E., 'Ask a foolish question: On the methodologies of cross cultural research', *Australian Journal of Cultural Studies*, 3:2 (1985), pp. 49–59.

Michell, L., 'Combining focus groups and interviews: Telling how it is; telling how it feels', in R.S. Barbour & J. Kitzinger (eds), *Developing Focus Group Research: Politics, Theory and Practice* (London, Sage Publications, 1999), pp. 36–46.

Milioni, D. L., 'Neither "community" nor "media"? The transformation of community media on the Internet', in J. Gordon (ed.), *Notions of Community: A Collection of Community Media Debates and Dilemmas* (Bern, Peter Lang, 2009), pp. 271–294.

Mishra, Vijay, 'Aboriginal representations in Australian texts', *Continuum*, 2:1 (1988), pp. 165–188.

Molnar, H. and Meadows, M., *Songlines to Satellites: Indigenous Communication in Australia, the South Pacific and Canada*, Leichhardt, Pluto Press, 2001.

Moran, A., 'Multiplying minorities: The case of community radio', in J. Craik, J. James Bailey and A. Moran (eds), *Public Voices, Private Interests: Australia's Media Policy* (St Leonards, Allen and Unwin, 1995), pp. 147–162.

Moran, K. C., 'Is changing the language enough? The Spanish-language 'alternative' in the USA', *Journalism*, 7:3 (2006), pp. 389–405.

Morgan, M., Interview at Woorabinda, Queensland, 19 October 2005.

Morris, C. and Meadows, M., 'Digital dreaming: Indigenous communication and the Internet', in G. Goggin (ed.), *Virtual Nation* (Sydney, UNSW Press, 2004), pp. 159–176.

Morris, C. and Meadows, M., 'Indigenising intellectual property', *Griffith Law Review*, 9:2 (2000), pp. 212–226.

Moylan, K., 'Towards transnational radio: Migrant-produced programming in Dublin', in J. Gordon (ed.), *Notions of Community: A Collection of Community Media Debates and Dilemmas* (Bern, Peter Lang, 2009), pp. 109–126.

Murdock, G., 'Thin descriptions: Questions of method in cultural analysis', in J. McGuigan (ed.), *Cultural Methodologies* (London, Sage, 1997), pp. 178–192.

Murdock, G. and Golding, P., 'Capitalism, communication and class relations', in J. Curran, M. Gurevitch and J. Woollacott (eds), *Mass Communication and Society* (London, Edward Arnold, 1977), pp. 12–43.

Murphy, P., 'Palm Island rioter Lex Wotton gets six years jail', *Australian Online*, 8 November 2008, available at http://www.theaustralian.news.com.au/story/0,25197,24616098-601,00.html <viewed 24 February 2009>.

Mushengyezi, A., 'Rethinking indigenous media: Rituals, "talking" drums and orality as forms of public communication in Uganda', *Journal of African Cultural Studies*, 16:1 (2003), pp. 107–117.

Nairn, R. G. and Coverdale, J. H., 'People never see us living well: An appraisal of the personal stories about mental illness in prospective print media sample', *Australian and New Zealand Journal of Psychiatry*, 39 (2005), pp. 281–287.

Nathan, D., Aboriginal Languages of Australia, 2007, available at http://www.dnathan.com/VL/austLang.htm <viewed 20 February 2009>.

National Ethnic and Multicultural Broadcasters' Council (NEMBC), *Submission to the House of Representatives Standing Committee on Communications Information Technology and the Arts Inquiry into Community Broadcasting*, 2006, available at http://www.aph.gov.au/house/committee/cita/community_broadcasting/subs/sub108.pdf <viewed 10 March 2009>.

National Ethnic and Multicultural Broadcasters' Council, www.nembc.org.au/ <viewed 22 February 2009>.

Nightingale, V. and Dwyer, T., 'Community attitudes and changing audiences', *Australian Journal of Communication*, 32:3 (2005), pp. 109–129.

NITV, *About National Indigenous Television*, 2009, available at http://nitv.org.au/ <viewed 24 February 2009>.

Ofcom, 'Communities are the stars', news release 9 March 2009, available at http://www.ofcom.org.uk/media/news/2009/03/nr_20090309a <viewed 23 March 2009>.

Ofcom, UK media regulator home page, available at http://www.ofcom.org.uk/ <viewed 24 February 2009>.

Ojo, T., 'Ethnic print media in the multicultural nation of Canada: A case study of the black newspaper in Montreal', *Journalism*, 7:3 (2006), pp. 343–361.

OLONieuws, 3 April (2007), p. 4, available at http://www.olon.nl/publiekdocs2/olonnieuws2007_03.pdf <viewed 3 March 2009>.

Onkaetse Mmusi, S., 'Impact of community broadcasting on rural development in South Africa', paper prepared for CODESRIA's 10th General Assembly on Africa in the New Millennium, Kampala, Uganda, 8–12 December 2002.

Onus, F., Personal communication, 19 August 2005.

OURMedia, home page, available at http://www.ourmedianetwork.org/ <viewed 3 March 2009>.

Parliament of the Commonwealth of Australia, *Community Television: Options for Digital Broadcasting*, Canberra, House of Representatives Standing Committee on Communications, Information Technology and the Arts, February 2007, available at http://www.aph.gov.au/House/committee/cita/community_broadcasting/firstreport/prelims.htm <viewed 24 February 2009>.

References

Paterson, B., 'Newspaper representations of mental illness and the impact of the reporting of events on social policy: The "framing" of Isabel Schwarz and Jonathan Zito', *Journal of Psychiatric and Mental Health Nursing*, 13 (2006), pp. 294–300.

Patterson, E. K., 'Through Torres Straits: Unique island settlements of wealthy and progressive ex-headhunters', *Digest of World Reading*, 1 March 1938.

PAW, 'Warlpiri Media Association Profiles', available at http://www.pawmedia.com.au/profiles.htm# <viewed 20 February 2009>.

Peissl, H and Tremetzberger, O., *Community Media in Europe: the legal and economic framework of the third audiovisual sector in UK, Netherlands, Switzerland, Niedersachsen (Germany) and Ireland*, Commissioned and published by the RTR (Austrian regulator for telecommunications and broadcasting), Austria, 2008, available at http://freie-radios.at/docs/1198689529_2008-Study-RTR-Community-Media-in-Europe-eng.pdf <viewed 20.7.09>.

Peters, B., 'Corporate media trends in Europe', Campaign for Press and Broadcasting Freedom, 18 July 2004, available at http://keywords.dsvr.co.uk/freepress/body.php?id=102&category=publications&finds=1&string=corporate%20media%20trends%20in%20europe <viewed 3 March 2009>.

Pickering, S., 'Common sense and original deviancy: News discourses and asylum seekers in Australia', *Journal of Refugee Studies*, 14:2 (2001), pp. 169–186.

Pietikäinen, S., 'Broadcasting Indigenous voices: Sami minority media production', *European Journal of Communication*, 23:2 (2008), pp. 173–191.

Pietikäinen, S. and Dufva, H., 'Voices in discourses: Dialogism, critical discourse analysis and ethnic identity', *Journal of Sociolinguistics*, 10:2 (2006), pp. 205–224.

Pimbert, M., Institutionalising participation and people-centred processes in natural resource management, IIED, London, 2004.

Pipol Fastaem, Solomon Islands Development Administration Planning programme (SIDAPP), People First Network, available at http://www.peoplefirst.net.sb/default.asp <viewed 3 March 2009>.

Polnigongit, W., 'Participation in community radio in Thailand: The case study of Mukdahan province's community enterprise radio station', in N. Chitty and S. Rattikalchalakorn (eds), *Alternative Media: Idealism and Pragmatism* (Penang, Southbound, 2007), pp. 127–140.

Polnigongit, W., 'Participation in community radio in Thailand: The case study of Mukldahan province's community enterprise radio', paper presented at the Alternative Media: Idealism vs pragmatism conference, Macquarie University, Sydney, 19–20 April 2005.

Pratt, A. and Bennett, S., 'The end of ATSIC and the future administration of Indigenous affairs: Current Issues Brief no. 4 2004–05', Canberra, Politics and Public Administration Section, Australian Parliamentary Library, 9 August 2004, available at http://www.aph.gov.au/library/pubs/CIB/2004–05/05cib04.htm#abolition <viewed 24 February 2009>.

Productivity Commission, *Broadcasting: Final Report*, Canberra, Ausinfo, 2000, available at http://www.pc.gov.au/projects/inquiry/broadcasting/docs/finalreport <viewed 24 February 2009>.

Prometheus Radio Project, 'Low Power Radio Triumphs over Big Broadcasters in Washington', News Alert, 8 October, 2009.

Project for Excellence in Journalism, *State of the News Media*, available at http://www.stateofthenewsmedia.org/2008/ <viewed 3 March 2009>.

Project for Excellence in Journalism and the Committee of Concerned Journalists, *The State of the News Media*, report produced in cooperation with the Pew Research Center for the People and the Press, 2004 and 2006, available at www.stateofthenewsmedia.com <viewed 1 April 2009>.

PY Media, Pitjantjatjara Yankunytjatjara Media Association home page, available at www.waru.org <viewed 24 February 2009>.

Ramırez, R., 'Appreciating the contribution of broadband ICT with rural and remote communities: Stepping stones toward an alternative paradigm', *The Information Society*, 23 (2007), pp. 85–94.

Ramirez, R., 'A model for rural and remote information and communication technologies: A Canadian exploration', *Telecommunications Policy*, 25 (2001), pp. 315–330.

Rankine, J. and McCreanor, T., 'Colonial coverage: Media reporting of a bicultural health research partnership', *Journalism*, 5:1 (2004), pp. 5–29.

Reese, S. D., Rutigliano, L., Hyun, K. and Jeong, J., 'Mapping the blogosphere: Professional and citizen-based media in the global news arena', *Journalism*, 8:3 (2007), pp. 235–261.

Rennie, E., 'The other road to media citizenship', *Media International Australia*, 103 (2002), pp. 7–13.

Rennie, E., 'Community television and the transition to digital broadcasting', *Australian Journal of Communication*, 28:1 (2001), pp. 57–68.

Response Ability, 'Media reporting of mental illness: Key research outcomes from 2002–2006', available at http://www.responseability.org/client_images/129984.pdf <viewed 24 February 2009>.

Riggins, S., (ed.) *Ethnic Minority Media: An International Perspective*, Newbury Park, Sage, 1992.

Rijavec, F., 'Careless, crude and unnecessary', *Online Opinion*, 19 July 2007, available at http://www.onlineopinion.com.au/view.asp?article=6127 <viewed 24 February 2009>.

Robie, D. 'Touching the heart of the Pacific', in D. Robie (ed.), *Nius Bilong Pasifik: Mass Media in the Pacific* (Port Moresby, University of Papua New Guinea Press, 1995), pp. 5–15.

Robinson, E., 'Flagship faces rough waters: US community radio in crisis', *Interadio*, 8:1 (1997), p. 17.

Rodriguez, C., '"Citizens" media and the voice of the angel/poet', *Media International Australia*, 103 (2002), pp. 78–87.

Rodriguez, C., *Fissures in the Mediascape: An International Study of Citizens' Media*, Cresskill, Hampton Press, 2001.

Rodriguez, C., Kidd, D. and Stein, L. (eds), *Making Our Media: Mapping Global Initiatives Toward a Democratic Public Sphere*, Cresskill, Hampton Press, 2010.

Romano, A., 'Journalism's role in mediating public conversation on asylum seekers and refugees in Australia', *Australian Journalism Review*, 26:2 (2004), pp. 43–62.

Roth, L., *Something New in the Air: The Story of First Peoples' Television Broadcasting in Canada*, Montreal, McGill-Queens University Press, 2005.

Roth, L. and Valaskakis, G., 'Aboriginal broadcasting in Canada: A case study in democratisation', in M. Raboy and P. A. Bruck (eds), *Communication for and against Democracy* (Montreal, Black Rose Books, 1989), pp. 221–234.

Roy Morgan Research, 'Image of professions survey: Nurses most ethical (again) – Politicians & journalists looked upon more favourably', Finding No. 4283, April 2008, available at http://www.roymorgan.com/news/polls/2008/4283/ <viewed 3 March 2009>.

Roy Morgan Research, *Aboriginal and Torres Strait Islander Needs Study: Final Report for Departments of Social Security, and Human Services and Health*, August, 1995.

Sawrikar, P. and Hunt, C. J., 'The relationship between mental health, cultural identity and cultural values in non-English speaking background (NESB) Australian adolescents', *Behaviour Change*, 22:2 (2005), pp. 97–113.

SBS, Special Broadcasting Service Online, available at www.sbs.com.au <viewed 24 February 2009>.

Schmidt, A., *The Loss of Australia's Aboriginal Language Heritage*, Canberra, Aboriginal Studies Press, 1993.

Schrøder, K. C., 'Beyond the pioneer days! Where is reception research going? Cross-fertilization of paradigms: A synthesizing approach to qualitative audience research', *Nordicom Information*, 3:16 (2001), pp. 23–36.

Schultz, J., 'The paradox of professionalism', in J. Schultz (ed.), *Not Just Another Business* (Leichhardt, Pluto Press, 1994), pp. 35–51.

Schulze, J. and Sainsbury, M., 'Kerry Stokes joins media frenzy', *The Australian*, 18 October 2006, available at http://www.theaustralian.news.com.au/story/0,20867,20600689-601,00.html <viewed 24 February 2009>.

Scifo, S., Radio Studies discussion forum, radio-studies@jiscmail.ac.uk, 2009.

Scifo, S., '"Student Radio" and "Student Press"', in K. Coyer, T. Dowmunt and F. Alan (eds), *The Alternative Media Handbook* (Abingdon and New York, Routledge, 2007), pp. 233–237.

Seale, C., Giampietro, G., Gubrium, J. F. and Silverman, D., 'Introduction: Inside qualitative research', in C. Seale, G. Gobo, J. F. Gubrium and D. Silverman (eds), *Qualitative Research Practice* (London, Sage Publications, 2004), pp. 1–11.

Servaes, J., 'Introduction', *Journal of International Communication*, 7:2 (2001), pp. 5–13.

Servaes, J. and Malikhao, P. 'Communication and sustainable development', background paper prepared for the 9th United Nations Roundtable on Communications for Development, Rome, 6–9 September 2004.

Shi, Y., 'Identity construction of the Chinese diaspora, ethnic media use, community formation and the possibility of social activism', *Continuum: Journal of Media and Cultural Studies*, 19:1 (2005), pp. 55–72.

Singh, M., *The Ethnic Broadcaster*, Autumn, 2002, available in summary form only at http://www.nembc.org.au/services/ethnicBroadcaster/Autumn_2002.htm#Barriers%20to%20Broadcasting <26 March 2009>.

Sinha, A., 'A holistic approach to communication research: An alternative methodology', *Media, Culture and Society*, 11 (1989), pp. 435–442.

Smith, B. L., 'Native American radio: Wolakota Wiconi waste', in A. Criswell (ed.), *More Than a Music Box: Radio Cultures and Communities in a Multi-Media World* (New York, Berghahn Books, 2004), pp. 95–108.

Spitulnik, D., 'Mobile machines and fluid audiences: Rethinking reception through Zambian radio culture', in F. Ginsburg, L. Abu-Lughod and B. Larkin (eds), *Media Worlds: Anthropology on New Terrain* (Berkeley and Los Angeles, University of California Press, 2002), pp. 337–354.

Sreberni, A., 'Media and global divides', keynote address at the International Association for Mass Communication Research Annual Congress, Stockholm, 24 July 2008.

Stevenson, J. H., *Community Radio Support in Other Jurisdictions*, report by the National Campus and Community Radio Association (NCRA/ANREC), 2006, available at www.tranquileye.com/free/community_radio_funding <viewed 3 March 2009>.

Stewart, G., 'Selling community: Corporate media, marketing and blogging', in J. Gordon (ed.), *Notions of Community: A Collection of Community Media Debates and Dilemmas* (Bern, Peter Lang, 2009), pp. 127–148.

Summerson Carr, E., 'Rethinking empowerment theory using a feminist lens: The importance of process', *Affilia*, 18:1 (2003), pp. 8–20.

Sydney Morning Herald, 'Believe me: I'm a journo', 2007, available at http://blogs.smh.com.au/sit/archives/2007/08/credibility_believe_me_im_a_jo.html <viewed 23 January 2009>.

Tacchi, J. and Price-Davies, E., 'A comparative study of community radio – designing a model for "access" radio in the UK', *Radio, Television and the New Media*, Australian Broadcasting Authority Annual Conference, Canberra, 3–4 May 2001.

Tacchi, J., Slater, D. and Hearn, G., *Ethnographic Action Research*, New Delhi, UNESCO, 2003.

Talk Black, Talkback commentary from callers to Bummera Bippera Radio, Cairns, streamed through radio 4K1G, Townsville, 7–11 November 2005, programme available daily live at http://www.4k1g.org/programs.htm <viewed 24 February 2009>.

Thede, N. and Ambrosi, A., (eds) *Video: The Changing World*, Montreal, Black Rose Books, 1991.

Thornley, P., 'Debunking the 'Whitlam myth' – The annals of public broadcasting revisited', *Media International Australia*, 77 (1995), pp. 155–164.

Thorpe, G., Address to the Engaging Audiences Symposium, Griffith University, Brisbane, 17 September 2008.

Thorpe, G., Interview at 4MBS, Brisbane, 2006.

Tomaselli, K. and Prinsloo, J., 'Video, realism, and class struggle: Theoretical lacunae and the problem of power', *Continuum*, 3:2 (1990), pp. 140–159.

Toyne, P., 'The Tanami network: New uses for communications in support of social links and service delivery in remote aboriginal communities of the Tanami', unpublished paper presented to the Service Delivery and Communications in the 1990s Conference, 17–19 March 1992.

Truglia, E., 'Community radio gridlock: Legal obstacles plague Latin American and Carribbean community radio', *Interadio*, 8:1 (1996), pp. 10–11.

Tsagarousianou, R., 'Rethinking the concept of diaspora: Mobility, connectivity and communication in a globalised world', *Westminster Papers in Communication and Culture*, 1:1 (2004), pp. 52–66.

UNESCO, 'India to establish 4000 community radio stations under new community radio policy', Communication and Information Sector's news service, 15 March 2007, available at http://portal.unesco.org/ci/en/ev.php-URL_ID=24250&URL_DO=DO_TOPIC&URL_SECTION=201.html <viewed 3 March 2009>.

Valaskakis, G., (1993) 'Parallel voices: Indians and others – Narratives of cultural struggle', *Canadian Journal of Communication*, 18:3 (1993), available at http://www.cjc-online.ca/viewarticle.php?id=179&layout=html <viewed 24 February 2009>.

van Vuuren, K., 'The value and purpose of community broadcasting', in J. Gordon (ed.), *Notions of Community: A Collection of Community Media Debates and Dilemmas* (Bern, Peter Lang, 2009), pp. 173–195.

van Vuuren, K., *Participation In Australian Community Broadcasting*, VDM Verlag, Saarbrucken, 2008.

van Vuuren, K., 'Community broadcasting and the enclosure of the public sphere', *Media, Culture and Society*, 28:3 (2006), pp. 379–392.

van Vuuren, K., 'Beyond the studio: A case study of community radio and social capital', *Media International Australia*, 103 (2002), pp. 94–108.

von Sturmer, J., 'Talking with Aborigines', *Australian Institute of Aboriginal Studies Newsletter*, 15 (1981), pp. 13–30.

Waru, 'ICTV', available at http://www.waru.org/organisations/ictv/ <viewed 24 February 2009>.

Wasko, J. and Mosco, V., *Democratic Communication in the Information Age*, Toronto and Norwood NJ, Garamond Press and Ablex, 1992.

West, D., 'Indigenous media', in *Voices from the Land: The 1993 Boyer Lectures*, ABC Books, Sydney, 1994.

White, R. A., 'Is "empowerment" the answer? Current theory and research on development communication', *Gazette: The International Journal for Communication Studies*, 66:1 (2004), pp. 7–24.

Wilkin, H. A. and Ball-Rokeach, S. J., 'Reaching at risk groups: The importance of health storytelling in Los Angeles Latino media', *Journalism*, 7:3 (2006), pp. 299–320.

Williams, R., *Marxism and Literature*, London, Oxford University Press, 1977.

Williams, S., personal communication with Ofcom representative, *The Radio Conference*, Lincoln, UK, 16 July, 2007.
Williams, W. H., Interview at the Garma Festival, Arnhem Land, 7 August 2005.
Willmot, E., *Out of the Silent Land*, Canberra, Australian Government Publishing Service, 1984.
Wilson, P. and Stewart, M., (eds) *Global Indigenous Media: Culture, Poetics and Politics*, Durham, Duke University Press, 2008.
Wilson, T. C., *Satellite Television in the Canadian Arctic 1974–1992: Cultural Replacement and Regeneration*, paper presented at the Post Colonial Formations Conference, Griffith University, Brisbane, 14–17 July 1993.
Wimmer, R. and Dominick, J., *Mass Media Research: An Introduction*, Belmont, CA, Wadsworth, 1987.
Worth, S. and Adair, J., *Through Navajo Eyes*, Bloomington, University of Indiana Press, 1973.
Yamada, H., 'Management of a small-scale community broadcasting FM station in Japan, Case study: FM West Tokyo', International Geographical Union, Commission on Communication Networks and Telecommunications, Commission Annual Conference and Pre-Congress meeting, Kwangju, 8–11 August 2000, English summary available at http://camp.ff.tku.ac.jp/YAMADA-KEN/Y-KEN/fulltext/00fm-igc.html <viewed 3 March 2009>.
Zhangazha, T., 'Community broadcasting has a big role to play', *Financial Gazette*, 23 May 2002, p. 1.

Appendix

Indigenous community radio and television audience focus groups (2006)

Radio Larrakia, Darwin
3KND, Kool 'n' Deadly, Melbourne
Bumma Bippera Media, Cairns
98.9 FM Murri Country, Brisbane
Radio Goolarri, Broome
CAAMA Radio, Alice Springs
TEABBA, Darwin
Umeewarra Media, Port Augusta, South Australia

Indigenous interviews were conducted at the following locations (2004–2006):
Batchelor College, Northern Territory
Remote Indigenous Broadcasting Services (RIBS) Festival, Alice Springs, Northern Territory
Laura Dance and Cultural Festival, Queensland
GARMA Festival, Gulkula, Northern Territory
Palm Island, Queensland
Townsville Cultural Festival, Townsville
Aboriginal Health Service, Townsville
Torres Strait Cultural Festival, Thursday Island
RIBS Festival, Woorabinda, Queensland
Yuendumu Sports Festival, Yuendumu, Northern Territory
'Surviving Cyclone' Festival, Maningrida, Northern Territory
Community visits to Beagle Bay, Djaridjin, and One Arm Point, Kimberleys, Western Australia
Anangu-Pitjantjatjara-Yankunytjatjara lands, 25th anniversary of lands hand-back, Umuwa, South Australia

Ethnic community radio audience focus groups

Macedonian programme, Plenty Valley FM, Melbourne, Victoria
Vietnamese programme, 3CR, Melbourne, Victoria
Sudanese programme, 3ZZZ, Melbourne, Victoria
Turkish programme, 3ZZZ, Melbourne, Victoria
Tongan programme, 5EB, Adelaide, South Australia
Serbian programme, TEN73 Border FM, Albury-Wodonga, New South Wales-Victorian border
Filipino/Tagalog programme, 104.1 Territory FM, Northern Territory
Indonesian programme, 104.1 Territory FM, Northern Territory
Chinese Youth programme, 4EB Brisbane, Queensland
Greek Seniors' programme, 4EB Brisbane, Queensland

Index

Aboriginal and Torres Strait Islander Commission, 54, 61, 65, 81
Aboriginal Invention of Television, 63
Aboriginal Peoples Television Network (APTN), 65, 153
Advisory committee, 28, 29, 30, 31, 144,
Alvarez, C., 46
AMARC (World Association of Community Radio Broadcasters), 46, 47
Anangu-Pitjantjatjara-Yankunytjatjara (APY), 63, 82, 88, 91, 93, 96, 99, 152, 155
Anderson, B., 157
Anderson, H., 7, 146
Ang, I., 18, 103
Atton, C., 18, 39, 41, 42, 129, 133
Audience research methods, 24–32
Audience-producer relationship, 17, 19, 53, 86, 130–131, 134, 136, 140, 146–149, 151, 153, 157
Australian Broadcasting Corporation (ABC), 23, 24, 54, 62, 77, 87, 93, 154
Australian Bureau of Statistics, 44, 54
Australian Communications and Media Authority (ACMA) 37, 72, 114, 118
Australian Competition and Consumer Commission (ACCC), 37
Australian Indigenous Communication Association, 7, 28
Australian Press Council, 43, 67
Avison, S., 133

Bailey, O. G., 19, 39, 41, 42, 136
Baker, R., 25
Ball-Rokeach, S. J., 19, 76
Barbour, R. S., 25, 27, 29

Barlow, D., 17, 18, 54, 60
Batchelor, 150, 154, 181
BBC, 72
Beagle Bay-Djaridjin,, 89, 93, 181
Bear, A., 17, 18, 54, 56
Beecher, E, 43, 44
Benhabib, S., 42
Bennett, S., 81
Bickford, S., 21, 40, 45, 88, 127, 136, 138
Biliki, R., 46
Bosch, T., 45
Brady, M., 30
Broadcasting for Remote Aboriginal Communities Scheme (BRACS), 63, 82, 86, 97, 98
Broadcasting Services Act 1992, 54, 57
Brough, M., 18, 74, 75
Browne, D. R., 18
Bumma Bippera Media, 31, 62, 88, 94, 97, 181

Camara, M., 44
Cameron, J., 26
Canada, 17, 38, 44, 46, 65, 68, 85, 143, 146, 153
Carpentier, Nico, 18, 19, 41, 42, 129, 131, 136, 138, 139
Castillo, A., 67
Catterall, M., 29
CB Online, 23, 57, 61, 66, 70, 114, 118
Central Australian Aboriginal Media Association (CAAMA), 62, 95–98, 146, 181
Centrelink, 73, 74, 116, 117, 120
Chand, A., 18, 75
Chinese Youth programme, 75, 103, 105, 106, 107, 110, 122, 148, 151, 181
Chitty, N., 42, 44

Chomsky, N., 43
Chowns, J., 37
Christian radio, 57, 127
Citizenship, 17, 21, 26, 39, 48, 53, 60, 66, 132–133, 135, 137, 139–140
Codes of Practice, 57, 64
Cohen, E., 18, 76
Community announcements, 75, 105
Community broadcasting
    as a key cultural resource, 20, 39, 53, 58, 70, 82, 85, 128, 132, 137, 143, 153, 157
    as a primary source of news and information, 19, 20, 21, 23, 37, 59, 60, 61, 66, 70–72, 74–75, 81, 92, 94–97, 100, 104–106, 108, 114–120, 122–124, 131, 132, 135, 144, 146, 151, 153, 155–156
    cultural and linguistic maintenance, 17, 45, 84–86, 105–108, 133, 157–158
    definitions of, 39–42, 46, 49, 55, 127, 131, 133, 140
    educational role, 22, 42, 44, 47, 54–58, 60, 74–76, 81, 91–93, 99, 100, 103, 106, 153
    maintaining networks and social cohesion, 20, 43, 46, 48, 53, 67, 72, 74–77, 81, 83–84, 89, 92, 104–105, 108–110, 113, 114, 120–124, 128, 136, 139, 144, 146, 148–149, 156
    promoting cross-cultural dialogue, 20, 29–30, 32, 45, 81, 92, 95, 97–98, 100, 144
    promoting music and dance, 19, 20, 21, 22, 29, 39, 45, 54–58, 71–74, 76, 81–83, 86, 89, 93, 98–99, 100, 104, 105, 108, 110–113, 118–124, 131, 132, 144, 146–148, 151, 153–156
    station accessibility, 20, 105, 117, 152
    theorizing, 129–140
Community Broadcasting Association of Australia (CBAA), 7, 71
Community Broadcasting Foundation (CBF), 7, 72, 156
Community Media Matters, 7, 21
Community public sphere, 26, 39, 41, 133, 134, 140
Community television, 60
Corker, J., 63
Couldry, N., 41

Council of Europe, 47, 104
Coupe, B., 18
Courier-Mail, 67
Coyer, K., 18, 42
Cultural bridge, 20, 23, 63, 65, 76, 92, 97, 100, 110, 111, 153
Cultural diversity, 17, 19, 27, 54, 57, 60, 67, 68, 78, 133
Culture, commitment, community, 21
Cunningham-Burley, S., 26
Curran, J., 130

Daniels, G. L., 18
Davies, N., 43
Davis, M., 43
Day, G., 127
De Cleen, B., 18, 42
De Wit, P., 37, 47
Deger, J., 61, 147
Department of Communication, Information Technology and the Arts, 7, 37
Deuze, M., 17, 18, 40, 43, 71, 76, 103, 145
Diaspora, 18, 24, 40, 49
Digital Dreaming, 63, 77
Digital radio, 38
Downing, J., 18, 19, 38, 39, 41, 42, 133
Dreher, T., 67
Dunn, K., 67
Durham, M. G., 43, 48, 129, 130, 135
Dwyer, T., 25

Eades, D., 30
Elghul-Bebawi, S., 41
Emerging communities, 73, 105, 108, 116, 148,
Empowerment, 32, 33, 40, 42, 46, 86, 130–132, 134–135, 140, 144–145, 153, 156
    community, 135–136
    media, 136–137
    society, 137–139
Ethnic Broadcaster, 69
Ethnic community broadcasting history, 66–70
Europe, 47–48, 54, 104, 156
European Broadcasting Union, 47
European Parliament, 47, 48
Everitt, A., 46, 47
Ewart, J., 7, 18

Index

Fairbairn, J., 40
Favelas, 40
Fenton, N., 18, 41, 42
Filipino/Tagalog programme, 106, 122, 181
Fine music stations, 22, 54, 55, 57, 58, 72, 73, 113
First level of service, 17, 19, 65
First Nations, 17, 40, 65, 152, 153
Flucker, D., 7, 30
Forde, S., 17, 18, 21, 24, 27, 38, 39, 42, 53, 59, 60, 61, 67, 71, 77, 127, 128, 132, 133, 157
Foster, L., 68
Foucault, M., 131
Foundation for Development Corporation, 40
Foxwell, K., 7, 135
Fraser, M., 68
Fraser, N., 41, 133
Fuller, L., 18, 42,

Galbally Report, 68
Gardiner-Garden, J., 37,
Geurts, J., 28,
Gibbs, A., 25,
Gibson, K., 26,
Ginsburg, F., 18, 61, 147
Girard, B., 39, 45, 46
Glaser, B. G., 27,
Goolarri Media, 65, 86, 87, 90, 94, 181
Gordon, J., 39, 42, 43, 46, 47
Greek Seniors' programme, 70, 105, 107, 108, 115, 116, 117, 122, 151, 152, 181
Green, L., 26,
Grossberg, L., 19, 129, 134, 135, 145
Grounded theory, 33, 127
Gurevitch, M., 130
Gutierrez, F., 19, 40
Guzman, I. M., 18

Hall, S., 132
Hamilton, J., 43
Hinton, R., 25
Hippocrates, C., 38, 66, 154
Hirner, W., 47
Hochheimer, J., 41, 54, 76, 128
Hollander, E., 37, 47
Horsfall, D., 27

House of Representatives Standing Committee on Communication, Transport and the Arts, 58
Howley, K., 18, 39, 42, 128, 129, 132
Hunter Institute for Mental Health, 7
Husband, C., 19, 38, 39, 41

Imparja Television, 63, 65, 96
India, 44, 70, 75
Indigenous community media history, 61–65
Indigenous Community Television (ICTV), 65, 77, 84, 85, 88, 92–94, 99, 150, 153, 155
Indigenous Remote Communications Association, 7, 28
Indonesian programme, 103, 111, 181
International Association for Mass Communication Research (IAMCR), 40
Ireland, 38, 47, 104
Ishikawa, S., 40, 46

Jakubowicz, A., 18, 66
Japan, 40, 44–46
Jayasuriya, L., 156
Johnson, F., 40
Joldersma, C., 28
Josiah, J., 46
Journalism, 18, 43, 44, 48, 67, 87

Kawakami, T., 44, 46
Kellner, D., 43, 48, 129, 130, 135
Kern European Affairs, 47
Kitzinger, J., 25, 27, 29
Kivikuru, U., 45
Klocker, N., 67
Knight, V., 38
Kobe earthquake, 44
Koori Mail, 65
Kulchyski, P., 20, 147

Land Rights News, 65
Langton, M., 20, 145, 152, 154, 158
Laura Cultural Festival, 83, 88, 90, 97, 181
Lewis, P., 17, 19, 37, 43, 46, 47, 48, 104, 120
Lin, Wan-Ying, 19, 75
Little, A., 127
Lopez-Vigil, J., 45

Luckman, S., 67
Lyons, G., 30

Macedonian programme, 70, 73, 120, 121, 122, 147, 181
MacLaran, P., 29
Maningrida, 87, 181
Manne, R., 38
Maori Television, 65, 85, 153
Marmot, M., 30
Marr, D., 67
Mattelart, A., 42
McCallum, K., 136, 143
McCauley, M. P., 18, 42, 46
McChesney, R., 43, 137
McNair Ingenuity, 21, 22, 23, 25, 26, 41, 60, 71, 113, 117, 143, 157
McNaughten, P., 27,
McQuail, D., 130, 135
Mdlalose, S., 44
Meadows, M., 7, 17, 18, 20, 21, 30, 38, 42, 45, 46, 53, 60, 61, 65, 74, 85, 88, 130, 132, 133, 135, 145, 147, 152, 154, 157
Medrado, A., 40, 131
Mental health, 74–76, 86–91
Mercer, C., 158
Michaels, E., 18, 20, 30, 31, 61, 63, 91, 147, 154, 155
Milioni, D. L., 48
Mishra, V., 154
Molnar, H., 18, 20, 30, 46, 61, 65, 85, 133, 147, 154
Moran, A., 17, 18, 19, 54, 56, 66,
Morris, C., 7, 30, 133
Moylan, K., 47, 103
Multiculturalism, 17, 68, 76, 77, 119, 156
Murdock, G., 25
Murri, 61, 62, 78, 82, 84, 89, 97, 181
Myers, G., 27

Namibia, 45
National Ethnic Multicultural Broadcasters' Council (NEMBC), 7, 73, 119
National Indigenous News Service (NINS), 23, 77
National Indigenous Radio Service (NIRS), 23, 65, 76, 83

National Indigenous Television service (NITV), 65, 77, 84, 87, 93, 150, 153, 155
National Indigenous Times, 65
National Multicultural Advisory Council, 68
Netherlands, 38, 47
New Zealand, 55, 65, 85, 118, 153
Ngaanyatjarra Media, 65, 85
Nichols, J., 43
Nightingale, V., 25

Ofcom, 22, 43, 46, 47
Ojo, T., 19
OLONieuws, 47
Onkaetse Mmusi, S., 45
OurMedia, 43
Out of the Silent Land, 63
Outback Digital Network, 64

Palm Island, 61, 62, 82, 84, 88, 89, 91, 94, 96, 98, 99, 146, 181
Patterson, E. K., 22
Peissl, H., 103
People First Network (PFNet), 46
Peters, B., 47
Philippines, 44
Pickering, S., 67
Pilbara and Kimberley Aboriginal Media (PAKAM), 62, 65, 85, 86
Pimbert, M., 144
Pintubi-Amatyerre-Warlpiri Media (PAW), 62, 65, 83, 85, 86, 91
Pipol Fastaem, 46
Pitjantjatjara-Yankunytjatjara (PY) Media, 62, 65, 82, 85
Policymaking, 26, 28, 143, 144
Politically progressive stations, 19, 39, 56, 57, 112
Polnigongit, W., 19, 44, 45
Pratt, A., 81
Price-Davies, E., 45, 46
Prinsloo, J., 132
Productivity Commission, 61, 63, 65
Project for Excellence in Journalism, 43, 71
Public sphere, 20, 21, 26, 39, 41, 44, 49, 53–54, 99, 104, 128, 131–134, 136–138, 140, 145

Qualitative research methods, 18, 19, 21, 25–28, 31–32, 37, 44, 57, 60, 71, 128, 131, 143, 157–158

Quantitative research methods, 18, 21, 25, 26–27, 37, 57, 60, 71, 113, 117–118, 128, 143, 157

Radio 104.1, Territory FM, 181
Radio 3CR, 112, 113, 121, 181
Radio 3KND, Kool 'n' Deadly, 92, 95, 146, 181
Radio 3ZzZ, 70, 181
Radio 4EB, 66, 110, 116, 117, 181
Radio 4K1G, 62, 89, 94, 96, 97, 99, 181
Radio 4ZzZ, 21, 22, 56, 181
Radio 5EB, 66, 181
Radio 98.9 Murri Country, 89, 92, 94, 95, 98, 147, 151, 181
Radio Adelaide, 5UV, 70, 22, 62, 69, 70, 181
Radio for the Print Handicapped, 7, 18, 57, 61, 72, 137
Radio Larrakia, 86, 181
Radio Plenty Valley FM, 181
Radio Sagarmatha, 44
Radio TEN73, 181
Ramirez, R., 27, 28, 143–144
Rattichalkalakorn, S., 42, 44
Reconciliation, 12, 24, 77, 152, 153,
Refugees, 18, 24, 48, 67, 69–70, 74, 77, 148
Remote Commercial Television Services (RCTS), 63
Remote Indigenous Broadcasting Services (RIBS), 61, 65, 82, 154, 155, 181
Rennie, E., 39
Reys, Ken, 7, 30
Riggins, S., 18
Rio de Janiero, 40
Robie, D., 46
Robinson, E., 46
Rodriguez, C., 18, 19, 39, 42, 129, 137, 138, 139
Romano, A., 67
Roth, Lorna, 17, 18, 30, 46
Roy Morgan Research, 30, 43

Sawricker, P., 74
Schmidt, A., 63
Scifo, S., 43, 46

Seale, C., 25
Seneviratne, K., 66
Serbian programme, 70, 107, 108, 112, 115, 116, 119, 120, 181
Shi, Yu, 18
Shroder, K. C., 24
Singh, M., 68
Social cohesion, 17, 40, 41, 42, 47, 48, 49, 100, 104, 120, 123, 134, 148–149
Social networks, 20, 82, 83, 144, 147
Song, H., 19, 75
South Africa, 45
Special Broadcasting Service (SBS), 23, 56, 62, 66, 70, 74, 93, 117, 119–120, 154, 157
Sri Lanka, 44
Stevenson, J. H., 47
Stockley, D., 68
Strauss, A. L., 27
Subscribers, 72–73,
Sudanese programme, 73, 105, 106, 108, 116, 118, 119, 121, 122, 148, 149, 181
Summerson-Carr, E., 134, 145
Surviving Cyclone Festival, Maningrida, 87, 181
Sydney Morning Herald, 47, 67

Tacchi, J., 26, 45, 46
Talk Black, 31, 62, 83, 86, 94, 95, 97, 150
Tanami Network, 64
Thailand, 19, 44
The Who, 22
Thornley, P., 17, 18, 54
Thorpe, G., 56
Thursday Island, 95, 181
Tomaselli, K., 132
Tongan programme, 70, 106, 107, 109, 111, 115, 116, 118, 122, 149, 181
Top End Aboriginal Bush Broadcasters' Association (TEABBA), 65, 86, 181
Torres Strait Cultural Festival, 85, 89, 92, 95, 99, 146, 181
Torres Strait, 22, 24, 28, 54
Townsville Cultural Festival, 62, 83, 94, 99, 151, 181
Toyne, P., 64
Tremetzberger, O., 103
Truglia, E., 45

Tsagarousianou, R., 18, 75
Turkish programme, 73, 107, 109, 111, 112, 113, 116, 118, 121, 181

UHF radio, 82, 153
Umeewarra Media, 61, 83, 90, 97, 99, 181
Umuwa, 84, 90, 91, 93, 181
UNESCO, 44
United Kingdom, 22, 46–48, 75
United States, 25, 38, 40, 46, 70, 75, 76, 103

Valaskakis, G., 17, 18
Van der Spek, J., 45
Van Vuuren, K., 7, 21, 30, 38, 128
Vietnamese programme, 70, 105, 109, 110, 112, 114, 115, 121, 124, 181
Volunteers, 21, 23, 46, 53, 54, 56, 59–60, 66, 69, 72, 123, 145, 154, 157
Von Sturmer, J., 30

Warlpiri Media, see Pintubi-Amatyerre-Warlpiri Media (PAW)

West, D., 154
White, R. A., 134
Whitlam, G., 22, 54, 60
Wilkin, H. A., 19, 76
Wilkinson, M., 67
Williams, S., 47
Williams, W. H., 98
Willmot, E., 63
Wilson, P., 18, 147
Wilson, T. C., 30
Woods, J., 22
Woorabinda, 62, 181

Yamada, H., 40, 46
Yuendumu, 63, 64, 83, 86, 87, 90, 91, 100, 146, 155, 181

Zhangazha, T., 45
Zimbabwe, 45

www.ingramcontent.com/pod-product-compliance
Ingram Content Group UK Ltd.
Pitfield, Milton Keynes, MK11 3LW, UK
UKHW051849210426
5322IPUK00025B/632